THE FUTURE
OF OLD NEIGHBORHOODS

REBUILDING FOR A CHANGING POPULATION

PUBLICATIONS OF THE JOINT CENTER FOR URBAN STUDIES
OF THE MASSACHUSETTS INSTITUTE OF TECHNOLOGY
AND HARVARD UNIVERSITY

This monograph is one of a series published under the auspices of the Joint Center for Urban Studies, a cooperative venture of the Massachusetts Institute of Technology and Harvard University. The Joint Center was founded in 1959 to organize and encourage research on urban and regional problems. Participants have included scholars from the fields of anthropology, architecture, business, city planning, economics, education, engineering, history, law, philosophy, political science, and sociology.

The findings and conclusions of this monograph are, as with all Joint Center publications, solely the responsibility of the author.

Other books published in the Joint Center series include:

Beyond the Melting Pot: *The Negroes, Puerto Ricans, Jews, Italians, and Irish of New York City.* NATHAN GLAZER and DANIEL PATRICK MOYNIHAN. M.I.T. Press; M.I.T. Paperback, MIT-13.

City Politics: *An Interpretation.* EDWARD C. BANFIELD and JAMES Q. WILSON. Harvard University Press.

City Politics in Washington, D. C. MARTHA DERTHICK. Harvard University Press.

A Communications Theory of Urban Growth. RICHARD L. MEIER. M.I.T. Press.

The Federal Bulldozer: *A Critical Analysis of Urban Renewal, 1949–1962.* MARTIN ANDERSON. M.I.T. Press.

The Future of Old Neighborhoods: *Rebuilding for a Changing Population.* BERNARD J. FRIEDEN. M.I.T. Press.

The Historian and the City. OSCAR HANDLIN and JOHN E. BURCHARD, editors. M.I.T. Press.

Housing and Economic Progress: *A Study of the Housing Experiences of Boston's Middle-Income Families.* LLOYD RODWIN. M.I.T. Press.

The Image of the City. KEVIN LYNCH. M.I.T. Press. M.I.T. Paperback, MIT-11.

The Intellectual Versus the City: *From Thomas Jefferson to Frank Lloyd Wright.* MORTON and LUCIA WHITE. Harvard University Press.

Law and Land: *Anglo-American Planning Practice.* CHARLES HAAR. Harvard University Press.

Location and Land Use. WILLIAM ALONSO. Harvard University Press.

Man's Struggle for Shelter in an Urbanizing World. CHARLES ABRAMS. M.I.T. Press.

The Myth and Reality of Our Urban Problems. RAYMOND VERNON. Harvard University Press.

Poverty and Progress: *Social Mobility in a Nineteenth Century City.* STEPHAN ALBERT THERNSTROM. Harvard University Press.

The Public Library and the City. RALPH W. CONANT, editor. M.I.T. Press.

Streetcar Suburbs. SAM B. WARNER, JR. Harvard University Press.

Urban Rail Transit: *Its Economics and Technology.* A. SCHEFFER LANG and RICHARD M. SOBERMAN. M.I.T. Press.

The View from the Road. DONALD APPLEYARD, KEVIN LYNCH, and JOHN R. MYER. M.I.T. Press.

The Zone of Emergence. ROBERT A. WOODS and ALBERT J. KENNEDY. Harvard University Press.

THE FUTURE
OF OLD NEIGHBORHOODS

REBUILDING FOR A CHANGING POPULATION

BERNARD J. FRIEDEN

PUBLISHED FOR

THE JOINT CENTER FOR URBAN STUDIES
OF THE MASSACHUSETTS INSTITUTE OF TECHNOLOGY
AND HARVARD UNIVERSITY

BY

THE M.I.T. PRESS
MASSACHUSETTS INSTITUTE OF TECHNOLOGY
CAMBRIDGE, MASSACHUSETTS

TO MY PARENTS

PREFACE

Housing conditions, the movement of people, the economics of rebuilding old neighborhoods, the social effects of urban renewal programs—these are some of the elements that have a bearing on the choice of public policies for the future of our cities. Research on these subjects must depend largely upon information from people close to the scene of events. Three cities were chosen for detailed examination in this study: New York, Los Angeles, and Hartford. Information was collected in 1961, and the findings in each of these cities should be re-examined in the light of changes since then. Public officials, housing specialists, and realtors in all three cities were generous in sharing their experience with me. Beyond the indebtedness acknowledged in citations within this study, several people are due for special thanks.

In New York, Milton Abelson, then with the Regional Plan Association, was particularly helpful. Staff members of the Federal Housing Administration and the New York Department of City Planning, and Louis Winnick and Frank Kristof of the New York Housing and Redevelopment Board, also helped generously.

For assistance in Los Angeles, I am most indebted to Henry A. Babcock; Leo Grebler and his associates at the University of California Real Estate Research Program; Arnold A. Wilken, Area Representative of the Housing and Home Finance Agency; and staff members of the Los Angeles City Planning Commission, the Los Angeles County Regional Planning Commission, and the Federal Housing Administration.

In Hartford, staff members of the Hartford Commission on the City Plan, the Capitol Region Planning Agency, the Federal Housing Administration, and the Hartford Area Transportation Study all provided special assistance.

My colleagues in the M.I.T. Department of City and Regional Planning offered good counsel in the formulation of research proposals and made many useful comments on an earlier draft of this study. I am particularly indebted to Lloyd Rodwin, who supervised my doctoral dissertation on which this book is based, and to Kevin Lynch, John T. Howard, Frederick J. Adams, and Charles Abrams. In addition, I want to thank Louis Winnick and Nathaniel Rogg for reviewing the manuscript and making many helpful suggestions.

I am grateful to the Joint Center for Urban Studies of M.I.T. and Harvard University—and to Martin Meyerson, its first director—for a research appointment that provided financial assistance and a stimulating atmosphere in which to work. Paul Kolp furnished important help, as a research assistant at the Joint Center, in developing statistical materials on race and housing.

An earlier version of Chapter 3 was published as an article in the *Journal of the American Institute of Planners,* "Locational Preferences in the Urban Housing Market," Vol. 27 (November 1961), pp. 316–324.

Finally, I am most indebted to my wife Elaine for her support and encouragement and for her own intellectual contributions to this study.

BERNARD J. FRIEDEN

Cambridge, Massachusetts
December 1963

CONTENTS

THE FUTURE
OF OLD NEIGHBORHOODS

REBUILDING FOR A CHANGING POPULATION

CHAPTER ONE

COMMUNITIES IN DECLINE

Vast and complex changes mark the current development of American cities. Large numbers of rural people are going to the big cities, while earlier city dwellers move to suburbia. The poor, the elderly, and racial and ethnic minorities, concentrated in central cities, are moving into old neighborhoods that the more affluent have left behind. As these groups lay claim to the old neighborhoods in their search for a place to live, city governments are experimenting with policies and programs to speed the rebuilding of these same areas.

The success of housing and renewal policies is blocked not only by conflicting interests, however, but by a poor understanding of changes under way in metropolitan regions. Population growth, mobility, rising incomes, and shifting housing preferences stir up intricate crosscurrents on the urban scene and make analysis and prediction difficult. The broad outlines of future prospects for old neighborhoods can be detected, but effective policymaking requires a more careful assessment of rates and directions of change.

It is clear that growth and decline go hand in hand in the modern metropolis. Of our dozen largest cities in 1950, eleven lost population between 1950 and 1960, while their metropolitan regions continued to grow. The same combination of central decline and over-all increase also characterized many smaller urban regions in the 1950's. Suburban growth has thus had an important side effect of reducing population in central areas.

Current interpretations of the American city emphasize the problems of obsolescence and decline in a period of generally buoyant expansion. The rebuilding of old areas has become a matter of national concern, with the federal government spending millions of dollars every year for urban renewal subsidies. And the picture

1

of urban problems that has emerged with this new interest is a grim one.

The "Gray Areas"

Many square miles of our cities consist of old neighborhoods where population decline appears imminent or has already begun. To recent analysts,[1] these are the "gray areas" of obsolescent housing destined to be vacated at an increasing rate in the near future. In their view, the old residential structures are rapidly outliving their usefulness and will shortly be ready for clearance and replacement. Further, according to this interpretation, economic and social forces are operating inexorably both to destroy the present usefulness of these parts of the city and to block efforts to rebuild them as new residential communities.

What is the nature of this hypothetical process that seems to ensure indefinite stagnation in the old residential areas? Changing public taste is expected to bring about a rapid obsolescence of buildings constructed to the standards of past generations, while the buildings themselves deteriorate with age. Residents will move out, leaving behind a set of partially occupied buildings. These semiabandoned structures are at the base of the gray areas hypothesis: their continued presence is expected to constitute a severe liability to the land they occupy. It is argued on the basis of current experience that such land can be cleared only at a high cost, for old structures are expensive to acquire despite their waning utilization.

Recent experience also suggests that desirable building sites will be available at a lower cost on vacant outlying land. Suburban sites are the overwhelmingly popular choice for new housing, and little evidence is at hand to suggest a sharp reversal of this trend. For most people in search of new housing, the attractions of the suburbs remain compelling, and a steadily growing metropolitan highway network promises to open up an increasing supply of suburban land with good accessibility to jobs and services.

The gray areas, in comparison, seem to offer few present or potential advantages. The central location of most of these areas was formerly a considerable asset for their development, but with the outward spread of jobs and services and with improved highway access to the suburbs, central locations no longer play a dominant role in the housing market. While a limited number of people want

2

to live near the center and are willing to pay enough for their housing to compensate for high land costs, the vast majority of those in the market for new housing choose suburban dwellings.

Thus the gray areas argument constitutes both an explanation of current population decline with its concomitant lack of new construction and a prediction of more widespread abandonment and stagnation in the coming decades. The argument rests on assumptions—drawn largely from current experience—about cost differentials between built-up and vacant land and assumptions about the extent of housing demand for inner locations. A further elaboration concerns the type of housing that people will choose. Multifamily housing can overcome high land costs through economies in the amount of land required for each unit. Yet, the mass market is for single-family houses, which require a lavish amount of land per unit. Although a certain portion of the population favors apartment living, it is expected that an increasing number in this group will want suburban locations.

On all these grounds, analysts of the gray areas foresee a bleak future. For the mass new housing market, the value of gray area land is expected to fall far short of its acquisition cost. The housing demand that remains for gray area locations is assumed to be too small to permit extensive rebuilding of the large residential sections that are becoming obsolete. In short, this hypothesis holds that the market for new housing will decisively reject locations in the declining neighborhoods in favor of suburban locations on vacant land.

As a result, new development in declining areas will require either tremendous public subsidies to wipe out current cost differentials between gray area sites and competitive vacant land, or a wait of many years until acquisition costs fall to low levels. Gray areas has become a pejorative term, synonymous with decay and stagnation.

Neighborhoods for Newcomers

This study will take issue with the basic perspective of the gray areas hypothesis and with many of its supporting assumptions. As a diagnosis of current trends, the gray areas view accurately identifies the *direction* of changes now under way. But it exaggerates the *rate* of change and thus leads to an ill-founded notion of the underutilization of older residential neighborhoods, with undesirable implications for public policy. The gray areas view thus poses a premature issue: how to accomplish the large-scale rebuilding of declining areas. These areas serve vital social purposes and will probably continue to do so for at least the next two decades: they provide housing for the poor and for the migrants now streaming into urban regions.

American cities have long been acquainted with migrations of the poor and the unassimilated. Traditionally, the big city has absorbed wave after wave of immigrant groups into American society. Although foreign immigration has now been reduced to a trickle, the movement of Negroes from the rural South to the central cities of the North presents a continuing challenge to public policy. The assimilation of newcomers is still an urgent problem in the city, and decent low-cost housing is a key requirement. The task of the next twenty years in most of our large cities is more properly one of renovating and preserving the old houses in order to prolong their usefulness during a period when they will be needed. Deteriorated areas that are truly ripe for clearance should be measured by the acre rather than by the square mile. The argument for selective clearance and gradual renewal will be developed and tested in the following chapters, but it can be summarized briefly here.

The use of old residential neighborhoods is closely linked to migration into urban areas. In the 1950's, record numbers of central-city residents moved out to the suburbs, leaving unoccupied living space in the older areas. At the same time migrants from the South and from Puerto Rico, like their counterparts from Europe fifty years ago, settled into old sections of the central cities.

Migration alone did not refill the vacant dwellings. High birth rates increased the size of minority groups already in the cities, and other families undoubled or moved into more spacious quarters. There was a general reduction in household size reflecting both a rising proportion of small households and an increase in dwelling space for the average household. On balance, most large central cities declined slightly in population in the 1950's, but their housing stock was still well utilized and vacancy rates were only moderate. Population loss thus had little to do with falling utilization of the housing stock. Instead, it made possible an upgrading of space standards for many families and enlarged the supply of housing for expanding low-income groups.

In time, urban minority groups—Negroes, Puerto Ricans, Mexican-Americans—will surely vacate the old neighborhoods in their search for better housing. But the present level of migration to the cities, the slow pace of minority movement from central cities to suburbs, and the high birth rates among incoming groups suggest that few cities will be ready for wholesale clearance within the next decade or two.

Housing in the declining areas is by no means uniformly substandard. Many of the structures do not conform to the tastes of the middle class today, but only a small proportion are seriously deteriorated or lack basic facilities. Moreover, much of the old housing has been improved. Private renovation in the 1950's upgraded a sizable proportion of formerly substandard units by combining small quarters into larger units and by installing new plumbing equipment. Since this housing is still very much in demand, any general clearance program would create considerable hardship unless alternate low-cost housing were provided. These circumstances argue for limiting clearance efforts to a scale consistent with the supply of vacant low-cost housing and removing only dilapidated or clearly substandard structures.

Public Policy Alternatives

Public policy is hemmed in by two types of constraints: the continuing need for old housing, which limits the amount of rebuilding that would be desirable at any given time, and the economics of developing new housing in the old areas, which limits the amount of new construction that can be financed without massive subsidies. Both constraints could be modified considerably by large-scale injections of government funds, either to provide subsidized housing alternatives for the poor who must otherwise occupy old housing or to make possible a profitable rebuilding by private interests. But given the present degree of government aid, or a moderate increase, the task of policymakers is to devise a course of action within the range of operations permitted by these dual constraints. The purpose of this study is to investigate the nature and extent of these limiting factors and suggest public policies consistent with them.

5

A first alternative for public policy is to await the gradual abandonment of declining areas and to defer rebuilding until few people are left and site acquisition costs have fallen to a low level. This policy is implicit in the gray areas hypothesis. It has some highly objectionable features, however. During the long period of abandonment, service costs would be high in relation to the number of people using local facilities. Streets, utilities, and public services would have to be maintained for a dwindling population. New capital investments in schools and environmental improvements would be difficult to justify against other claims on public funds since the life of many of these facilities would be short, geared to the life expectancy of the old housing. In all likelihood, public services would be cut back to minimum levels despite the needs of the people who remained.

In time, high vacancy rates would reduce acquisition costs sufficiently so that large-scale clearance and rebuilding could begin. Yet most areas would still be far from vacant at this point; perhaps half the dwelling units would still be occupied. The remaining residents are likely to be those with the greatest attachment to the community. They would have to be relocated, with all the well-known hardships that have already beset large redevelopment projects.

A second alternative is to rebuild declining areas gradually, so that new housing develops at the same time that demand for the old units declines. This pattern of change avoids the problems of underutilization by attracting new occupants throughout the transition period. A high level of services can be provided for the total population, while capital investments can be related to new housing as well as old. Further, residents would leave the area at times of their own choosing. The limited clearance of deteriorated and predominantly vacant structures would displace some people from time to time; but if they wished to remain in the area, they could move into other buildings with a longer useful life. Some old residents might move into the new buildings. Continual rebuilding would also broaden the range of residential choice for prospective tenants by offering them new housing and good local services at inner locations as well as in the suburbs.

In some cases, the physical constraints of gradual rebuilding will run counter to the desired direction of change. When the new func-

6

tion of an area requires a radically different land-use pattern with a complete reorganization of streets and utilities, rebuilding by small sections may prove impractical. Or if the new development is incompatible with housing—heavy industry, for example—partial redevelopment would deteriorate the environment still further for remaining residents. In general, a policy of slow rebuilding would involve more complex physical planning problems than a clean sweep, but only rarely are these problems likely to make a gradual approach unworkable. Where no compelling reasons dictate a choice of large-scale clearance, gradual rebuilding offers clear advantages in avoiding the problems of slow decline and subsequent dislocation.

A third alternative has actually characterized public policy in many big cities during the 1950's: the large-scale clearance of minority areas in an effort to rebuild them with expensive new developments intended for a middle- or upper-class market. In view of the continuing need for low-cost housing, this has been a socially objectionable policy. Regardless of the urban renewal objectives embodied in these programs, their result has generally been a self-defeating one of uprooting communities and shifting slum conditions to other neighborhoods. As these effects have become better understood, public policy has shifted toward improving old areas for their present occupants—an approach more in keeping with the second alternative of gradual rebuilding.

Feasibility of Gradual Rebuilding

A gradual replacement of worn-out housing may be socially desirable, but is it economically feasible? New construction could take many forms: shopping areas, factories, housing, community facilities. This study is limited to the feasibility of attracting new housing, with the assumption that supporting activities—shopping, schools, public facilities—will follow the housing pattern. It thus omits any consideration of industrial development or other forms of nonresidential construction which may replace old housing in many areas.

The feasibility of attracting new housing to old residential areas, as I define it, depends upon two sets of requirements. First, economic preconditions must be such that large public subsidies will

7

not be necessary to aid in purchasing cleared land for new housing. That is, the value or earning power of cleared land for new housing must be commensurate with its acquisition cost. Second, the demand for housing sites must be great enough to utilize all cleared land that is not needed for environmental improvements (schools, public works) within a reasonable number of years. This would mean that the surrounding environment must be improved sufficiently so that it will not obstruct new development and will, in fact, attract residents willing to pay the cost of new housing. To meet these requirements, it will be necessary to experiment with various types of neighborhood plans involving different proportions of clearance and rehabilitation and different treatments of the environment.

The current lack of new development in older areas does not necessarily mean that the economic prerequisites for rebuilding are missing. Even when an area meets the basic conditions for attracting new housing, further public action is usually necessary. In many cases, the present stagnation of older areas results from a failure to capitalize upon basically favorable economic circumstances.

Meeting the final conditions for rebuilding—upgrading the environment and replanning the neighborhood—will surely involve sizable outlays of public funds for new community facilities, for assistance in rehabilitation, and for general overhead. These expenditures will bring obvious benefits in terms of improved living conditions and prolonged usefulness of old residential areas. In each locality, these social benefits will have to be weighed against the costs involved and against alternative welfare policies. Except for a brief glance at cost levels, I shall not analyze the issues involved here in any detail. My concern in this part of the study is to determine whether the declining areas offer a reasonable economic basis for attracting new housing, provided that satisfactory environmental improvements are made.

Influence of Regional Structure

The first precondition for attracting new housing—a balance between site cost and re-use value—depends in part upon the characteristics of individual metropolitan regions. The structure of a region influences this balance in several ways:

8

1. The older areas, which are generally near the center of the region, may or may not derive special advantages from their location. Depending upon the strength and functional significance of the downtown core, the value of inlying housing sites may be considerable.
2. Alternate vacant sites may or may not be competitive with clearance areas, depending upon their respective locations and the regional transportation system.
3. The density of existing development, which influences its earning power and therefore the cost of site acquisition, varies considerably in the old residential areas of different regions, as well as within regions.

Aside from structural influences, regional differences in housing preferences, in public acceptance of high densities, and in the cost of new construction affect the feasibility of rebuilding declining areas.

New housing can be feasible in the declining areas under many different regional circumstances; no unique combination of factors is required. My detailed analyses cover three contrasting regions—New York, Los Angeles, and Hartford—in detail. Site costs and potential re-use values for new multifamily housing are roughly in balance in the declining sections of all three central cities. Housing demand need not favor central locations in order to bring land values in line with site costs. Centrality has little significance in the Los Angeles housing market; yet land costs are commensurate with potential returns from new housing in the aging inner areas of Los Angeles.

A factor of special significance in establishing current relationships between site costs and re-use values is the density of development before and after rebuilding. The density of existing housing in clearance areas has a major effect on land cost, with cost usually rising in direct relation to density. The density of new housing also affects the maximum land price that is feasible for new development: the higher the density, the higher the price that can be paid. When new buildings are developed at higher densities than existing structures on the site, as is generally the case in Los Angeles, the economics of new development permit an easy conversion of old housing to new. When preferences in the housing market dictate a

9

moderate reduction in density, as in parts of New York, such a change may also be possible. Only a radical downward break with the densities of the past is likely to create a wide gap between high site costs and low re-use values.

Demand for New Apartments

The second precondition for rebuilding calls for a balance between the amount of land to be cleared of deteriorated housing and the amount of land that can be utilized by new housing in the clearance areas. The cost of sites that must be cleared of old structures is generally too high to permit the use of the land for single-family houses. Thus the size of the market for new apartments is a basic factor in establishing the rate at which cleared sites can be rebuilt. Where the total demand for new apartments is small and cannot be increased, the rate of rebuilding must be slow.

Few large cities have so limited a demand for new apartments that a rebuilding of their declining areas is not feasible on these grounds alone. Only a portion of the demand can be attracted to the old areas, however, depending in part upon consumer locational preferences as well as upon the price of competitive sites and the comparative cost of developing and operating new housing in the old areas and alternate locations.

To judge how much of this new housing could occupy cleared sites in the declining neighborhoods requires a careful analysis of locational characteristics of the housing market in each metropolitan region. In two of the three regions that I have analyzed in detail, a sufficient amount of new apartment construction could potentially be drawn into the old locations to permit a reasonably rapid replacement of deteriorated housing. At current land consumption rates for such new housing, New York could rebuild its deteriorated areas in nine years. In Los Angeles, fourteen years would be required.

Of the three regions studied in detail, only Hartford would be unable to rebuild its cleared land in a reasonable time. Hartford's situation may be representative of small cities where the total current demand for new apartments is quite limited. Even if a significant part of this demand could be satisfied within the declining areas, the pace of land utilization would be slow, and several decades would be required before sites cleared of deteriorated housing could be rebuilt.

A glance at the sizable volume of apartment construction in large urban regions indicates that many have the raw material for a rebuilding program. In addition to New York and Los Angeles, the metropolitan regions of Chicago, Philadelphia, Washington, San Francisco, San Diego, Atlanta, Miami, Minneapolis, and Seattle all have been building a large number of apartment units in recent years.[2] The housing markets of these regions warrant a close examination to determine the extent to which new multifamily construction could serve as a basis for rebuilding their deteriorated areas in the near future.

Variations in Public Policy

Public policies for rebuilding can differ considerably in various cities, depending upon the presence or absence of the conditions necessary to attract new housing to the old residential areas. Where these preconditions are weak, as in Hartford, limited action to strengthen them may be possible through the general physical planning of the region. Changes in regional structure—the transportation system and the functional importance of the center—plus changes in the regulation of building on competitive sites may create additional demand for housing locations in the old neighborhoods. Federal action in the fields of housing and tax policy may foster demand for new apartments by reducing cost differentials that now favor homeownership. Barring such changes, the rebuilding of declining sections in these regions will have to proceed very slowly until such time as land costs fall, or rebuilding will have to be accomplished with the aid of sizable public subsidies.

In the large cities that already meet the prerequisites for rebuilding, public action will have to be taken to create the final conditions for integrating new and old housing. Individual neighborhoods will require many different types of treatment to provide satisfactory settings for new housing, and experimentation will be necessary to develop appropriate planning techniques. The gradual transformation of old areas will not be simple to manage, but with an economic basis assured, public policy can focus on detailed techniques for initiating and maintaining a steady rebuilding process.

11

CHAPTER TWO

THE CENTRAL CITY IN THE 1950's

PART 1: THE NATIONAL SCENE

The connection between migration and the fate of old neighborhoods is well enough established to take on the status of an urban American tradition. Thus the narrator of Philip Roth's *Goodbye, Columbus* visits the old Jewish section of a city and finds it now the heart of the Negro area:

> The neighborhood had changed: the old Jews like my grandparents had struggled and died, and their offspring had struggled and prospered, and moved further and further west, towards the edge of Newark, then out of it, and up the slope of the Orange Mountains, until they had reached the crest and started down the other side, pouring into Gentile territory as the Scotch-Irish had poured through the Cumberland Gap. Now, in fact, the Negroes were making the same migration, following the steps of the Jews, and those who remained in the Third Ward lived the most squalid of lives and dreamed in their fetid mattresses of the piny smell of Georgia nights.[1]

This dual movement of old groups and new provides a source of housing for the migrants and a market for the old structures. Currently, both movements are operating at record levels, with newcomers moving into the old neighborhoods almost as rapidly as their former residents desert them. Many central cities regard the loss of their former residents to the suburbs as a civic tragedy. Remaining occupants of the old areas, however, as well as the newcomers, have been well served by the great move to the suburbs in the 1950's. For the thinning out of population in central areas caused a gradual improvement of living conditions, with more interior space per person and an easing of the housing shortage of the early 1950's.

Still, the improvement has been modest, representing an inching up of housing standards rather than a dramatic rise. In most large cities, the gains of the past decade are tenuous as yet, and could be set back considerably by unwise public policies. Large-scale programs to clear the old residential areas pose a particular threat to the presently improving situation. As the housing market has been operating, the production of new units has barely taken care of new household formation, with just enough of a surplus to create a slight expansion in the general housing supply. If future production maintains the same relationship to growing demand, the destruction of a large number of old units would undo much of this expansion and plunge cities once again into a period of shortage and overcrowding.

To gauge the results of population shifts of the 1950's and their implications for the aging neighborhoods of American cities, I have looked briefly at the recent experience of central cities in the dozen largest metropolitan areas. Following this general survey, I have investigated New York, Los Angeles, and Hartford in more detail to determine the nature of the changes in their populations and in the occupancy of their housing and to discover the character of their declining sections. Specifically, I have attempted to discover: (1) whether the old housing is still utilized; (2) whether the new migrants are following close on the heels of their predecessors in leaving the older parts of the cities; and (3) whether new private construction shows any signs of replacing the old structures in these locations.

Migration to the City

The United States is now involved in a migration of historic proportions: the movement of Negroes from the rural South to the urban areas of the North. In the 1950's, net migration of nonwhites from the South was 1,457,000, only slightly less than that of 1,597,000 in the 1940's.[2] Figures on earlier migrations from Europe lend dramatic historical perspective to the current migration. The great Irish and German migrations of the 1850's each brought less than one million people to the United States in a decade. Peak Jewish migrations from 1900 to World War I were at the rate of

13

approximately one million per decade, while the Italian migration of 1901–1910 reached two million, but with a considerable backflow occurring simultaneously.[3] Thus the scale of the contemporary Negro migration exceeds that of most of the great European migrations of the past. In relation to total population, and to the housing resources of the big cities, this current migration is of course more limited in scope than the earlier ones. Nevertheless, it is one of the most striking population shifts of our time and perhaps the greatest challenge to the contemporary American city.

Nor is this movement of Negroes the only migration to the cities at the present time. Net migration from Puerto Rico to the mainland was 430,000 in the 1950's,[4] and other internal migrations of rural whites to the big cities are as yet uncounted. Taken together, these vast shifts in population have created problems that most of our big cities have not had to face since the early 1900's.

Are these migrations temporary phenomena destined to halt in the near future? The evidence does not support such an assumption, although the question is certainly debatable. Negro and Puerto Rican migrations have been large for some time. Yet several decades of out-migration from the South and from Puerto Rico have not even begun to exhaust the pool of remaining potential migrants. After years of exodus, more Negroes remain in the South and more Puerto Ricans remain on the island than ever before—thanks to high rates of population increase. Further industrial development in the South, however, and the achievement of a better balance between jobs and population, may well slow the pace of future out-migration, as it has already begun to do in Puerto Rico. A shrinking of low-skill employment in the big cities—which may be expected as a byproduct of automation—is also likely to discourage future migration. As the economic pull of the city weakens in relation to opportunities in rural areas over the next few decades, this movement of people will surely subside, but the change will probably come slowly unless the urban economy dips suddenly into a recession.

Natural increase has already begun to supplement migration as a factor in the growth of minority groups within the cities. The new migrants are young, and once settled in the big cities they tend to have large families. Whether or not migration rates drop, recent arrivals and their children will swell population pressures on the

14

urban housing stock. If these groups succeed in raising their incomes quickly, they may be able to take care of their increasing housing needs by moving outside the old residential areas. If the experience of earlier Negro arrivals is repeated, however, the newcomers will be slow to disperse from central cities to suburbs. The numerical growth of Negro population outside the central cities has been sizable, but it has been countered by ever-increasing concentrations in the core. In the twelve largest metropolitan regions, the proportion of nonwhites living in central cities actually increased from 77.8 per cent of total nonwhite population in 1930 to 80.7 per cent in 1950. Decentralization in the 1950's was extremely limited: as of 1960, 80.2 per cent of the nonwhites remained in central cities.[5]

Figure 2.1 traces the sharply contrasting distribution of whites and nonwhites from 1930 to 1960 in the central cities and suburban rings of the 168 metropolitan areas defined in the 1950 census. Both groups expanded greatly during these three decades. White population, however, leveled almost to a standstill in the central cities while increasing rapidly in the suburbs. The net result was a redistribution of white population by 1960, with the majority now living in suburban territory. The number of nonwhites has grown quickly throughout the metropolitan region, but growth has been faster in central cities than in outlying locations; nonwhites have thus concentrated increasingly in the core.

On balance, then, nonwhite increases have more than replaced white losses due to out-migration. Total central-city population increased steadily from 41.2 million in 1930 to 49.4 million in 1950 and 53.6 million in 1960. On the basis of numbers of inhabitants alone, the demand for central-city housing obviously increased during this period.

In the late 1950's, a series of population projections were prepared for the Commission on Race and Housing. These have been plotted on Figure 2.1 and indicate continuing population increase in the core cities to a total of 58.9 million in 1975. Comparison of these projections with actual population figures for 1960 further confirms the likelihood of mounting demand for central-city housing: as of 1960, white population in the central cities was within the projected range, but nonwhite population was even higher than the maximum projection.

15

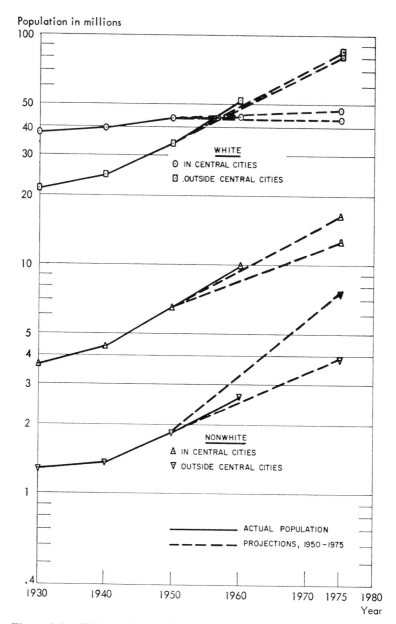

Population in millions

WHITE
O IN CENTRAL CITIES
☐ .OUTSIDE CENTRAL CITIES

NONWHITE
△ IN CENTRAL CITIES
▽ OUTSIDE CENTRAL CITIES

――――― ACTUAL POPULATION
― ― ― ― PROJECTIONS, 1950 –1975

Year

Figure 2.1.   White and nonwhite population in central cities and outlying
sections of 168 standard metropolitan areas, 1930–1960, with
projections to 1975.

Data cover the 168 standard metropolitan areas and their central cities as defined in the
1950 census. Corrections have not been made, however, to take account of (*a*) annexations

16

Despite the aggregate trends, many central cities lost population in the 1950's. The twelve largest metropolitan regions in 1960 differ in their experience from the 168 areas charted in Figure 2.1. As shown in Figure 2.2, nonwhite population in the twelve regions grew more rapidly in both central cities and suburbs, and whites left the core cities at a faster rate. Thus white population in the central cities dropped from 21.0 million in 1950 to 18.7 million in 1960, and nonwhite increases did not fully offset this decline. As a result, total central-city population in the twelve regions fell from 24.3 million to 23.9 million in the 1950's.

The central cities of these regions were the twelve largest in the country in 1950. By 1960, all but Los Angeles had lost population, while their metropolitan areas continued to expand. Population losses were relatively small, however, ranging from below 5 per cent in six of the cities up to 13 per cent in Boston (see Table 2.1). Nonwhite population, on the other hand, showed sizable rates of growth, reflecting heavy in-migration from the South as well as rapid natural increase among Negro families already in the cities by 1950.

The characteristic central-city combination of nonwhite expansion and white withdrawal may suggest a causal connection, but there is probably less in this situation than meets the eye. Middle-class dispersal to the suburbs is a long-standing trend that proceeded rapidly in the 1950's even in such cities as Minneapolis, where the Negro population is small. Similarly, a supply of housing left vacant by whites seems to have no major significance in drawing Negroes to particular cities; cities with tight housing supplies, such as New York, draw large numbers of migrants who crowd together in single rooms.

to central cities between 1930 and 1960, and (*b*) changes in metropolitan area boundaries resulting from new census definitions between 1950 and 1960. For 1960, area boundaries are those of the Standard Metropolitan Statistical Areas that had been created from the 168 Standard Metropolitan Areas of 1950. The net effect of these data limitations is a small overstatement of (*a*) the increase in white central-city population from 1930 to 1960, and (*b*) the increase in white population outside the central cities from 1950 to 1960.

Sources: Federal Housing Administration Division of Research and Statistics, Market Analysis Section, *Nonwhite Population Trends in Standard Metropolitan Areas, in Central Cities, and Outside Central Cities, 1930–1950* (August 15, 1953); Paul F. Coe, "Nonwhite Population Increases in Metropolitan Areas," *Journal of the American Statistical Association,* Vol. 40 (1955), Table 2, p. 288; *U.S. Census of Population: 1960, Number of Inhabitants, United States Summary,* Final Report PC (1)–1A, Table 33; *U.S. Census of Population: 1960, General Population Characteristics,* Final Report PC (1) series, volumes for separate states, Table 21; Davis McEntire, *Residence and Race* (Berkeley: University of California Press, 1960), Table 5, p. 22.

Population in millions

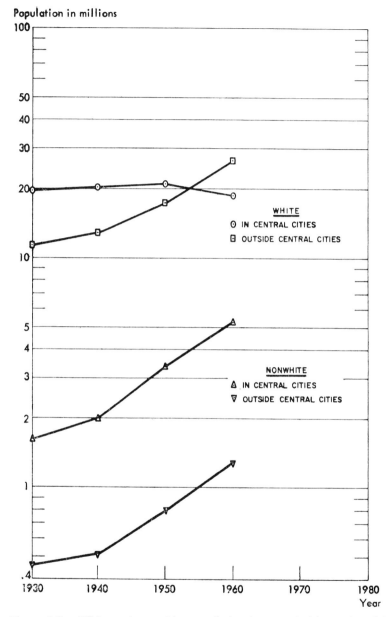

Figure 2.2. White and nonwhite population in central cities and outlying sections of twelve largest standard metropolitan areas (as of 1960), 1930–1960.

Data cover the following Standard Metropolitan Areas, as defined in the 1950 census: New York–Northeastern New Jersey, Los Angeles, Chicago, Philadelphia, Detroit, San Francisco–

18

Table 2.1. Population Changes, 1950–1960, in Twelve Largest Cities of 1950

	Total Population 1950	Per Cent Change 1950–1960	Nonwhite Population 1950	Per Cent Change 1950–1960
New York	7,891,957	−1.4	775,516	+47.2
Chicago	3,620,962	−1.9	509,437	+64.4
Philadelphia	2,071,605	−3.3	378,968	+41.2
Los Angeles	1,970,358	+25.8	211,585	+97.2
Detroit	1,849,568	−9.7	303,721	+60.4
Baltimore	949,708	−1.1	226,053	+45.3
Cleveland	914,808	−4.2	149,544	+69.3
St. Louis	856,796	−12.5	154,448	+39.9
Washington	802,176	−4.8	284,313	+47.3
Boston	801,444	−13.0	42,744	+60.2
San Francisco	775,357	−4.5	81,469	+66.8
Pittsburgh	676,806	−10.7	82,981	+22.6

Sources: Calculated from *U.S. Census of Population: 1950,* Vol. 2, *Characteristics of the Population,* Part 1, United States Summary, 1953, Table 86; *U.S. Census of Population: 1960, General Population Characteristics,* Final Report PC (1) series, 1961, volumes for each state, Table 20; *U.S. Census of Population: 1960,* Supplementary Reports PC(S1)–7, "Rank of Cities of 100,000 or More: 1960," June 16, 1961.

Implications for Housing

How have these population shifts affected the utilization of housing in the big cities? In 1950, housing was in short supply in all major cities. Gross vacancy rates (including substandard units) were below 3 per cent in eleven of the twelve largest cities (Table 2.2). More to the point, net rates of sound vacant units were well below 2 per cent in all but Los Angeles.

By 1960, vacancy rates were beginning to reach the 5 per cent level that housing economists have long considered the desirable minimum to facilitate normal turnover and mobility. The significant measure of vacancies is the proportion of sound housing units available for rent or sale. In terms of this measure, only three cities —Los Angeles, Detroit, and San Francisco—had achieved a satis-

Oakland, Boston, Pittsburgh, St. Louis, Washington, D. C., Cleveland, and Baltimore. Central-city population figures have not been corrected to take account of changes resulting from annexations. San Francisco and Oakland have been treated as a single central city.

Sources: Federal Housing Administration Division of Research and Statistics, Market Analysis Section, *Nonwhite Population Trends in Standard Metropolitan Areas, in Central Cities, and Outside Central Cities, 1930–1950* (August 15, 1953); Donald J. Bogue. *The Population of the United States* (Glencoe: Free Press, 1959), Table 7–21, p. 148; *U.S. Census of Population: 1960, Number of Inhabitants, United States Summary,* Final Report PC (1)–1A, Tables 31, 32, 33, 37; *U.S. Census of Population: 1960, General Population Characteristics,* Final Report PC (1) series, volumes for separate states, Tables 13, 21, 25, 27.

Table 2.2. Selected Housing Characteristics, 1950–1960, in Twelve Largest Cities of 1950

	Nonseasonal Dwelling Units 1950	Per Cent Vacant 1950	Nonseasonal Housing Units 1960	Per Cent Vacant 1960	Per Cent of Nonseasonal Units Vacant and Available in Sound Condition		Number and Per Cent of Nonseasonal Units with 1.01 or More Occupants per Room			
							1950		1960	
					1950	1960	Number	Per Cent	Number	Per Cent
New York	2,406,169	1.8	2,735,272	3.0	1.1	2.0	386,167	16.7	325,060	12.2
Chicago	1,105,692	1.5	1,212,264	4.5	0.8	3.7	163,007	15.2	135,880	11.7
Philadelphia	599,126	2.3	647,914	5.0	1.3	3.4	56,405	9.8	45,206	7.3
Los Angeles	697,620	4.2	933,354	6.1	2.7	4.9	65,822	10.0	72,007	8.2
Detroit	521,988	1.7	552,050	6.7	1.0	5.6	51,787	10.2	45,126	8.8
Baltimore	277,527	3.1	289,734	4.9	1.8	3.7	31,675	12.0	29,010	10.5
Cleveland	270,846	1.6	282,358	4.4	0.9	3.4	26,645	10.1	27,686	9.8
St. Louis	262,873	1.7	262,383	5.2	0.7	3.8	53,521	20.4	40,842	16.4
Washington	229,609	2.0	262,287	3.9	1.2	3.0	31,035	14.1	31,157	12.4
Boston	221,974	1.7	237,596	5.5	0.9	3.9	27,261	12.7	17,956	8.0
San Francisco	265,614	2.7	291,975	6.1	1.5	4.9	19,481	7.3	19,060	6.5
Pittsburgh	193,780	1.4	195,646	3.7	0.8	2.7	32,437	16.7	19,622	10.4

Sources: Calculated from *U.S. Census of Housing: 1950*, Vol. 1, *General Characteristics*, Part 1: U.S. Summary, 1953, Tables 27, 29; *U.S. Census of Housing: 1960*, Advance Reports, *Housing Characteristics: States*, HC(A1), Table 1; *U. S. Census of Housing: 1960*, Vol. 3, *City Blocks*, Series HC(3), 1961, Table 1. Units classified as vacant and available in sound condition are year-round, nondilapidated units available for rent or sale.

factory level by 1960, but the rest had improved notably since 1950. New York continued to have a tight housing supply, with only 2 per cent vacant and available, but the others all reached rates of 2.7 per cent or more. *In no case did vacancy levels climb enough to suggest a city-wide surplus of housing.*

Still another test of the adequacy of the supply is the number of persons per room in occupied housing units. Table 2.2 presents comparative information for 1950 and 1960 on the number of units with more than one person per room. In all twelve cities, the *proportion* of units with more than one person per room declined from 1950 to 1960. From a social welfare point of view, city housing policies should aim also at a reduction in the *absolute* extent of overcrowding. Of the twelve cities, eight reported fewer units with more than one person per room in 1960 than in 1950, two reported about the same number, and two more reported an increase in absolute number.

This comparison requires qualification, however. As a result of changes in the types of units enumerated in the census, many single-room dwellings were counted in 1960 but not in 1950. In cities where a considerable number of families live in one-room units, as in New York, 1950 figures understate the extent of overcrowding. Consequently, the 1950–1960 increase in residential space per person was probably greater in a number of large cities than the census data show.

The changing character of urban households has had much to do with this improvement in space standards. Families have "undoubled" to occupy separate quarters; parents have kept their large apartments after grown children have left. Further, a process of increasing residential specialization has been under way. Families with young children have chosen to live in the suburbs, while newly married couples and older people have concentrated in central cities. The resulting drop in average household size is evident in Table 2.2: even while total population declined in eleven of the twelve central cities, the number of housing units generally increased between 1950 and 1960.

Along with population shifts, there has been a striking physical adaptation of the old housing to meet changing needs in the cities. Two common types of alteration are the conversion of large apartments into smaller ones and the merger of small units to make more

21

Table 2.3. Changes in Housing Inventory, 1950–1959, in Twelve Largest Metropolitan Regions

Region (Standard Consolidated Area or Standard Metropolitan Statistical Area)	1950 Dwelling Units Changed by Conversion or Merger, 1950–1959		Dwelling Units Substandard in 1950 and Renovated (In sound condition with all plumbing facilities) in 1959			
			Nondilapidated units lacking one or more plumbing facilities in 1950		Dilapidated Units in 1950	
	Conversion	Merger	Total reported 1950 and 1959	Per cent renovated in 1959	Total reported 1950 and 1959	Per cent renovated in 1959
New York SCA	95,215	91,582	184,985	53.8	110,670	56.4
Chicago SCA	34,246	51,996	145,680	53.1	47,676	58.1
Philadelphia SMSA	29,330	38,374	59,514	53.9	24,651	55.9
Los Angeles–Long Beach SMSA	11,331	15,712	19,500	63.2	31,394	62.3
Detroit SMSA	14,353	30,932	47,738	63.3	17,969	62.8
Baltimore SMSA	15,834	34,359	36,534	69.1	10,343	83.2
Cleveland SMSA	6,314	12,160	15,665	52.9	13,081	35.1
St. Louis SMSA	11,115	25,137	86,057	45.2	20,686	38.9
Washington, D.C. SMSA	5,802	25,806	17,849	53.1	2,844	44.4
Boston SMSA	15,686	17,290	34,251	60.7	18,344	65.3
San Francisco–Oakland SMSA	8,603	19,652	18,333	39.4	15,542	66.9
Pittsburgh SMSA	16,962	68,599	90,567	52.0	22,152	44.7

Source: U.S. Census of Housing: 1960, Vol. 4, Components of Inventory Change, Final Report HC(4), Part 1A, for respective metropolitan regions, Tables 3 and 5.

spacious quarters. The dominant trend of the 1950's was the merger rather than the conversion. Table 2.3 presents information on remodeling and rehabilitation in the dozen largest metropolitan regions. Except in the New York area, consolidations exceeded conversions by a sizable margin.

Aside from an easing of housing shortages and overcrowding, the quality of old housing also improved in the last decade. *In cities of over 100,000 population, 2.6 million units — 20 per cent of the housing stock — were substandard in 1950. By 1960, a combination of renovation and demolition had reduced this number to 2.0 million, or 11 per cent of the total.*[6] Here, too, the extent of improvement was striking. In the dozen largest metropolitan areas, more than half the substandard units of 1950 that were surveyed in 1959 had been put into sound condition through repairs or plumbing additions (Table 2.3). Powerful forces have been at work in the private housing market to improve conditions in the cities. Public policy could make a major contribution toward raising environmental standards by nurturing and promoting this type of rehabilitation in the old areas.

Extent of Housing Improvement

Does this reallocation and remodeling of the old housing represent merely a first reaction to the availability of surplus housing, soon to be followed by a sharp drop in the demand for the old buildings? A closer look at the distribution of housing gains will demonstrate that large numbers of families have not yet shared in the general improvement of the 1950's and that newly arrived migrants are still overcrowded and badly housed. Certainly the need for more space and better housing — at prices the poor can afford — is far from satisfied. This social need is likely also to mean a sizable effective demand for the old housing, provided that the incomes of presently disadvantaged groups rise enough to permit them to leave overcrowded and substandard quarters.

Negroes and other minorities improved their housing in the 1950's, but less so than the white population. Their gains were primarily in the improvement of housing quality; overcrowding was not reduced significantly by 1960. Comparative information on 1950–1960 changes in housing quality and occupancy is available by race for eight of the twelve largest metropolitan regions.

Table 2.4. Substandard Housing* in Selected Metropolitan Areas, 1950 and 1960

Metropolitan Area 1950: Standard Metropolitan Area 1960: Standard Metropolitan Statistical Area or Standard Consolidated Area	Whites† 1950 Substandard dwelling units Number	Per cent of total	1960 Substandard housing units Number	Per cent of total	Units Occupied by: Nonwhites 1950 Substandard dwelling units Number	Per cent of total	1960 Substandard housing units Number	Per cent of total	Whites with Spanish Names 1950 Substandard dwelling units Number	Per cent of total	1960 Substandard housing units Number	Per cent of total
New York (SMA–SCA)	348,000	9.9	228,000	5.4	86,000	33.8	108,000	23.0				
Chicago (SMA–SCA)	256,000	17.6	121,000	6.8	91,000	59.3	69,000	25.4				
Philadelphia (SMA–SMSA)	89,000	10.0	34,000	3.1	53,000	42.8	25,000	13.8				
Los Angeles (SMA–SMSA)	112,000	8.2	66,000	3.2	14,000	19.0	11,000	6.2	23,000	32.2	14,000	8.6
Detroit (SMA–SMSA)	76,000	10.1	33,000	3.6	22,000	29.3	15,000	10.3				
St. Louis (SMA–SMSA)	123,000	28.1	60,000	11.1	43,000	75.0	32,000	39.4				
Washington, D.C. (SMA–SMSA)	27,000	8.0	17,000	3.7	25,000	33.9	17,000	13.6				
San Francisco–Oakland (SMA–SMSA)	60,000	9.1	41,000	5.0	14,000	25.6	15,000	14.9	4,000	16.1	4,000	7.9

* Substandard units are either dilapidated or lacking one or more plumbing facilities.
† Including whites with Spanish names.

Sources for Tables 2.4 and 2.5: Davis McEntire, *Residence and Race* (Berkeley: University of California Press, 1960), Tables 14 and 15, pp. 123, 127; *U.S. Census of Housing: 1950,* Vol. 1, *General Characteristics,* volumes for each state, Tables 17, 21a; *U.S. Census of Housing: 1960,* Vol. 1, *States and Small Areas,* Final Reports HC(1) series, volumes for each state, Tables 12, 15, 38, 41.

Boundaries of the metropolitan areas are the same for 1950 and 1960, with the following exceptions:

1. Chicago Standard Consolidated Area of 1960 includes two counties outside the 1950 Standard Metropolitan area. These counties had a 1960 population of 144,489, including 212 nonwhites, of a total of 6.8 million in the Standard Consolidated Area.
2. St. Louis Standard Metropolitan Statistical Area of 1960 includes one county outside the 1950 Standard Metropolitan Area. This county had a 1960 population of 66,377, including 855 nonwhites, of a total of 2.0 million in the Standard Metropolitan Statistical Area.

The data, presented in Tables 2.4 and 2.5, cover each region as a whole rather than the central city alone, but figures for nonwhites basically describe the central cities where they are concentrated.

Within these regions, nonwhites as well as whites generally made both proportional and absolute gains in reducing the extent of substandard conditions in their housing. In terms of overcrowding, however, nonwhites made only small proportional gains; the *number* of overcrowded units increased consistently both for nonwhites and for Mexican-Americans (the latter enumerated only in Los Angeles and San Francisco–Oakland). Since census coverage expanded in 1960 to include many single-room units that were not counted in 1950, much of this statistical increase may reflect no more than a definitional change; but it is clear in any case that reductions in overcrowding were very limited for the nonwhite population.

The rate of improvement in housing during the 1950's and the extent of the remaining problem make it clear that the goal of a decent home for every American family is still far from achievement. Yet the migration of the poor to the cities, which seemingly accounts for much overcrowding and continuing use of substandard housing, in itself represents an improvement at the national level. Negroes leave shacks in the rural South that are lacking plumbing, heating, and even electricity; although their first homes in urban slums may be little better, within a few years many find adequate housing and almost all find a life that offers better opportunities than the one they left behind. Nationally, 45 per cent of housing occupied by nonwhites was substandard in 1960.[7] In metropolitan regions covered in Table 2.4, the typical range varies from 10 to 25 per cent.

While the migration continues, an important task for public policy in the big cities is to help the poor find decent housing. When the poor are Negroes, the problem takes on an additional dimension. *It is evident from the experience of the 1950's that housing abandoned by the white middle classes in their move to the suburbs has not been reallocated equally to Negroes and whites.* One of the great challenges to American democracy is to remove barriers of racial prejudice, and to make housing available to all racial groups on equal terms. Racial segregation, as well as poverty, has limited the housing gains of Negroes in metropolitan areas.

Table 2.5. Overcrowded Housing* in Selected Metropolitan Areas, 1950 and 1960

Metropolitan Area 1950: Standard Metropolitan Area 1960: Standard Metropolitan Statistical Area or Standard Consolidated Area	Whites† 1950 Overcrowded dwelling units		Whites† 1960 Overcrowded housing units		Nonwhites 1950 Overcrowded dwelling units		Nonwhites 1960 Overcrowded housing units		Whites with Spanish Names 1950 Overcrowded dwelling units		Whites with Spanish Names 1960 Overcrowded housing units	
	Number	Per cent of total	Number	Per cent of total	Number	Per cent of total	Number	Per cent of total	Number	Per cent of total	Number	Per cent of total
New York (SMA–SCA)	436,000	12.4	361,000	8.6	62,000	24.4	105,000	22.3				
Chicago (SMA–SCA)	170,000	11.7	151,000	8.5	55,000	35.9	74,000	27.3				
Philadelphia (SMA–SMSA)	64,000	7.1	53,000	4.9	27,000	21.9	30,000	16.3				
Los Angeles (SMA–SMSA)	133,000	9.7	163,000	8.0	16,000	22.7	30,000	17.4	27,000	37.2	42,000	26.9
Detroit (SMA–SMSA)	72,000	9.6	80,000	8.6	19,000	25.3	26,000	17.5				
St. Louis (SMA–SMSA)	73,000	16.6	64,000	11.8	20,000	35.2	23,000	28.0				
Washington, D.C. (SMA–SMSA)	31,000	9.3	29,000	6.2	21,000	28.7	29,000	22.6				
San Francisco-Oakland (SMA–SMSA)	51,000	7.8	49,000	6.0	16,000	29.8	19,000	19.7	5,000	21.7	8,000	16.5

* Overcrowded units defined as those with 1.01 or more occupants per room.
† Including whites with Spanish names.

Sources: See Table 2.4.

Segregation and the Housing Problem

The vast increase in Negro population during the 1950's was not distributed generally throughout metropolitan areas. It was concentrated in the central cities, and within these cities it was concentrated in areas where the previous population was predominantly Negro. Washington, D. C. is a particularly striking example of the residential *apartheid* in the American city. Between 1950 and 1960, the nonwhite population of the metropolitan area grew by 157,000. Eighty-five per cent of this increase took place in the central city. By 1960, nonwhites were a majority in Washington, with 54.8 per cent of the population — a proportion far higher than in any other large American city.

In this predominantly nonwhite city, one might naturally expect to find most people living in racially mixed neighborhoods, with Negroes spreading into new locations as they grow in number. The opposite is true: the bulk of the nonwhite population lives in neighborhoods that are virtually all-colored, while most whites live in areas that Negroes have barely entered. Further, nonwhite growth during the 1950's increased the degree of racial segregation by building up Negro concentrations in areas that were already heavily Negro and adding only slightly to Negro population in mixed areas.

The extent of racial segregation in a city is not easy to measure. Of the various measurement techniques that have been proposed, the most applicable one in general use requires classifying small areas of a city — census tracts, generally — according to their proportion of nonwhite population. The proportion of total nonwhite population living in tracts that are predominantly nonwhite then indicates the degree to which residential areas are segregated. In Washington, the proportion of total nonwhite population living in tracts that were more than 75 per cent nonwhite rose from 37.3 per cent in 1940 to 51.8 per cent in 1950 and 70.7 per cent in 1960.[8] If the increase in Negro population over this period had followed the locational pattern of Negroes already in Washington in 1940, the proportion of nonwhites in highly segregated tracts would have remained constant. But from decade to decade, Negro population grew faster in segregated neighborhoods than in mixed areas. Thus nonwhites have become increasingly concentrated in segregated

27

areas not only in Washington but in almost every American city for which information is available.[9]

This characteristic growth pattern means that incoming Negro migrants settle in areas that are heavily Negro, while relatively fewer Negroes break out of segregated neighborhoods into districts with a higher proportion of whites. The bulk of the white population continues to live in areas where Negroes are barely noticeable. Even in Washington, where Negroes are a majority, 44.6 per cent of the white population lived in tracts that were less than 10 per cent nonwhite in 1960, and 79.3 per cent in tracts that were less than 50 per cent nonwhite.

The forces underlying this increase in segregation are well known. For the newcomers, segregation may well be voluntary in part, but Negroes who have long been in the city still cannot move about freely. Social mobility has a different meaning for Negroes than for whites: whites can move to the suburbs or choose any of a number of city neighborhoods to live in when their incomes rise and their housing standards change; Negroes are severely limited in their choice of neighborhood and consequently in their choice of housing. Because of this limited residential mobility, Negroes compete for housing in a restricted market where good housing is scarce and where, for any given level of housing, prices are higher than in the white market.[10] The effects of racial discrimination in housing are profound and go far beyond questions of mere physical shelter. Segregation in housing becomes a basis for other kinds of segregation, particularly in the assignment of children to school districts, and a bar to social and economic progress as well as personal fulfillment. For all these reasons, as well as on general grounds of social justice, the Negro housing problem is an urgent matter for public attention.

One way to alleviate this problem is to promote the movement of Negroes into housing vacancies created by the white migration to the suburbs. And, clearly, one way to maintain the walls of discrimination is to destroy surplus housing in the declining white areas while Negroes are still concentrated elsewhere in bad housing and segregated neighborhoods. As vacancies develop in the central cities, property owners will find themselves under economic pressure to deal with any potential tenants or purchasers, regardless of race or social status. If the vacant units are in sound condition or can be renovated, policies designed to prolong their life can ultimately improve housing conditions for Negroes and break down neighborhood segregation.

It may be argued that saving vacant housing in the core cities for Negroes will solve their shelter problems at the expense of reinforcing central-city segregation and that the first goal of public policy must be to achieve a more balanced distribution of Negroes between cities and suburbs. Two points are important in considering this issue. First, the extreme segregation of Negroes *within* central cities has already been noted; there is much room for achieving a more balanced racial composition of neighborhoods within the cities themselves as well as between cities and suburbs. Second, for some disadvantaged groups of Negroes, better housing is still likely to be a more pressing priority than racial integration.

Lorraine Hansberry has drawn a memorable picture of the difference in outlook between the first and second generation of Negro city-dwellers. To the generation that moved from the South, the important goals were physical security and decent living conditions, but their children are driven by different needs. In *A Raisin in the Sun,* the older generation cannot grasp the change:

> You something new, boy. In my time we was worried about not being lynched and getting to the North if we could and how to stay alive and still have a pinch of dignity too. . . . Now here come you and Beneatha — talking 'bout things we ain't never even thought about hardly, me and your daddy. You ain't satisfied or proud of nothing we done. I mean that you had a home; that we kept you out of trouble till you was grown; that you don't have to ride to work on the back of nobody's streetcar — You my children — but how different we done become.[11]

Perhaps the issue of housing *versus* segregation can best be regarded as a succession of needs, with the migrant newcomer needing safe and sanitary housing and the more urbanized Negro needing residential mobility. From this perspective, there is no real conflict: public policy should aim both at improving housing conditions for Negroes and reducing segregation in the city. Both objectives are important and both are related, but it would be premature to concentrate entirely on enlarging the range of locational choice for Negroes while so many are still badly housed.

Constraints on Rebuilding

Despite the fears of many cities about losing their middle classes and despite their inclination to regard population decline as a symbol of municipal decay, both these developments have been necessary in order to achieve reasonable vacancy levels and to relieve overcrowding. Unless the patterns of population movement and housing development change radically in the near future, large cities will have to continue to lose population if they are to provide decent living conditions for the migrants of the mid-twentieth century.

The extent of substandard housing remaining in 1960 and the clear need to retain much of the old housing in central cities for the use of the poor and the newcomers set major constraints on rebuilding declining areas. Yet a certain amount of reconstruction will surely be desirable, even if only to remove substandard housing that can make no contribution to raising living standards. The economics of rebuilding, however, set further constraints on how much can be accomplished and how it can be done.

PART 2: THREE CASE STUDIES

Of the three metropolitan regions I have surveyed in detail, New York, the great urban center of the East Coast, is the traditional absorber of immigrants and an exaggerated prototype of the older American cities now being transformed to meet new ways of life; Los Angeles, the giant metropolis of the West Coast, is an equally extreme symbol of the new American city; and Hartford is a small metropolitan area representative of the many American cities whose rates of growth have been sufficiently moderate to retain considerable flexibility for future development.

The three study areas contrast in a number of structural features that relate in theory to the demand for new housing in central locations — the locations now being abandoned in the push to the suburbs. The body of theoretical literature on this subject is reviewed in Appendix C, and relevant characteristics of the three study areas are presented in detail in Chapter 3. Briefly, structural features of major interest are the strength of the downtown core and the access advantages of declining locations over competitive vacant sites for new housing. New York is a center-oriented region;

Los Angeles is extremely decentralized; and Hartford has a moderately strong core but a large supply of vacant land highly accessible to the center.

These regions all have their declining sections, differing in extent but similar in many ways. All are characterized by central location, a concentration of old housing, the thinning out of former residents, and a rapid growth of low-income groups. Further, all these sections are still well utilized, and their new low-income occupants show few signs of joining the march to the suburbs in the near future. Declining areas in the three regions display varying ability to attract new housing. I shall discuss their prospects for rebuilding in Chapters 4 and 5.

New York Region: Population Shifts

The decade from 1950 to 1960 was one of profound and sweeping change for the New York metropolitan region. The major central cities — New York, Newark, Jersey City — all lost population. Data cited in Appendix A indicate a combined drop of 166,000 from a 1950 population of 8.6 million in the central cities of the New York region, which represented a loss of 1.9 per cent. When population change is analyzed separately for whites and nonwhites, a more striking picture of massive residential shifts becomes clear. The push to the suburbs involved a net out-migration of 1,294,000 non-Puerto Rican whites from New York City alone. Movement to the city from outside the area was smaller, consisting of a net in-migration of 163,000 nonwhites and 274,000 Puerto Ricans. High birth rates among Puerto Ricans and Negroes accounted for further gains in the City, while natural increase among remaining whites helped counter the huge white out-migration. Three boroughs of New York City — Manhattan, the Bronx, and Brooklyn — plus the declining cities of Newark and Jersey City, on balance lost a total of 1,002,000 non-Puerto Rican whites but gained 443,000 Puerto Ricans and 340,000 nonwhites.[12]

Are Negroes and Puerto Ricans likely to disperse rapidly from the central locations they now occupy? *Relative* diffusion of the Negro population has been under way for some time,[13] and a similar pattern is detectable among Puerto Ricans, but two qualifications are important. First, the decentralization has been solely relative, with Negro and Puerto Rican populations continuing to grow in

31

absolute terms in *all* central cities and boroughs. Second, even the relative dispersal has been proceeding at a glacierlike pace, except for shifts within the central cities themselves.

Appendix Table A.1.3 depicts the regional decentralization of Negroes from 1950 to 1960. Manhattan's share of the regional total dropped markedly from 37.9 per cent to 25.5 per cent, while New York City outside Manhattan increased its proportion of the total from 35.8 to 44.4 per cent, and the two New Jersey cities also registered proportional increases. According to migration estimates, Manhattan even had a net out-migration of 40,000 nonwhites. But the proportional decentralization has not yet been reflected in absolute numbers. Manhattan and the remainder of the central cities all *gained* Negro population; and the position of the central cities relative to the entire region barely changed at all, moving from 83.2 per cent of total regional Negro population in 1950 to 81.1 per cent in 1960.

Information on the Puerto Rican population is not available at the regional level, but relative shifts from Manhattan to the Bronx and Brooklyn seem to be under way. Between 1956 and 1960, Manhattan's share of total Puerto Rican enrollment in New York City schools fell from 43.4 to 36.9 per cent while the Bronx and Brooklyn gained correspondingly (Table A.1.4). Once again, the shift was purely relative, however, for Puerto Rican school enrollment *increased* in Manhattan during this period.

At the neighborhood level, Negroes remained highly segregated in New York City. Four large concentrations contained over 80 per cent of the City's Negro population in 1960: Harlem, the traditional center of Negro life in Manhattan; the Morrisania section of the Bronx; the Bedford-Stuyvesant area of Brooklyn; and a newly expanding settlement in the South Jamaica–St. Albans section of Queens.[14] Harlem passed its population peak and began to thin out in the 1950's; Morrisania continued to grow, but at a slower rate than in previous decades; Negro population continued to multiply rapidly in the other two neighborhoods. Of these high-growth areas, South Jamaica–St. Albans contains much good housing, but the Bedford-Stuyvesant section of Brooklyn is one of the worst slums in the City. Here continued concentration of Negroes encourages both substandard living conditions and racial segregation. In general, the degree of segregation has declined slightly since

1950, but in 1960 62.7 per cent of New York's nonwhites still lived in neighborhoods where they constituted more than 50 per cent of the population.

This limited dispersal suggests that an increasing proportion of the expanding Negro and Puerto Rican population will continue to locate outside the old central areas. Yet the limited scope of recent decentralization also suggests that in the near future prospects for a further depopulation of the declining areas will depend primarily upon the continuing drift to the suburbs of white, non-Puerto Rican residents. It is also clear that minority groups still constitute a large reservoir of potential demand for housing in the declining neighborhoods and that a turnover of the newly vacated units to Negroes and Puerto Ricans can help them to achieve both better living circumstances and a less segregated way of life.

Population and Housing Demand in the New York Region

The housing demand that a given population generates depends directly upon its organization into households. Provided that there is adequate earning power for each household to afford a separate dwelling unit, the more households in a population, the more dwelling units it will occupy. Changing population totals do not in themselves indicate even the direction of change in housing units required. When population declines, a shift to smaller average household sizes can nevertheless produce a demand for increased housing resources. This has been the experience of areas losing population in the New York region.

White and nonwhite components of the population generate very different housing demands in the New York area. Appendix Table A.1.5 illuminates some of the significant differences between the two populations. The white population is an older one, with a smaller proportion below the age of 18 and a greater proportion aged 65 and over in the region at large and in the central-city areas of population loss. Differences between the two racial groups have become more pronounced since 1950, with notable increases in the proportion of nonwhites under 18 and the proportion of whites 65 and over. In addition, the age distribution of the white population in the central cities has climbed upward from that of the white population in the region at large during the 1950's, with a substantially smaller proportion under 18 and a larger proportion 65 and over.

White population in the old neighborhoods has come to consist more and more of small households, generating a demand for many housing units. This change is part of a long-term trend noticeable in New York since the end of the nineteenth century.[15] Its immediate significance is clear: it accounts for continued use of old housing, even when total population declines. But its long-range importance for the use of old housing is still more important. Reductions in household size result only in part from changes in the number of children per family. They result also from rising incomes, which enable grown children to set up their own households earlier, older people to live in their own quarters, and relatives other than the immediate family to move out on their own. Among poor people, members of the "extended family" are often part of the household: an elderly uncle, unmarried brother-in-law, a cousin who is not steadily employed. Rising incomes have had much to do with the long-term reduction in household size in New York and elsewhere. But many groups in the population — particularly the newly arrived Negroes and Puerto Ricans — still lack the income to permit a general undoubling into small households. As their incomes rise in the future, they will generate additional demands for old housing.

As of 1960, changing household size resulted in continued use of old housing. The best evidence is the low vacancy rate. The New York region outside the central cities had a vacancy rate of 3.7 per cent in 1960. The central cities had lower vacancy rates, except for Newark with 5.2 per cent (Table A.1.8). These rates include vacant units in substandard condition. The vacancy reserve of housing in sound condition that could be used for relocating displaced people is much lower (Table A.1.9); in Brooklyn and the Bronx it has increased only slightly since 1950.

Further, only part of this reserve consists of housing within the means of low-income families. The Manhattan vacancy reserve of 2.5 per cent undoubtedly includes many apartments in new luxury buildings not yet fully rented at the time of the 1960 census. Numerous surveys in Manhattan have shown higher vacancy rates in new buildings than in old. Surveys of vacancies in old-law tenements (built before 1901) have indicated a decline

34

from 16 per cent in 1944 to 0.1 per cent in 1954.[16] Additional evidence of a severe shortage of low-cost housing in New York appears in the experience of families receiving City welfare aid and living in single furnished rooms: of 14,000 families in this category in 1960, 10,000 paid rents ranging from $60 to $200 per month for "essentially slum accommodations."[17]

With the possible exception of Newark, the declining sections of the New York region appear still to be heavily utilized as residential areas. As of 1960, the vacancies left by families moving to the suburbs were well filled; and the slow rate of decentralization among low-income minorities ensures a steady demand for the old housing for some time to come.

Why have New York's declining areas remained so fully occupied? Their high degree of occupancy is particularly striking in view of the age and deterioration of much of the housing stock. More than one third of the nontransient dwelling units in Manhattan in 1960 were in old-law tenements built before 1901; 20 per cent of the nontransient units in Brooklyn and 7 per cent of those in the Bronx in 1960 were also in old-law tenements. In New York City as a whole, 16 per cent of the housing units were classified as deteriorating or dilapidated in the 1960 Housing Census. Substandard conditions were still more evident in the other central cities, with 29 per cent of the housing units in Newark and 19 per cent of those in Jersey City deteriorating or dilapidated.[18]

One reason for the continued utilization of old housing in New York is that, as in most big cities, the old units have made possible a raising of housing standards. Although vacancy reserves are still low in New York, overcrowding has been reduced notably since 1950. Units with more than one occupant per room have declined in absolute number as well as in proportion to total housing in all central cities of the region (Table A.1.9). In this sense, intense use of the old areas reflects a general desire for more residential space and reflects also the failure of the housing market to provide alternate low-cost housing capable of meeting this need.

Beyond this typical situation for big cities, New York has some special characteristics that promote continued use of the central areas. Rent control is one of these special factors. In New York City, rents are still controlled by law in many apartments completed before the end of World War II. Rent levels in controlled apartments are substantially lower than those in typical postwar units. The effects are likely to (1) encourage people to remain in old central housing rather than move to the suburbs, and (2) encourage older couples who no longer need large apartments to hold them rather than look for expensive smaller apartments in new buildings.

Although the metropolitan structure of New York may be expected to produce more clear-cut effects in the market for new housing, it is likely also to influence the utilization of older housing. The New York region exemplifies a structure that is theoretically highly favorable for inlying housing: the core is a powerful magnet, and vacant sites for new development are far removed from the center. These factors can make old housing in central areas more attractive than it would be in a region with a weaker core or with highly accessible vacant land.

Rebuilding the Declining Areas

A full consideration of prospects for rebuilding the old areas will be postponed until later chapters, but a few observations are in order here. Areas that have declined in population cover a large part of the central cities. Tabulations for small statistical districts in New York City indicate that declining areas blanket all of Manhattan, large parts of Brooklyn and the Bronx, and the inner parts of Queens.[19] These sections differ considerably. Some are occupied by old-law tenements with densities exceeding 250 dwelling units per acre of residential land; others by brownstones at lower densities; and still others in Brooklyn, the Bronx, and Queens by small structures with densities ranging from 20 to 100 units per acre. Some, in and near Manhattan, have obvious access advantages to the central business district; others, in mid-Bronx and Brooklyn, involve fairly long trips to the core. Some have high proportions of deteriorated housing, and some have such major social problems as juvenile delinquency and broken families. All these characteristics play a part in determining the attractiveness of such areas for new housing. The greater the access advantages, the better the surrounding environment, and the fewer the social problems — the more attractive these areas are likely to seem to developers of new housing.

How much new construction went into these areas in the 1950's?

36

Newark and Jersey City had relatively little new housing — 6,500 private units and 9,000 units of public housing — but new construction boomed in New York City (Table A.1.10). The declining boroughs of Manhattan, the Bronx, and Brooklyn together attracted 136,000 new units of private housing, while public construction added another 60,000 units.

This new private housing is not spread evenly throughout the declining areas. In Brooklyn and the Bronx, much of the new construction is not in declining sections but in newer areas farther out where the surrounding environment is in better condition. Similarly, many new private apartment buildings in Manhattan are in "desirable" locations, on streets where adjoining buildings are in good condition. Newark and Jersey City have fewer desirable sections where new housing can locate. Although publicly sponsored renewal programs could conceivably alter the situation in the New Jersey cities, their present lack of good environments may have had much to do with their small volume of new private construction in the 1950's.

At typical densities for new development in the three declining boroughs of New York City, new private construction in the 1950's covered some 700 acres of net residential land. Had this construction been integrated into plans for rebuilding old neighborhoods, it would have constituted a basis for extensive renewal. I estimate the total land area occupied by deteriorated housing in New York as 1,145 acres (Appendix B), using a definition that limits deteriorated housing to structures that are in dilapidated condition or are deteriorating and lacking plumbing facilities. *Thus the volume of new private construction in the 1950's might have served as a basis for clearing 60 per cent of the land now occupied by deteriorated structures if the developers could have been induced to use these sites rather than alternate locations.*

Public housing construction in the 1950's occupied an estimated 700 additional acres of net residential land in Manhattan, the Bronx, and Brooklyn. *New public and private housing together utilized considerably more land than the total area now covered by deteriorated housing in these three boroughs.*

The question of *how much* new private housing can conceivably be attracted to sites cleared of deteriorated structures is reserved for later analysis. Even this brief look at new construction suggests, however, that the demand for housing sites located in the declining boroughs of New York is at a high level and that population losses from these boroughs do not indicate a drying up of the demand for *new* housing, provided that suitable environments are available for new construction.

Los Angeles Region: Population Shifts

Los Angeles has not experienced the spectacular population shifts of New York in the 1950's, but similar changes on a smaller scale have created areas of decline even in this newer, more dynamic region. Changes in the Los Angeles area are more difficult to chart, since the sprawling City of Los Angeles contains rapidly growing sections as well as declining ones. Thus the central city as a whole continued to expand in the 1950's, but one can detect traces of the same declining area syndrome noted in New York. Central-city growth was small in comparison with growth elsewhere in the region: population increased 25.8 per cent in the City of Los Angeles and 77.8 per cent in the rest of the region. Within the central city, nonwhite population almost doubled, while white population increased only 17.2 per cent (Appendix Tables A.2.1, A.2.2).

Areas of population loss were concentrated in a zone surrounding downtown Los Angeles and extending to the north and northeast. The Los Angeles County Regional Planning Commission compiles data for thirty-five statistical areas comprising the County. The three statistical areas that lost population from 1950 to 1960 constitute this central zone; their location is described in Table A.2.7. Total population loss in the three areas from 1950 to 1960 was 66,000, or about 12 per cent of the 1950 total.

As in New York, the components of population change in these loss areas were a net increase in minority group population and a larger net decrease in whites of native American background. The three statistical areas consist of eleven communities in the City of Los Angeles and three in unincorporated territory of the County; some population information is available for the eleven City communities. Seven of these had substantial minority-group populations in 1950, with Negroes, other nonwhites, and Mexican-Americans constituting more than 20 per cent of their population. In three of the seven cases, minority groups accounted for more than 50 per cent of the total population. No information is available for the Mexican-American population since 1950, but non-whites registered gains in almost all these communities since 1950, while total population declined.[20]

The major expansion of nonwhite population has not been in these communities, however. Other parts of central Los Angeles have attracted far greater numbers of nonwhites in the past decade. Exposition Park, Green Meadows, and West Adams have all experienced more significant absolute growth in the nonwhite population. These other central communities would have been counted among the declining areas if not for their large gains in minority population.

In Los Angeles, as in New York, decentralization of minority groups was negligible in the 1950's. The central area of the City of Los Angeles accounted for a slightly smaller *share* of the region's total Negro and Japanese population in 1960 than in 1950, but both groups *doubled in absolute size* within the central part of the City during this time.

Racial segregation is strong in Los Angeles, having increased substantially from 1950 to 1960. In the typical American pattern, nonwhite population grew much faster in segregated neighborhoods than in racially mixed areas. In 1950, racial minorities were less segregated in Los Angeles than in many other cities; 36.7 per cent lived in communities that were less than 25 per cent nonwhite, although another 48.5 per cent lived in areas that were 50 per cent or more nonwhite. By 1960, only 25.5 per cent lived in the mixed communities, while 68.9 per cent were in predominantly nonwhite areas.[21] In terms of the quality of their housing, nonwhites were better off in Los Angeles than in New York in 1960, but from the point of view of racial segregation their situation was comparable to that of nonwhites in New York.

Population and Housing Demand in the Los Angeles Region

Age and household characteristics of the population again help to explain the utilization of housing in the declining areas. The nonwhite population is younger than the white, both in the City of Los Angeles and in the metropolitan region (Table A.2.5). For both racial groups, the City population was older than that of the region at large in both census years. Thus the City population of

39

both groups is likely to generate a great demand for housing in relation to its size. As in New York, the white central-city population is likely to be a particularly great consumer of housing, with a significantly higher proportion of old people and a lower proportion of children than the nonwhites. The low incomes of nonwhite groups and their restricted choices in housing also limit the amount of residential space they can command at present and suggest an increasing demand for old housing as their incomes rise in the future.

Central-city housing was utilized less fully in Los Angeles than in New York in 1960: gross vacancy rates were 6.1 per cent in the City of Los Angeles and 3.0 per cent in the City of New York. But housing in the declining areas was utilized more fully than housing elsewhere in the City. City Planning Department estimates for the eleven declining communities indicate a vacancy rate of 4.7 per cent as of October 1960, compared with a rate of 5.4 per cent for the rest of the City.[22] These vacancy figures include substandard units. Vacancy rates for sound units are somewhat lower (4.9 per cent for the entire City), so that Los Angeles has probably not yet achieved a satisfactory vacancy surplus for starting large-scale clearance of its old areas.

Information on residential crowding also suggests that the removal of old low-cost housing would be premature under present circumstances. Between 1950 and 1960, the number of units with more than one occupant per room *increased* by 11 per cent. This increase, in the face of rising vacancy rates over the same period, probably indicates that vacant units are largely in the high-cost brackets and that low-cost housing is still in short supply. Housing in the declining areas of Los Angeles thus retains considerable social value, but the situation is not one of extreme housing shortage, as in New York. If present trends continue, Los Angeles will have a surplus of old housing ready for replacement long before New York.

Prospects for Rebuilding in Los Angeles

The declining sections of Los Angeles are not as diverse in character as those in New York. Like their counterparts.in New York, they are centrally located, but they do not extend out as far from the core. Densities of existing housing are more homogeneous,

40

with single-family houses on small lots predominating. Net residential densities are mostly 8 to 10 units per acre, while declining areas in New York range from more than 250 units per acre in parts of Manhattan to less than 50 in parts of Queens.

Whether these characteristics will facilitate the rebuilding of declining areas in Los Angeles remains to be seen. Their central location is likely to count for less in the housing market than central locations in New York, since the core of Los Angeles is less important functionally than the core of Manhattan. On the other hand, low densities of existing development are likely to mean low site acquisition costs. The implications of both these factors will be investigated in later chapters, but a preliminary look at new construction trends in the declining areas furnishes some insight into prospects for rebuilding.

Information on new residential construction is not directly available for Los Angeles areas of decline, but data on net changes in the number of dwelling units suggest a fair amount of building activity. Eight of the eleven communities had net increases in dwelling units from 1956 through 1960, with a total increase of 3,284 units.[23] This net increase includes conversions as well as new construction, minus mergers and demolitions; it consists entirely of private housing. Total new construction probably exceeds the net increase in dwelling units, since a number of units were demolished for nonresidential development and freeway construction in these areas. Detailed information for the Westlake section just outside downtown Los Angeles shows 1,914 new units (including conversions) constructed from 1955 through 1960, 1,728 demolitions, and a resulting net increase of 186 units.[24]

The performance of Los Angeles' declining areas is not in the same class as New York's building boom of the 1950's, but it does indicate continuing interest in these areas on the part of developers. At typical densities for new construction in this part of the region, 4,000 new units would occupy a net land area of some 80 acres. I estimate the total land area occupied by deteriorated housing in the City of Los Angeles as 2,755 acres (Appendix B), but much of this land lies outside the declining sections. Still, it is clear that rebuilding blighted housing in the declining areas will require attracting new development that now locates elsewhere in the region.

The extent to which new development *can* be attracted into these areas is the subject of Chapters 4 and 5.

Population and Housing Changes in the Hartford Region

The Hartford region presents a clear-cut case of population loss coupled with racial change in the central city and substantial population growth in the suburbs. Central-city shifts in population from 1950 to 1960 closely parallel those in the central areas of New York and Los Angeles. A loss of 28,000 whites was partly balanced by an increase of 12,000 nonwhites, with a net loss of 16,000 for the City of Hartford. Despite a doubling of the nonwhite population in the central city from 1950 to 1960, the Negro minority showed only weak signs of a relative decentralization. The City of Hartford had a somewhat smaller share of the region's Negro population in 1960 than it had in 1950, but even in relative terms dispersal was minor (Table A.3.3).

Within the central city, the growth of Negro population brought with it a substantial increase in racial segregation. In 1950, most Negroes lived in census tracts of mixed racial composition: only 39.8 per cent of nonwhites were in tracts where they constituted a majority. By 1960, 69.3 per cent of the city's nonwhites lived in segregated tracts.[25]

The age differences between white occupants of the central city and the total white population widened significantly, with fewer children and more old people in the center than in the region at large in both 1950 and 1960. Age differences between whites and nonwhites in the central city also sharpened between 1950 and 1960, with a significantly higher proportion of nonwhites under 18 and whites over 65 in 1960 than in 1950. Thus, as in New York and Los Angeles, whites remaining in the central city in 1960 were likely to be heavy consumers of dwelling units, while nonwhites were likely to consist of larger households generating proportionately less demand for separate units at this time, but constituting a reservoir of demand when incomes rise in the future.

Vacancy rates in Hartford, however, indicate less immediate need for the old housing than in New York. The gross vacancy level in Hartford was a moderate one (5.1 per cent), falling between the levels that prevailed in New York and in Los Angeles in 1960. According to the indicators of housing utilization, Hartford made real progress in raising housing standards from 1950 to 1960, and, like Los Angeles, is now approaching a situation where some clearance and replacement of old units may soon be justifiable in social terms. The net vacancy rate for sound housing units was 4.1 per cent in 1960, and the number of units with more than one occupant per room declined significantly since 1950. So far, the old housing is still well utilized, but population pressure on the housing supply is clearly easing in Hartford.

New Construction in Hartford's Declining Areas

Declining sections of Hartford consist primarily of low multifamily structures with densities of 15 to 20 units per net acre. As in the other cities, the declining areas are centrally located; and some consist of neighborhoods currently being abandoned by ethnic groups remaining from earlier migrations. One large area of decline in Hartford was formerly an Italian section, but Italian residents are now on the move to better housing elsewhere in the region. The value of the central location of declining parts of Hartford and the significance of their existing densities will be explored in later chapters dealing with the feasibility of developing new housing in the old areas.

The pattern of new construction during the 1950's does not suggest much promise for the rebuilding of Hartford. Advance tract information from the 1960 Housing Census reported a total of 57,625 housing units in the City of Hartford, an increase of 5,196 over the number of dwelling units counted in the 1950 census. Within the City of Hartford, several outlying tracts gained population during this period. If we exclude those housing units in these tracts, the net increase in housing units for City areas of population loss totaled 2,656 from 1950 to 1960.[26] Part of this increase reflects the change in census definition from "dwelling unit" to "housing unit," but the bulk of it represents new private housing. At typical new construction densities for the old areas, 2,000 new units would use about 40 acres of land. My estimate of land area now occupied by deteriorated housing in Hartford is 185 acres (Appendix B). Once again, if land cleared of substandard housing in the declining areas is to be absorbed by new construction in a reasonable period of time, new housing will have to be diverted from alternate locations in the region. Whether the pace of new

43

construction in the old areas can be accelerated in this way is the subject of the following chapters.

The Three Study Areas: General Findings

The declining areas of New York, Los Angeles, and Hartford all show signs of life, both in utilizing existing housing and in attracting new housing. The old housing is indeed still needed and occupied in all three study areas. In the declining parts of New York City, the 1960 situation was essentially one of housing shortage. Only the New Jersey central cities of the region showed signs of underutilization of the housing stock. Los Angeles and Hartford had more excess housing in their declining areas, but their vacancy rates were moderate and suggest no massive abandonment of the central city in either region. The economic implications of these vacancy levels will be investigated in Chapter 4, which analyzes information on site acquisition costs in the declining areas. *Social implications are already clear: the old housing is decidedly useful and has made possible an improvement in living conditions in all three cities during the 1950's.*

Although this study will go no further in explaining present occupancy characteristics of the declining areas, it has suggested some of the reasons for different findings in New York than in the other regions. The condition of the housing seems to have little to do with the results. If housing quality were a guide, vacancy levels should be higher in New York than in Los Angeles or Hartford. More than 15 per cent of the housing units in New York City were classified as deteriorating or dilapidated in the 1960 Housing Census; in Hartford, 9.3 per cent of the units were so classified; and in Los Angeles, 8.8 per cent.[27] Vacancy rates, however, were in reverse order: 6.1 per cent in Los Angeles, 5.1 per cent in Hartford, and 3.0 per cent in New York.

A variety of individual factors can operate significantly in determining the extent of demand for centrally located housing. Rent control in New York City helps to slow decentralization; age and income distributions and household characteristics condition the demand for dwelling units; the extent of in-migration of low-income people conditions the size of the market for blighted housing. In addition to all these influences, the structure of the region may also play a part in creating demand for central housing. New York, with its strong central concentration of employment and its lack of vacant land for development near the center, is an example of a region that should theoretically have a center-oriented market for new housing. Inasmuch as old housing is a substitute for new, whatever center-orientation exists may appear in the market for older central housing as well.

In addition to checking on the utilization of existing housing, this study has also surveyed decentralization tendencies among new migrant groups in the cities. Slight proportional changes in the central concentration of these groups were noticeable in all three areas, but even in this relative sense the dispersal has been very slow. In absolute numbers, minority groups expanded significantly in the declining areas between 1950 and 1960. If recent trends are a guide to the future, these newcomers will continue to maintain a demand for the old housing in declining areas, but it is possible that the continued dispersal of other residents will create some surplus of old housing. To a limited extent, a surplus has already developed in Los Angeles and Hartford. So far, this surplus is desirable as a vacancy reserve to facilitate normal turnover and mobility in the housing market. Within the near future, however, Los Angeles and Hartford may be in a position to start clearing their old housing. For New York, this times lies further in the future, but the eventual development of a housing surplus can be foreseen even in New York.

New residential development of the 1950's has served as a rough guide to prospects for rebuilding the areas of population loss. In all three study areas, there has been some new development in declining sections, but the findings do not indicate that a rebirth of these areas is under way. New development does not penetrate the old areas evenly in any region. Even the building boom in New York has bypassed some inlying areas, and the more limited new development in Los Angeles and Hartford is by no means distributed equally among the various declining sections.

The significance of this new construction is that central locations still attract some residential development, even while the general movement of population proceeds outward from the center. Though some parts of the declining areas receive no new housing, these areas on the whole are not stagnant. Chapter 3 will look more closely into locational patterns of the demand for new housing in each of these regions to determine the extent to which the generally central location of the old areas constitutes an asset in the housing market. The insights of this phase of the study will provide a basis for judging what market advantages such areas offer for new housing in each of the three regions.

REBUILDING THE DECLINING AREAS: LOCATIONAL PREFERENCES FOR NEW HOUSING

Housing in the declining areas is still too useful to be replaced, both in the regions selected for this special study and in the dozen large cities covered in the brief national survey. Yet, as I have noted, changes in population and the utilization of old residential structures may soon open up possibilities for replacing surplus housing, provided that present occupants continue to evacuate the declining sections of cities more quickly than new migrants arrive on the scene. As the old housing is abandoned, can the declining areas attract new private housing to replace it?

Some new development has already been noted in areas of population loss within the three study regions, but it is far from clear whether economic conditions are really favorable for such development in comparison with possibilities elsewhere in the city or suburbs. What are the economic conditions that confront the developer in declining neighborhoods? I have previously suggested two preconditions for rebuilding these areas: (1) the value of cleared land for new housing must be commensurate with its acquisition cost, and (2) the demand for housing sites must be great enough to utilize all cleared land that is not needed for environmental improvements (schools, public works) within a reasonable number of years.

This chapter and Chapter 4 will investigate the first of these preconditions. Achieving a balance between re-use value and site acquisition cost depends upon maintaining a favorable relationship between advantages to the developer of building in declining areas and his costs in these locations. This chapter is concerned with the advantages; Chapter 4 considers the costs.

47

Since my objective is to assess the prospects for renewing the declining areas, the present physical environment must be considered temporary and subject to varying degrees of change in the course of renewal. Only the location of the old areas remains fixed. This location is generally a central one within the metropolitan region. Thus the rebuilding problem is closely linked to the question of whether central location is an asset in the housing market. The theoretical literature on this question (Appendix C) presents persuasive evidence that the center is less in demand for housing now than it was formerly; and a preliminary look at the three study regions has reinforced this conclusion by documenting the movement of the white middle classes from the center to the suburbs and the incipient decentralization of new minority groups as well. But all this evidence does not establish that the public has decisively rejected central locations. There are also signs of life in the form of new construction in areas of population loss. The suburban exodus could conceivably reflect dissatisfaction with housing and environmental conditions in the center rather than with the central location as such.

This chapter will evaluate the strength of the public's preferences for central housing locations and the influence of this strength on the developer's choice of sites. I shall examine certain assumptions about the relationship between metropolitan structure and demand for central locations in the context of the experience of New York, Los Angeles, and Hartford. To the extent that preference patterns are consistent with theoretical expectations, the findings can be applied to other regions with similar characteristics and can serve as a basis for coordinating general metropolitan planning with renewal objectives for centrally located areas.

The working hypotheses developed from a survey of the literature can be summarized briefly. Metropolitan features that have been considered influential are: (1) the strength of the core, which may be defined in terms of the employment, shopping, recreational, and cultural activities it offers; (2) the transportation system of the region, which determines traveltimes from various locations to the core; and (3) the proximity to the core of vacant sites that may be competitive with locations in declining areas. These factors in turn are likely to influence the density preferences of consumers, which play a significant role in determining the economic feasibility of constructing housing in central locations.

As these factors operate in theory, central preferences will be strongest in a metropolitan region with a strong core, with substantial traveltime savings from inlying locations to the core, and with vacant land relatively inaccessible. In such a region, people would theoretically accept high residential densities in order to gain the advantages of living close to the core. As the core weakens, as traveltime advantages from inner locations diminish, and as vacant land becomes more accessible, central preferences will weaken and people will find less reason to accept high-density housing for the sake of living close to the core.

In reality, many other factors are also involved in the choice of residential locations, and people differ considerably in their subjective evaluation of various factors. Such considerations as the prestige of particular areas, the quality of the environment, social character of the neighborhood, and local school system all enter into locational decisions in the housing market. Nevertheless, most theoretical works emphasize structural factors within the region as basic organizers of the residential pattern and regard these other considerations as modifying elements. Such an analysis is particularly significant for this study, for "environmental" factors can be manipulated to a certain extent through renewal programs, while structural factors are less changeable. The main question is whether the structural setting is favorable for rebuilding provided environmental conditions are modified appropriately.

In addition to estimating the strength of central preferences, it is important to determine whether they encompass those declining areas that are not immediately adjacent to the core but lie somewhat farther away. The "gray areas" problem, according to Chester Rapkin, is one of "massive deterioration in neighborhoods that lack locational advantages."[1] This chapter will investigate the extent to which central preferences involve such areas. Another objective is to quantify the concept of strong and weak cores and to measure the degree of central preference associated with cores of varying strengths. Finally, it will be useful to determine the ways in which locational preferences enter into the market for new housing: to what extent do they affect rents, vacancy rates, and densities? The results will help resolve some of the perplexing questions of

49

urban renewal: To what extent can older areas capitalize on their central locations as an asset in attracting new housing? How strong a core is necessary to stimulate housing demand for inlying sites? How far out does a strong core extend its influence on the housing market?

Three Regional Structures

New York and Los Angeles represent polar types of regions with respect to core strength: New York is a highly center-oriented region; Los Angeles is an extremely decentralized region; and Hartford is midway between the two in the strength of its core, but unlike either New York or Los Angeles, it has a plentiful supply of vacant land starting as close as 7 or 8 miles (20 minutes traveltime) from the downtown area. Table 3.1 summarizes the main characteristics of each region.

Differences in core strength are defined clearly in terms of employment: the Manhattan central business district contains 37 per cent of all jobs in the entire metropolitan region, while downtown Los Angeles provides only 9 per cent of the employment in its region. Employment in offices and financial institutions is particularly significant, since income in these fields is high enough to enable large numbers of employees to afford new housing. Downtown employment in these typically core-oriented activities accounts for 61 per cent of total employment in offices and financial institutions in the New York region, while downtown Los Angeles employs only 15 per cent of the total office and financial force in its region. New construction in the central business district adds a dynamic perspective to this picture of core employment strength: unparalleled office expansion in the Manhattan business area, which accounts for the overwhelming majority of office expansion in the New York region, produced 44.7 million square feet of new office space between 1947 and 1960. In Los Angeles, new construction of 2.5 million square feet in and near the core represents only 16 per cent of total regional office growth over the same time span. During the same period, 6.5 million square feet of office space (42 per cent of the region's total) were built in the newly developing business area extending some 7½ miles along Wilshire Boulevard to the west of the downtown area.

Aside from employment opportunities, the core may influence

50

Table 3.1. Selected Characteristics of Three Study Areas

	New York	Los Angeles	Hartford
1. Population, 1960 Census	14,759,429	6,742,696	525,207
2. Persons Entering Core Area on Business Day	3,316,000 (1956)	679,000 (1960)	not available
3. Total Employment in Central Business District (CBD)	2,475,900 (1956)	244,500 (1960)	49,480 (1960)
4. Per Cent of Regional Employment in CBD	37.0 (1956)	9.4 (1960)	24.9 (1960)
5. Per Cent of Regional Office Employment in CBD	61.3 (1956)	15 (1960 est.)	not available
6. Square Feet of New Office Space Constructed in CBD, 1947–1960	44.7 million	2.5 million	not available
7. Per Cent of Regional Retail Sales in CBD, 1958	13.0	4.2	20.8
8. Per Cent of Change in CBD Retail Sales, 1954–1958	+9.0	−5.3	+3.4
9. Miles from CBD to Nearest Large Tracts of Vacant Buildable Land	20	15	7–8

Regional definitions: New York, N.Y.–Northeastern New Jersey Standard Consolidated Area (identical with 1950 Census Standard Metropolitan Area); Los Angeles–Long Beach Standard Metropolitan Statistical Area; Hartford Standard Metropolitan Statistical Area.

Sources: New York: (2) Regional Plan Association, *Bulletin 91,* "Hub-Bound Travel in the Tri-State Metropolitan Region," April 1959, p. 10; (3), (4), (5) Edgar M. Hoover and Raymond Vernon, *Anatomy of a Metropolis* (Cambridge: Harvard University Press, 1959), p. 260; (6) John McDonald, "The $2-Billion Building Boom," *Fortune,* Vol. 61 (February 1960), p. 119; (7), (8) *U.S. Census of Business: 1958,* Vol. 7, Central Business District Report, New York, N.Y., Area — BC58 — CBD55, Tables 1A, 4A, and Retail Trade, BC58-RA1, United States Summary, Table 8.

Los Angeles: (2), (4), (5), (6) Los Angeles Central City Committee and Los Angeles City Planning Department, "Economic Survey: Los Angeles: Centropolis 1980" (December 12, 1960), pp. 19, 26, 30, 38; (3) Los Angeles City Planning Department, using generous CBD definition to include all major employment in and near downtown core; (7), (8) *U.S. Census of Business: 1958,* Vol. 7, Central Business District Report, Los Angeles–Long Beach, Calif., Area — BC58 — CBD43, Tables 4A, 5A.

Hartford: (3), (4) Hartford Area Transportation Study, Connecticut Highway Department, using generous CBD definition to include all major employment in and near downtown core; (7), (8) *U.S. Census of Business: 1958,* Vol. 7, Central Business District Report, Hartford, Conn., Area — BC58 — CBD35, Tables 4, 5.

locational preferences for new housing by means of its shopping and entertainment functions. Retail sales figures are the best available indicators of shopping opportunities in the central business districts. The relative core strength of New York compared with Los Angeles is evident once again, with downtown sales amounting to 13 per cent of regional sales in New York and only 4 per cent in Los Angeles. Downtown retail trade is still more significant in the Hartford area, where retail sales in the central business district are 21 per cent of regional sales. In recent years, all three downtown areas have failed to keep pace with regional percentage increases in retail sales, but New York and Hartford have registered slight absolute gains downtown while Los Angeles sales have declined 5 per cent.

Downtown entertainment and cultural activity varies still more strikingly than retail sales in the three core areas. Little need be said about either the strength or vitality of Manhattan as a cultural center: its significance is international, and its strength has grown recently even in the generally moribund categories of the legitimate theater and movie houses. In the former field, the number of playing weeks in professional theaters has increased by an estimated 30 per cent or more in the face of a major national decline.[2] Downtown Los Angeles plays a negligible role in the region's entertainment. Restaurants and night clubs are decentralized; musical and theatrical performances are given either in Los Angeles outside the downtown area or in the centers of outlying communities; movie theaters are located primarily outside the downtown core. In Hartford the situation is mixed: the main auditorium for musical and theatrical events is just outside downtown, but restaurants and movie theaters are largely decentralized.

Location of New Housing

The method of this analysis is to study locational patterns of new housing in the three regions for indications of central preference and for evidence of the way in which this preference registers in the housing market. To facilitate price comparisons of similar housing units and to obtain a sample with wide geographic coverage, attention will be limited to rental apartments. The characteristics of greatest interest are the general location of new apartments within each region, the *rents* in comparable units located in zones of different traveltime to the core, and locational variations in *vacancy rates* and *densities*.

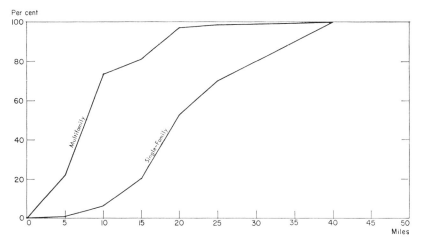

Figure 3.1. Cumulative percentage of new single-family and multifamily dwelling units within 5-mile distance zones from center of New York region, 1957–1960.

Source: Regional Plan Association, "New Homes in the New Jersey–New York–Connecticut Metropolitan Region," 1957–1960; based on building permit data for counties in the region. Total new single-family units: 158,761; total new multifamily units: 145,921. Public housing excluded.

Where, then, do developers locate new housing? Figures 3.1 to 3.3 represent graphically the locational distribution of new multi-family and single-family dwelling units (excluding public housing) within the study regions for roughly comparable time spans within the period 1956 to 1960. If consumers were totally indifferent to the location of new housing, one might expect to find similarities in the location of single-family houses and apartments. The amount of land needed for single-family units generally dictates the choice of a site on vacant land; distant zones where the bulk of single-family housing has been built contain large vacant tracts. If locations closer to the center offered no advantages in marketing apartments, developers might locate them in the same general areas where single-family subdivisions appear: land costs are typically cheaper in these areas than they are closer to the core, and the newness of such areas provides certain market advantages in itself. Yet in all three regions new apartments are located significantly closer to the core than new single-family developments. Since central locations involve higher costs, they must reflect some degree of public preference within the rental market. An additional factor, however, may be the

53

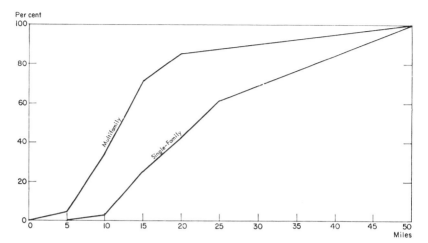

Figure 3.2.   Cumulative percentage of total increase in single-family and multifamily dwelling units within 5-mile distance zones from center of Los Angeles region, October 1956 to March 1960.

Source: Los Angeles County Regional Planning Commission, distribution of dwelling types in 35 statistical areas of Los Angeles County for October 1956 and April 1960; Security First National Bank, Los Angeles, building permit data for Orange County, fourth quarter, 1955 through first quarter, 1959. Total increase: 148,730 single-family units; 128,726 multifamily units.

developer's desire to remove new apartments from areas where they would be in competition with single-family houses.

In New York, almost 75 per cent of the new apartments lie within 10 miles of midtown Manhattan. In Los Angeles, about 35 per cent of the new apartments lie with 10 miles of the core, but 70 per cent are within the 15-mile zone. Part of this difference results from limitations in the Los Angeles data. Los Angeles information shows net increases in dwelling units rather than total new units within each statistical area; some new construction close to the core has been countered by the demolition of older housing for nonresidential building and for the construction of freeways. Nevertheless, the pull toward the center appears to be greater in New York than in Los Angeles: the cumulative curve of apartment construction rises more steeply over the inner half of the metropolitan region in New York than in Los Angeles. Differentiation between multifamily and single-family locations is also greater in New York, with wider distances separating the two curves.

To understand the shape of the multifamily curves, it is necessary to take into account differences in the transportation systems of the

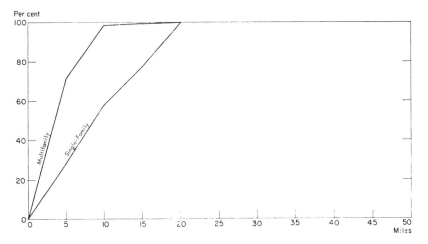

Figure 3.3. Cumulative percentage of new single-family and multifamily dwelling units within 5-mile distance zones from center of Hartford region, 1958–1960.

Source: Connecticut Public Works Department Housing Division, building permit data for towns in region. Total new single-family units: 10,919; total new multifamily units: 1,590. Public housing excluded.

two regions. Forty minutes of peak-hour traveltime via the New York City subway system and via rail and bus service to the New Jersey portion of the region corresponds approximately to 10 miles from the core. Forty minutes of peak-hour automobile traveltime via the Los Angeles street and freeway network corresponds roughly to 15 miles from downtown Los Angeles. Thus within 40 minutes of traveltime, there are very similar proportions of the new apartment housing in both New York and Los Angeles.

This approach to determining the pull of the center is not complete, however, without some consideration of the increasing costs that developers encounter as they move in from outlying vacant land and approach the cores of these two regions. The economic analyses in Chapter 4 demonstrate that cost differentials are many times greater as one approaches the center of New York than they are as one approaches the center of Los Angeles. Thus although new apartments are distributed similarly with respect to traveltime in both New York and Los Angeles, New York developers incur a much higher cost to achieve this distribution than do developers in Los Angeles. The pull of the center, as reflected in market advantages to the developer, must therefore be substantially greater in New York than in Los Angeles.

The Hartford region shows less differentiation than either New York or Los Angeles. Distances separating the multifamily curve from the single-family curve are smaller in Hartford than in either of the other regions. The primary reason for this is the nearness of vacant land: single-family houses are feasible on vacant tracts 7 or 8 miles from downtown. Traveltimes are quite short in the Hartford region. During peak commuting hours, trips to points 5 miles from the core average some 20 minutes when weighted according to current proportions of automobile commuters and bus riders. To go 5 miles farther in most directions requires a total of some 25 minutes by car, and the number of bus riders diminishes to negligible proportions.

The pulling power of downtown Hartford appears to be quite substantial, for 70 per cent of new apartment units are located within 5 miles of downtown Hartford rather than a few miles farther out where extensive single-family development occurs. Since the savings in traveltime to the core are relatively small, other factors must explain the apparent market advantages of these inlying locations. One influence of some importance in the Hartford area is not a market advantage but a limitation resulting from public policy: relatively little outlying land is zoned for apartments and local developers consider suburban zoning restrictions difficult to change. A more significant market advantage is the network of public bus transportation available within the 5-mile limit that thins out significantly beyond it. Still another is the demand for walk-to-work housing near some of the large insurance firms just outside the core.

Rent Differentials and Traveltime

The locational pattern of new multifamily housing in all three study areas, as it differs from the single-family pattern, suggests that all three cores exercise material pulling power in the market for new apartments. This pulling power must consist of advantages to the developer in renting his units. The most likely advantages would take the form of higher rents in more central locations; greater ease of renting, which would be reflected in lower vacancy rates in more central locations; or public acceptance of higher densities, which would enable builders to economize on development costs in central sites having high land values. These three characteristics can be used to measure the extent of central preferences in the housing market.

For a study of rent differentials at different locations, ideal data would consist of rent levels in identical apartments that differ only in their location with respect to the core. The approach of this study has been to eliminate major qualitative differences within the housing sample by including only units built since 1950,[3] separating apartments into size categories according to number of bedrooms, adjusting rents to take into account the presence of special features (such as air conditioning) or the absence of features normally included in new housing in the region (free parking space in the Hartford area), and selecting new housing only in neighborhoods that local realtors consider to have "good environments for renting." To eliminate the additional factor of differing transportation systems in the three regions, units were classified according to peak-hour traveltime from the core by the dominant means of commuter transportation: subways and commuter railroads traveltime in New York; automobile traveltime in Los Angeles; and averages of bus and automobile traveltime weighted according to the proportion of bus riders and auto users in different parts of the Hartford area.[4]

The resulting patterns of rents and traveltimes appear in Figures 3.4 to 3.6, where efficiency apartments (without separate bedroom), one-bedroom, and two-bedroom units are shown separately. Information for New York and Hartford, drawn from extensive inventories of rents in all units in a large sampling of new developments, is presented in the form of median rents and median traveltimes to the core for all units, grouped according to 10-minute time zones. The Los Angeles sample consists of rents for individual apartments based largely on advertised vacancies that were subsequently checked in the field. Los Angeles information is presented as a plotting of individual unit rents, since the number of units covered is too small to permit the use of medians as a reliable index.

New Yorkers pay a far greater premium to live close to the core than do residents of either Los Angeles or Hartford. For one- and two-bedroom apartments, New Yorkers pay more than twice as much near the core as they do on the fringe of the sample; for efficiency apartments, they pay more than one and one-half times

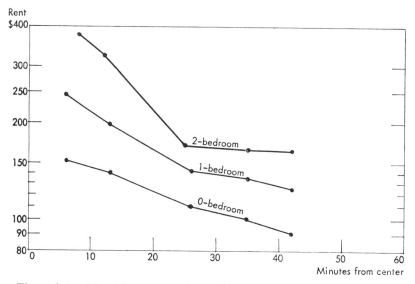

Figure 3.4. Monthly rents and traveltimes from center of New York region.

Source: City of New York Department of City Planning, rental inventory of 14,152 dwelling units in 136 apartment developments constructed 1958–1959 in New York City. Data grouped within 10-minute time zones from center, with median rent and median time indicated for each group.

as much in central locations as they do on the fringe. To determine whether these rent differentials between central and outlying locations reflect differences in room size, additional information was obtained on the number of square feet per apartment in a sampling of new two-bedroom apartments constructed between 1955 and 1960. Ten new buildings in the sample were located in the upper East Side of Manhattan, averaging about 12 minutes in traveltime to the core; nine were in Queens, averaging about 35 minutes in traveltime to the core. Rents per square foot for the Manhattan group averaged $4.27 per month, compared with an average of $2.35 in Queens. On the rent curve for two-bedroom apartments in Figure 3.4, rents for apartments 12 minutes from the core are twice as high as rents in apartments 35 minutes away. The control sample corresponds closely, with square foot rentals 12 minutes from the core 1.8 times as high as square foot rents 35 minutes away.[5] (Certain differences in physical equipment and levels of service do exercise limited influence upon these rent differentials, however. These factors will be discussed more fully in Chapter 4.)

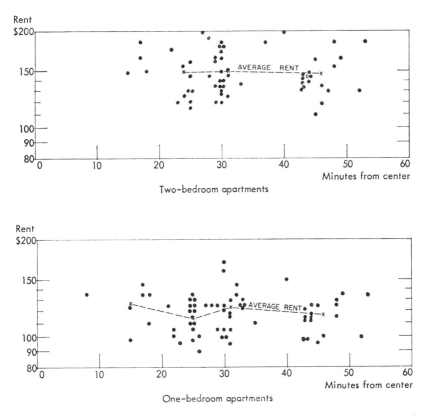

Figure 3.5.   Distribution of monthly rents and traveltimes from center of Los Angeles region.

Source: Sample of 126 dwelling units in 115 apartment developments of similar construction type completed 1950–1961. Information from: Henry A. Babcock Consulting Engineers, Los Angeles; Federal Housing Administration, Los Angeles; Prudential Insurance Company of America, Los Angeles; William Walters Real Estate, Los Angeles; *The Los Angeles Times* advertisements, April 16, 23, and 30, 1961.

In Los Angeles, no significant locational differences in rent are detectable for either of the two apartment-size categories in our sampling. Hartford rents show a clear tendency to increase near the center—rent curves for all three apartment sizes tilt upward toward the center—but the differentials are very slight, amounting to 4 to 6 per cent increases for central locations in the relatively narrow time band covered by the sample.

These regional differences must be seen in relation to the strength of the core. New York, with 37 per cent of its employment in the core, shows extreme central preferences in its rent structure. Hart-

59

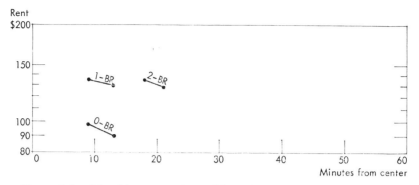

Figure 3.6. Monthly rents and traveltimes from center of Hartford region.

Source: Rental inventory of 619 dwelling units in 14 apartment developments constructed 1947–1960. Information from Federal Housing Administration, Hartford; and Rowlson Real Estate and Insurance, Hartford. Data grouped within 10-minute time zones from center, with median rent and median time indicated for each group.

ford, with 25 per cent of its employment in the core, has some noticeable central preference influencing the housing market despite the small time savings achieved by inlying housing. Los Angeles, with 9 per cent of its employment in the core, has no distinguishable central orientation in its rent structure, although considerable time savings to downtown are possible from central locations.[6]

In absolute numbers, Los Angeles has five times as many jobs downtown as Hartford. Nevertheless, the small Hartford core acts as a magnet influencing rent levels, while the larger Los Angeles core exerts no such influence. Differences in the over-all regional distribution of employment probably account for these contrasting rent patterns. The Los Angeles housing sample has been drawn from neighborhoods in the western sector of the Los Angeles region, extending out from the core to take in the central Wilshire Boulevard area, Hollywood, Beverly Hills, West Los Angeles, Westwood, and Santa Monica. These districts, and the adjacent Culver City area, contain 350,000 jobs in themselves (compared with 245,000 downtown). If employment in nearby noncentral areas is added to this total, the number of jobs outside the core that are readily accessible from the western sector comes to 664,000.[7] This large number of jobs scattered about the sector and its environs undoubtedly sets up powerful crosscurrents in the housing market that negate the influence of downtown jobs on rent levels in this sector. Housing locations anywhere in this sector offer easy access

60

to a large number of jobs; those sites that offer special access advantages to the core can command no higher rents than more outlying locations which offer special access advantages to a number of other employment centers.

Similarly, retail shopping in and near the western sector upsets the pull of downtown shopping. Retail sales within major shopping areas in the western sector totaled 302.7 million dollars in 1958, compared to 365.4 million downtown. Total retail sales in the sector plus nearby San Fernando Valley shopping areas amounted to 436.3 million dollars; there were 1,594 retail stores, compared with 1,460 downtown, including 54 general merchandise stores and 13 department stores, compared with 42 general merchandise and 4 department stores downtown.[8]

The magnetic pull of Hartford's smaller core meets little interference from other centers of employment and shopping within the sector where the housing sample is located. The Hartford sample is drawn from neighborhoods situated west of downtown lying predominantly within a 1-mile band on either side of Farmington Avenue in Hartford and West Hartford. Within this sector, the pull of downtown dominates both employment and shopping opportunities. Indexes of accessibility to total employment and to retail trade (prepared for a regional transportation study using the gravity-model approach) were made available for locations included in the housing sample.[9] These indexes were derived by dividing the region into small zones, obtaining figures for total employment in each zone, dividing the employment in each zone by a function of traveltime from the location in question to the employment zone, and summing all results for a particular location. The resulting index reflects general accessibility from a particular location to jobs and shopping everywhere in the region. For locations included in the sample, the general accessibility indexes to both total employment and employment in retail trade correspond directly to traveltimes to the core. In Los Angeles, no general accessibility index was available, but the extent of employment and retailing within the sector included in the housing sample indicates quite clearly that traveltime to the core does not correspond to general accessibility to *all* jobs and *all* retailing in the region.[10]

Scope of Rent Gradients

Since the New York housing sample extends over a broad geographic range, its characteristics can help answer the question of whether central preferences affect only a limited area near the core itself or whether they spread their effects over the housing market in an extended gradient. Figure 3.4 illustrates an extended rent gradient for the sampling within the City of New York. To push the analysis still farther out from the core, two independent samplings of new rental units in Westchester County were also obtained. Their median rents and median traveltimes (within 10-minute time zones) are plotted in Figure 3.7, along with a repetition of the New York City rent gradients for one- and two-bedroom apartments. Although the Westchester units lie several miles beyond the outer edge of the New York City sample, their traveltimes from midtown Manhattan via commuter railroad fall within the same range as traveltimes to housing in outlying parts of the city served by slower subway trains. The Westchester rent curves tilt consistently upward toward the core, furnishing additional evidence of the extended rent gradient in the New York region. As far out as the Westchester sample extends (to the 40–49-minute time zone), greater centrality still appears to bring higher rents.

The level of rents in Westchester is also of some interest in illustrating the unpredictable effect of commuting costs upon the housing market. Although traveltimes from the core to Westchester are the same as traveltimes by subway to the upper Bronx and lower Brooklyn, commuting costs are much higher to Westchester: $25 or more per month for rail fare alone, compared with subway fares of $6 per month. Thus one might expect to find lower rents in Westchester as compensation for higher travel costs. Yet for dwelling units with comparable traveltimes (but with slightly lower densities), Westchester rent medians range from $5 to $20 per month higher than New York City rent levels. As several theoretical works recognize, commuting costs are a highly subjective matter. For Westchester residents, life in the suburbs evidently offers advantages that justify both higher rents and higher commuting costs than they would have to pay in Brooklyn or the Bronx. As a result, Westchester rent gradients are higher than those for comparable traveltimes in the City, *but central preferences operate in both locations.*

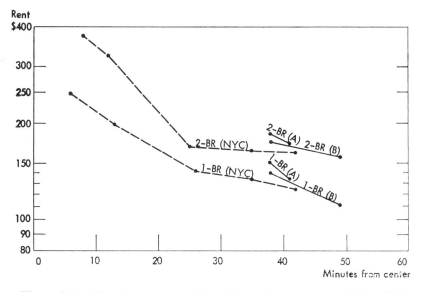

Figure 3.7. Monthly rents and traveltimes from center of New York region, for apartments in Westchester County and New York City.

Sources: Westchester sample A: survey of 600 units in 11 developments completed 1959–1961; information from Federal Housing Administration, New York. Westchester sample B: survey of 1614 units in garden apartment developments completed 1945–1961, Apartment Owners Advisory Council, White Plains. New York City: see Figure 3.4. Data grouped within 10-minute time zones from center, with median rent and median time indicated for each group.

While the New York rental pattern is an extended gradient rather than merely a peak near the core and a horizontal line farther out, the gradient is nevertheless much steeper near the core than in outlying areas. For one-bedroom units, rents increase by about 13 per cent as traveltime diminishes from 42 to 26 minutes. Yet the next time saving of only 13 minutes (from 26 to 13 minutes median time) brings a rent increase of 40 per cent (from $142 to $200). Clearly, minutes saved are worth more to the rental market near the core than they are farther away, but the reasons are not at all evident. One factor to consider is that apartments near the outer margin of development suffer from the competition of new single-family houses nearby. This competition may hold down rents in outlying locations, but closer in, single-family homes are less important as a competitive force.

Another feature of the New York region that helps explain the

63

steepness of rent gradients near the core is the lack of suitable environments for new rental housing in areas about 15 to 25 minutes from the core. These are the "gray areas" of decaying housing and unsightly industry in the older parts of Brooklyn and Queens near Manhattan, upper Manhattan, and the lower Bronx. As a result, for many people the next practical alternative to living in a new building 10 to 15 minutes from the core is to move 25 minutes away; the gradient of choices is discontinuous in this part of the range. High rents near the core probably reflect in part the unavailability of close substitutes for housing 15 minutes or less from the core.

The transportation facilities of the region may also play a distinct role in raising rent levels near the core. New Yorkers who live close to the Manhattan business area find bus lines or even taxis feasible for commuting, while those who live farther away must descend to the far less pleasant subway system. In this sense, transportation choices change abruptly as distances from the center of Manhattan increase.

Basic explanations for the rising slope of the rent curve near the center undoubtedly derive largely from subjective consumer preferences and from the premiums that different groups of people will pay in order to save traveltime. Probably consumers have sorted themselves out along the rent gradient so that those who live near the center value traveltime savings very highly. Recent interviews with residents of new downtown apartments in several cities have suggested that the downtown occupant places high value on having the activities of the core close at hand. In addition to his trip to work, he makes numerous other trips to core facilities for shopping or entertainment.[11] Time savings multiply in importance as the number of trips to the core increases for an individual. Whether for actual time savings on a large number of trips or solely for the psychological satisfaction of having downtown facilities nearby, the New Yorker who lives close to the core pays considerably more in rent to save a few minutes in traveltime than does the commuter who lives farther out. Conversely, a New Yorker who lives close to the core can save much more on his rent bill by moving a few minutes farther away, if he can find an environment he likes, than can the New Yorker who lives 30 minutes from the core.

The Pattern of Vacancy Rates

The first aggregate analysis of the location of new multifamily housing showed strong central tendencies in all three study areas; yet rental patterns indicate that only in New York can developers reach substantially higher rent levels by building close to the core rather than farther away. Rent differentials resulting from central locations are small in the Hartford area and apparently nonexistent in Los Angeles. Developers must find other types of market advantages in central locations in Los Angeles and Hartford. One of these advantages is the greater ease in renting new apartments, which reduces the risk of income loss through high vacancy rates. In the opinion of developers and realtors consulted in all three study areas, new apartments are a safer investment in good inlying locations than in good outlying locations: they rent more quickly at the start, and long-run vacancy experience is more favorable in central locations. To the extent that information on vacancy rates is available, it confirms these opinions in all three areas.

In Los Angeles, where rent differentials show no central orientation, vacancy rates in comparable buildings decrease steadily as locations become more central. A large sampling of idle electricity meters in apartments of similar quality located in fifteen different areas of the region indicates the following average vacancy rates for 1959 and 1960, arranged according to the distance of each area from the core:[12]

Miles from core	0–5	6–10	11–15	16–25
Average vacancy rate (per cent)	4. 4	5. 8	7. 3	7. 7

Comparable vacancy information is not available for New York, but various surveys of new apartments indicate lower vacancy rates in Manhattan than elsewhere in the City, at least before the luxury housing boom in Manhattan reached its peak in the early 1960's. A 1959 survey of all postwar apartments completed in New York City through the end of 1958 indicated a City-wide vacancy rate of 2.9 per cent.[13] A different survey of postwar units in Manhattan indicated an average vacancy rate of 1.6 per cent from 1952 to 1956.[14] These results are in accord with the general opinion in real estate circles that Manhattan vacancy rates in new housing are below those in the rest of the City. At the regional scale, little information is at hand to test the equally general opinion that vacancy rates in the City are below those in new housing farther from the center of the region. According to the 1960 Housing Census, vacancy rates for standard rental units (with all plumbing facilities) were 2.0 per cent in New York City and 4.0 per cent in the rest of the New York State part of the region.[15]

Little information is available for the Hartford region. The best approximation of over-all vacancy rates in standard apartments that can be gleaned from advance reports of the 1960 Housing Census is 4.2 per cent for towns within 5 miles of the core and 4.5 per cent for the remainder of the Standard Metropolitan Statistical Area.[16]

Densities and Central Preference

Another type of advantage to the developer is the willingness of people to live at high densities. This acceptance of high density affects development cost rather than rental income, and its benefits are limited by the increase in construction and operating costs per apartment as the type of structure shifts from walk-up to elevator buildings and from light to heavy construction. Nevertheless, high densities add to the developer's flexibility, permit him to reduce land cost per unit, and within the limits of a particular building type may facilitate economies of scale by allowing more units on a given site without necessitating a shift to a more expensive type of construction.

Density preferences within a housing market undoubtedly have strong bases in local tradition and in prestige associations with different building types, as well as in functional conveniences or inconveniences of living in neighborhoods and structures of different densities. One of the hypotheses in this study is that the same factors that condition central preference — strength of the core, distance to vacant land, time savings from central locations — will contribute to acceptance of high densities in central areas. High central densities are complementary to strong central preferences, in theory, and density patterns of the three study areas should therefore be consistent with their rental and vacancy patterns.

Figure 3.8, which plots average densities and average traveltimes to the core for buildings grouped by 10-minute time intervals, confirms these expectations in the three study areas. New York densities far exceed those of Hartford and Los Angeles across the entire

66

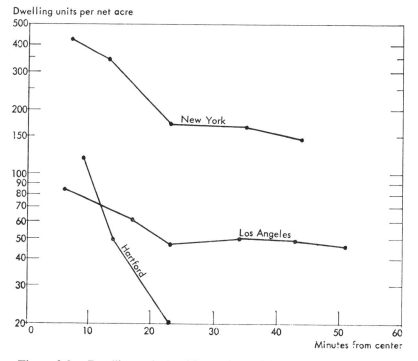

Figure 3.8. Dwelling unit densities and traveltimes from centers of three study regions.

Sources: Sample of 37 apartment buildings constructed in New York City 1954–1961, from New York Department of City Planning; sample of 23 apartment developments constructed in Los Angeles region 1958–1961, from Los Angeles County Department of Building and Safety and Prudential Insurance Company; sample of 14 apartment developments constructed in Hartford region 1947–1960, from Federal Housing Administration and Rowlson Real Estate and Insurance. Data grouped within 10-minute time zones from center, with average density and average time indicated for each group.

range covered by the sample. Density levels in New York entail obvious inconveniences: limited light and air, few ground-level facilities for recreation, auto and subway congestion, parking spaces available only in garage structures at considerable extra cost (more than $50 a month in Manhattan). Normal density standards furnish some perspective on the extent of consumer tolerance of high densities in New York. Maximum recommended densities of the American Public Health Association are 95 dwelling units per net acre in thirteen-story buildings and 75 in six-story buildings.[17] Manhattan residents in new thirteen-story buildings typically live at net densities ranging from 300 to over 500 units per acre. New six-

67

story buildings in areas from 25 to 50 minutes from the core are generally developed at about 150 dwelling units per acre.

In terms of light and air, these densities are not quite as oppressive as the comparison with standards suggests. Density statistics used here apply to single buildings or small developments, most of which pirate light and air from adjacent streets not counted in their own net acreage or from air space over neighboring buildings. In addition, the high densities of new buildings in central locations partly reflect their high proportion of efficiency and one-bedroom apartments. So far as ground facilities and traffic congestion are concerned, however, these are indeed oppressive densities by any standards other than those that dominate the New York housing market. To find new apartments at lower densities, the New Yorker must increase his commuting costs by moving to outlying areas served by commuter railroads. His rent in these suburban areas will be slightly more than he would pay for an apartment with comparable traveltime via subway in outer Brooklyn or the Bronx. For shorter traveltimes to the magnetic core of Manhattan, New Yorkers pay a cost in terms of high density as well as high rent.

The downtown core also exerts strong influence on density patterns in the Hartford region. All the new apartment developments over two stories high are located within 15 minutes of downtown, where densities of new buildings typically range from 35 to 70 dwelling units per net acre. The density curve declines sharply away from downtown, for new housing 20 minutes away lies in the zone where vacant land is readily available and developers find little advantage in exceeding a density of 20 units per acre for garden apartments. The steepness of the Hartford curve thus reflects primarily the small size of the region, plus the pull of downtown that causes occupants to accept higher densities in central locations in exchange for savings in traveltime.

Los Angeles showed no evidence of central orientation in the rent levels of new apartments, but some indication of central preference in the pattern of vacancy rates. A sampling of densities in new apartment construction reinforces the vacancy pattern in demonstrating some degree of central orientation. This sample consists entirely of the predominant type of apartment structure in the Los Angeles area: two- and three-story buildings of frame and stucco construction. Within the limits imposed by this type of building, densities are somewhat higher near the core than in outlying areas, but limitations of the sample conceal an important emerging trend. Tall elevator structures (four stories and higher) have been uncommon in Los Angeles for some time. A few were built in the 1920's and 1930's, primarily in central areas. A recent revision of zoning height limits has triggered construction of tall luxury buildings, with about ten major developments completed or under construction in the western sector from 1955 to 1960, and many more planned. None of the recent developments are near the downtown core; all within the western sector are in the Beverly Hills and Westwood areas, about 35 to 40 minutes in traveltime from the core.

Since these new elevator structures are still exceptional in Los Angeles, they were not included in the relatively small density sample of representative construction. They are significant, however, as an emerging characteristic of new apartment housing in the region. If they were included in a density curve of all new apartment development, the curve would probably reach a peak in the 35- 40-minute time zone, where a small rise in density is evident in the curve of ordinary construction. In an over-all perspective, the density patterns of new housing in Los Angeles suggest limited preference for central sites, with locational preferences currently shifting to a new noncentral orientation.

Conclusions

Analysis of locational preferences in the market for new housing within the three study areas confirms the theoretical approach, at least as far as apartment development is concerned. *New York shows clear and substantial central preferences; Hartford has similar tendencies, but their effects are undercut by the proximity of vacant land; Los Angeles presents an ambiguous picture suggesting only weak central preferences that have little or no effect on rent levels.*

One object of this analysis was to learn whether the public has rejected central locations for new housing. The answer depends upon metropolitan characteristics. In New York, with its strong center and lack of accessible vacant land, occupants of new apartments prefer central locations to the extent of paying sizable rent premiums and living at extremely high densities near the core. In

Hartford and Los Angeles, where the regional structures are not so oriented toward the center, central housing is less in favor; but people pay slight rent premiums and accept higher densities at central locations in Hartford, and inlying housing in Los Angeles is occupied more fully than outlying units of comparable quality.

What do these findings mean for attracting new housing to the declining areas? In terms of the strategy of renewal planning, they corroborate what has long been recognized on an intuitive basis: strengthening the downtown core is an important means of stimulating market demand for inlying housing. They also underline the importance to the housing market of traveltime differentials between various parts of the region and the downtown core. Transportation systems that change traveltime relationships between central and outlying locations (for trips to the core) can alter the demand for new housing in these locations. New highways that decrease traveltimes from vacant land without creating proportional effects in central locations can reduce the attractiveness of inlying areas for new housing.

Locational preferences in the housing market furnish important guides for renewal policies in old neighborhoods, for housing preference patterns play a key part in determining maximum feasible cost levels for new development. Cities in which central preference is an important factor in the housing market can undertake renewal programs on central sites even if costs to the developer are higher than in more outlying areas. *The only relevant standard is that costs must be commensurate with market advantages in a given location.* Where central preference is weak or nonexistent, the successful renewal of areas near the core requires keeping development and operating costs competitive with those in outlying locations. The pattern of locational preferences in a housing market establishes the extent of leeway within which developers' costs can rise above levels prevailing in other parts of the region. Further research into existing cost structures is necessary, however, in order to learn whether a given preference pattern permits or obstructs the rebuilding of older areas or whether contemplated public policies will succeed in reshaping the locational pattern of new housing.

The relevance of locational preferences for determining renewal prospects is particularly clear in New York. The initial rental sample

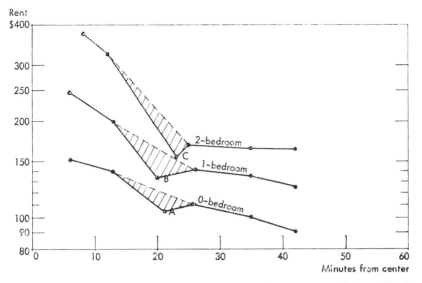

Figure 3.9. Monthly rents and traveltimes from center of New York region, including poor environments in 15 to 25 minute zone.

Source: City of New York Department of City Planning rental inventory of buildings completed 1958–1959; 14,152 dwelling units in 136 apartment developments in "good environments" plus 2,500 units in 15 developments in "poor environments." Median rents and median times of poor environment sample plotted at A, B, and C.

there eliminated housing located in poor environments that might have adverse effects on rent levels. As a result, the sample contained very few units with traveltimes of 15 to 25 minutes to the core; this time zone consists largely of the "gray areas" of New York, with decaying housing and inferior environments. Rental information for these units in poor environments has now been added in Figure 3.9 to the previously established rent gradients. Median rents and median times are plotted for the new sample at points A, B, and C.

Not only are these rents below the original gradients at the same location, but they are even below rents in more outlying locations. The depressed rent levels at these locations most likely reflect their undesirable environment. Renewal programs that provide new housing in an improved environment should be able to achieve rent levels in the range shown by the shaded areas, raising them toward the extrapolated gradients for good environments. (As implied earlier in this chapter, however, major housing programs in these locations may also reduce rent levels in more central areas by providing close substitutes for central housing where none now exist.)

71

At the very least, improved environments should be able to raise rents to the level found in the vicinity of 25 minutes from the core. This analysis suggests that development and operating costs in areas within the 15–25 minute zone can safely exceed comparable costs farther from the core, but they should not be far above costs at the 25-minute interval.

For a full analysis of renewal potential, locational patterns of costs as well as preferences should be investigated. Locational preferences can be understood in terms of the metropolitan factors that have been identified in this analysis. The extent to which cost patterns correspond to locational preferences in the three study regions is the subject of Chapter 4.

CHAPTER FOUR

THE ECONOMICS OF NEW HOUSING IN OLD NEIGHBORHOODS

Central locations offer important advantages for new housing in New York, slight advantages in Hartford, and negligible advantages in Los Angeles. Taken alone, these market characteristics neither promote nor retard the construction of new housing in central areas. If development costs were equal throughout a region, locational preferences alone would determine where new housing could earn the greatest return on investment. But development costs vary within urban regions: land costs differ from site to site, and real estate taxes differ in each taxing jurisdiction. Developers have a certain degree of flexibility in coping with cost differences. They can adjust densities to take into account different land costs, and they can vary building types to achieve different construction and operating costs per dwelling unit. The object of these adjustments is always to produce a housing unit that will yield a satisfactory return on investment, a unit whose rental income will exceed yearly costs by an amount sufficient to compensate the investor.

Wherever such adjustments succeed in producing a satisfactory return on investments, new housing is feasible. To evaluate the prospects for developing new apartment housing in the declining parts of the study regions requires bringing together three separate elements that enter into the investor's calculations: *cost levels* confronting developers, the *rents* they can obtain with particular kinds of dwelling units, and their *methods for adjusting the type of housing they build* to yield a satisfactory return within the limits established by cost factors and market characteristics. Rent information gathered for Chapter 3 was used to establish rent levels for this investigation. In this chapter, rent data are combined with informa-

73

tion on land, development, and operating costs to see whether developers can work out acceptable densities and structural types to produce a satisfactory return on new housing in the declining areas. Cost and market conditions can best be understood by looking first at areas within each region where construction has been active and then applying the findings to the declining areas.

This analysis produces surprising results. Despite the widespread view that new private development is not economically feasible in the declining "gray areas," *the three study regions all meet the first requirement for rebuilding. Site costs and re-use values are roughly in line in all three — although the Hartford case is marginal.* These results are the more striking because only New York displays clear and strong central preferences in the new housing market. Nevertheless, the balance of land costs and re-use values is clearly favorable for rebuilding the old areas of Los Angeles as well as New York, and favorable with only slight qualifications in Hartford.

New York Development Costs

According to the findings of the New York Metropolitan Region Study, the cost of developing new apartments in most of the built-up sections of New York City — including the declining areas — is so high that necessary rents will price such apartments out of the reach of all but the wealthiest groups. Edgar M. Hoover and Raymond Vernon observe:

> Members of the middle income group who insist upon tolerable structures are effectively excluded; this group could not afford to exploit the access advantages of such locations by rebuilding. Such an operation . . . is too costly except for the very rich.[1]

To demonstrate that this conclusion is incorrect requires working through the cost and return analyses that every developer must make, and determining what rent levels are necessary to produce a satisfactory return on investments in the declining areas and whether such rents are obtainable. New housing must conform to normal investment expectations and offer returns competitive with those at other locations that developers now find attractive.

Several components of development cost are more or less constant throughout the New York area, as well as throughout the Los Angeles and Hartford areas, and therefore have little influence on the developer's choice of building locations within the region. Construction costs for comparable apartment structures vary so slightly that developers consider them approximately equal throughout the New York area. Building code requirements within the various jurisdictions of the region offer no significant opportunities for structural variations that might reduce the cost of new apartment buildings in particular locations. Operating costs are also more or less constant throughout the region, depending on building type and level of service rather than location. The major elements that vary with location are *property taxes* and *land costs;* the extent to which they influence the locational pattern of new housing depends upon their importance within the total cost structure for new buildings and the extent to which they vary within the region. Zoning regulations, which vary with location, also limit the ability of a developer to make adjustments to cost and market conditions; this constraint will be considered later in discussing public policies affecting the rebuilding of old neighborhoods.

Property Tax Levels

Contrary to the popular impression that real estate taxes are highest in the central city and grade off to significantly lower levels in the suburbs, information for the New York region indicates that tax differences are not major ones and do not follow a center-oriented pattern. Table 4.1 presents a comparison of estimated tax rates in the five boroughs of New York City and five other cities in the region, using estimates of assessment to market value by the New York State Board of Equalization and Assessment.

These rates are somewhat higher than actual rates because the equalization ratios are based on 1952 and 1957 market values, which have subsequently risen. For purposes of comparison, however, they do indicate that central areas suffer from no major tax burden in comparison with outlying sites. Rates in several Westchester cities are higher than those in New York City. Within New York City, differences are minor between Manhattan and the Bronx, Brooklyn, or Queens. For a new dwelling unit with a market value of $10,000, Manhattan taxes at these estimated rates will be $75 per year higher than Queens taxes — a difference that can be overcome by a monthly rent $6 higher in Manhattan than in Queens. Manhattan apartments of course command a rent premium far

75

Table 4.1.   Property Tax Rates for Communities in New York Region, 1959

Community	Estimated Tax Rate (Per cent of full market value)
City of New York:	
Manhattan	3.86
Bronx	3.70
Brooklyn	3.41
Queens	3.11
Richmond	2.73
Westchester County:	
Mount Vernon	4.36
New Rochelle	4.07
Rye	3.78
White Plains	3.35
Yonkers	3.27

Source: New York State Department of Commerce, "Real Property Taxes in Cities of New York State, 1959," M-575-r, based on equalization ratios established by State Board of Equalization and Assessment. Tax rates include city, county, and school-district taxes due in 1959.

higher than that needed to wipe out this tax differential. The only tax difference that appears significant in Table 4.1 is the gap between Richmond and the other boroughs of New York City. Despite an apparently favorable tax level, Richmond has been too inaccessible from the core of the region to attract more than a small amount of new apartment housing. The major alternatives for new apartment locations (within the New York State portion of the region) are Manhattan, Queens, Brooklyn, the Bronx, or Westchester County. Among these alternative locations, tax differences are minor.

To check on the accuracy of this comparison and its applicability to new construction, information was obtained from real estate developers on the proportion of assessed value to development cost for new apartment buildings in areas of recent construction activity.[2] These ratios, applied to 1959 nominal tax rates, produced the following estimated tax rates:

Manhattan	3.18 per cent
Bronx	3.19
Brooklyn	3.20
Queens	3.20
White Plains	3.10

According to this information, gaps between tax levels are still narrower than they appeared in Table 4.1. Within New York City, differences are negligible. The White Plains rate is so close to those in the New York City boroughs that the total tax differential for a $10,000 dwelling unit would amount to a maximum of $10. *Tax levels, then, do not seem to constitute an obstacle to rebuilding the inner parts of the New York Region.*

Land Costs in the New York Region

Land costs in New York follow the pattern of rents and densities observed in Chapter 3. Rents and densities are much higher in the center of the New York region than in outlying locations. Land costs for inlying apartment sites reflect the high rent-earning capacity of central land and in the late 1950's were many times higher than costs in other parts of the region. In Manhattan, most land in areas of active apartment development sold at this time for prices ranging from $20 to $70 per square foot.[3] Prime sites in Greenwich Village cost $60 per square foot at the time information was gathered, while less favored Village sites were $30 to $40. Good sites on the Upper East Side brought prices of $60 to $70 per square foot; other sites, away from the prime locations, cost $20 to $30 per square foot. In all these cases, site acquisition prices included the cost of existing buildings on the land.

In the other boroughs of New York City, land prices seldom exceed $10 per square foot for apartment sites. The best locations in Brooklyn, Queens, and the Bronx brought $10 in 1960, but most apartment sites in these boroughs cost less than $5 per square foot. Average locations in Brooklyn and the Bronx were sold for $3 to $4 per square foot; in Queens, they ranged from $3 to $5. These sites were also covered with existing buildings, but typically the densities were much lower than in Manhattan.

Apartment sites in Westchester County are generally in built-up areas, readily accessible to commuter railroad stations. Here the prices were generally $4 to $5 per square foot at the time of the survey. Site acquisition for Westchester apartment houses generally requires clearing existing structures of low or moderate density.

Vacant land in the New York region sells at lower prices, but little of it is easily accessible to public transportation. The Bronx, Brooklyn, and Queens all have some vacant land far removed from subway connections that sold for $1 to $3 per square foot in the late 1950's. In Westchester County, garden apartment developers paid from $1 to $2 per square foot for vacant land within driving distance of commuter railroad stations. These prices represent actual sales of land to apartment developers; they are thus fully in line with development opportunities in locations where new construction has been active.

How do land prices in the old neighborhoods compare with those in areas of building activity? Many redevelopment projects in New York have been located in areas of Manhattan highly accessible to the core (15 minutes or less in traveltime) where little unsubsidized housing has appeared in recent years. Land for these projects has cost from $20 to $40 per square foot,[4] a price level corresponding to the lower end of the $20 to $70 range noted previously for areas of Manhattan where new apartment construction has been active. Manhattan locations farther from the core offer lower land prices: site acquisition costs have ranged from $9 per square foot for land in Harlem to $15 per square foot for a site on the Upper West Side near Central Park. Site acquisition costs for public housing projects in Manhattan have been still lower, ranging mostly from $7 to $11 per square foot for locations 15 to 20 minutes from the core.[5] *With the exception of highly accessible locations near the core, land prices in the inactive areas of Manhattan are clearly lower than typical prices in active construction areas.* Whether they are low enough to match the earning capacity of this land remains to be seen.

Land costs in the declining areas of other boroughs are below Manhattan levels. Redevelopment sites near the commercial core of downtown Brooklyn, some 25 minutes from midtown Manhattan, cost from $6 to $9 per square foot, but advance acquisition estimates for one prime site were $24 per square foot. Away from this secondary commercial core, public housing site costs reflect price levels in the declining areas. Land costs for most housing projects outside Manhattan have ranged from $3 to $7 per square foot for built-up sites near public transportation and accessible to the core in 20 to 35 minutes. These prices are somewhat higher than the $3 to $4 range found in typical active areas in Brooklyn and the Bronx and the corresponding $3 to $5 prices in Queens. Some addi-

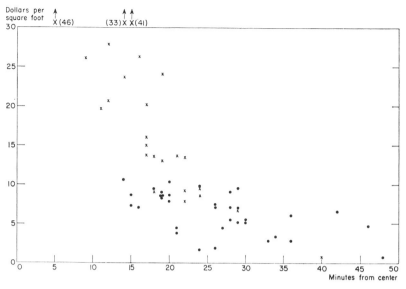

Figure 4.1.   Site acquisition costs and traveltimes from center of New York City. Public housing project: •; urban renewal project: x; all are post-1950 projects requiring site clearance.

tional market advantage would therefore seem to be necessary to attract investment to these more expensive locations.

Figure 4.1 brings together information on land prices for redevelopment and housing project sites, excluding housing projects built on vacant land. Land prices in these old areas decline as traveltime from the core increases, but prices vary considerably for any given degree of accessibility. In addition to traveltime from the core, the earning power of previous development is a major factor influencing cost levels. Figure 4.2 presents public housing land costs per square foot as a function of dwelling units per acre on the site before clearance, using only those project sites that were predominantly residential before acquisition. The obvious relationship between density and earning power calls attention to existing density as a critical factor influencing the cost of sites in declining areas. In Manhattan, public housing sites were previously built up at densities between 100 and 200 dwelling units per acre of total project area. Projects in the Bronx, Brooklyn, and Queens generally use sites that had been developed at densities of between 20 and 100 dwelling units per acre.

79

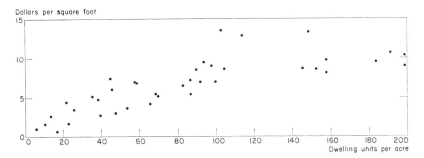

Figure 4.2.   Site acquisition costs and prior density of development, New York City public housing projects (post-1950) in residential areas.

The Adjustment of Cost Factors

How significant are the differences in land costs within the New York region? Prices for apartment sites in Manhattan are often twenty times as high as those in the outer boroughs. Sixty dollars per square foot is a typical price for Manhattan luxury apartment sites, while apartment land in outer Brooklyn and the Bronx sells for as little as $3 per square foot. But the costs that matter for apartment developers are not prices per square foot; they are development costs per unit and yearly operating outlays. It was noted in Chapter 3 that new apartments are developed at much higher densities in the center of the New York region than in outlying areas. Thus the land cost per dwelling unit need not be twenty times higher on $60-land than it is on $3-land. By reducing the amount of land per unit in central locations, the developer can hold down the land cost per unit even where land prices are high. Also, higher densities on small, expensive sites make possible significant economies of scale in building and operating a large number of apartments in a single undertaking.

The developer's ability to adjust costs in this way is limited by a number of factors. If he could build central housing at twenty times the density of outlying housing, he could equalize land costs per unit; but high densities bring extra costs of their own. Tall buildings mean heavy and expensive construction, including much unproductive interior space for corridors and elevator shafts and such expensive service features as extra elevators and underground parking levels. High densities thus raise unit construction and operating

80

costs at the same time that they reduce unit land costs. In addition, people may be unwilling to accept high densities if they entail loss of light and air, and zoning laws set an upper limit on both density and land coverage. As a result, New York developers do not build in Manhattan at twenty times the densities they use in Brooklyn; they build at about three times the Brooklyn densities — 400 to 500 dwelling units per acre on expensive Manhattan land, compared with 150 on cheap land in the other boroughs.

This higher density reflects not only taller building types and fuller land coverage but also a high proportion of small units. As Table 4.2 indicates, efficiency apartments constitute only a small proportion of new units in outlying locations but account for a major share in the center of the region. Two-bedroom apartments, on the other hand, represent one fourth of all new units in outlying areas but shrink to half that proportion in the center.

Of the two methods for increasing density, taller structures make possible major density increases, while shifts in apartment-size distribution allow only small supplementary gains. Thus increases in density typically bring about the higher unit construction and operating costs that are characteristic of tall buildings. As a result, the first problem of selecting an optimum density is one of balancing economies in unit land cost against increased unit construction and service costs.

In adjusting development costs, however, the objective is not to minimize unit cost but to achieve a satisfactory return per unit investment. Part of the cost adjustment, therefore, may represent a strategy for increasing unit rent rather than merely holding down costs. Certain high-cost locations allow a developer to reach a "luxury" submarket, where he can obtain higher rents by providing such special construction features as outdoor balconies, central air conditioning, and decorative lobbies and exteriors. Special service features — doormen, elevator operators, superior property maintenance — also bring higher rents. Construction and service costs thus play a dual role in the cost adjustment process: they are partially determined by the choice of density, but they are also determined in part by independent decisions to vary the facilities and services in order to reach different rent levels. As this type of variation suggests, developers may overcome high land costs not merely by raising densities to economize on development costs but also by

81

Table 4.2. Size Distribution of New Apartments by Traveltime from Core, New York City, 1958–1959

Minutes from Core:	0–9		10–19		20–29		30–39		40–49	
	Number	Per cent	Number	Per cent	Number	Per cent	Number	Per cent	Number	Per cent
Efficiency (0-bedroom) Apartments	750	44.0	1,443	33.4	439	21.0	1,013	21.8	215	15.5
One-Bedroom	686	40.3	2,074	48.0	1,033	49.5	2,259	48.6	798	57.5
Two-Bedroom	203	11.9	728	16.8	496	23.8	1,187	25.5	348	25.1
Three-Bedroom or Larger	65	3.8	78	1.8	119	5.7	191	4.1	27	1.9
Total	1,704	100.0	4,323	100.0	2,087	100.0	4,650	100.0	1,388	100.0

Sources: Rental inventory used in Chapter 3, Figure 3.4. Traveltime calculations described in Chapter 3, footnote 4.

entering a distinct luxury market where a superior product can command a rent premium.

Examples of Cost Adjustment

The cost adjustment process must take account of all these factors — *density, construction cost, operating cost* — as variables that are manipulated to produce an acceptable investment "package." In Table 4.3, a number of examples are given to illustrate the ways in which New York developers adjust costs in a variety of locations with differing land prices within the region. Columns 1 through 5 describe costs and their adjustment in areas where apartment construction has recently been active. On the basis of these current practices, feasible development alternatives have been prepared for hypothetical locations in the declining areas; these alternatives are presented in columns 6 through 8. Information on current cost levels and development practice in different parts of the region was derived from a series of interviews with New York realtors and public officials and from published cost analyses of recent apartment buildings.[6]

Discussions with realtors indicated that a yearly return of approximately 15 per cent on equity investment after payment of interest and amortization is necessary to attract risk capital into most apartment developments in the New York area. The case examples all produce returns of about 15 per cent according to the stated assumptions. These assumptions are conservative with respect to financing and property taxes. In practice, the equity share is often less than one third of development cost, and the land assessment is lower than those assumed here. On the other hand, no specific allowance has been made for vacancies, so that the indicated rates of return are not likely to differ greatly from realistic conditions.[7]

Column 4 describes the basic New York apartment house: six stories, undistinguished in appearance, with minimum physical features (no balconies, plain lobbies, red brick facing) and minimum service. This type of building, found in large numbers in Brooklyn, the Bronx, and Queens, provides the cheapest new apartments available in the area. Rents are typically $40 per room, with three and one-half rental rooms a normal size for a one-bedroom apartment. This type of structure is a reasonable investment on land

Table 4.3. New York Region: Financial Calculations for One-Bedroom Apartments

Location:	1 Manhattan	2 Manhattan	3 Queens	4 Brooklyn-Bronx	5 White Plains (Westchester)	6 New York Declining Area	7 New York Declining Area	8 New York Declining Area
Traveltime from Downtown	5–9 min.	10–19 min.	25–34 min.	35–39 min.	40–44 min.	15–24 min.	15–24 min.	15–24 min.
Land Cost per Square Foot	60.00	20.00	10.00	3.50	4.50	5.00+	9.00	4.50+
Building Type	15-story el.	12-story el.	6-story el.	6-story el.	6-story el.	6-story el.	6-story el.	3-story
Dwelling Units per Acre	500	350	160	150	120	150	150	50
Square Feet per Dwelling Unit	87	124	272	290	363	290	290	871
Land Cost per Dwelling Unit	5,220	2,480	2,720	1,015	1,634	1,500	2,610	4,000
Construction Cost per Dwelling Unit	16,000	13,000	10,000	8,500	9,000	9,000	9,000	8,000
Total Investment per Dwelling Unit	21,220	15,480	12,720	9,515	10,634	10,500	11,610	12,000
Equity Share (⅓)	7,073	5,160	4,240	3,172	3,545	3,500	1,161*	1,200*
Mortgage (⅔, 6%, 20 years)	14,147	10,320	8,480	6,343	7,089	7,000	10,449*	10,800*
Yearly Operating Cost	660	420	350	350	350	350	350	300
Tax Rate	.0318	.0318	.0320	.0319	.0310	.0319	.0319	.0319
Yearly Taxes	675	492	407	303	330	335	370	382
Total Yearly Cost	1,335	912	757	653	680	685	720	682
Yearly Rent	3,600	2,520	2,100	1,680	1,800	1,800	1,680	1,680
(Monthly Rent)	(300)	(210)	(175)	(140)	(150)	(150)	(140)	(140)
Cash Surplus over Cost	2,265	1,608	1,343	1,027	1,120	1,115	960	998
Less Yearly Interest and Amortization (8.5% of mortgage)	1,202	877	720	539	603	595	758*	783*
Net Cash Return	1,063	731	623	488	517	520	202	215
Return on Equity	15.0%	14.2%	14.7%	14.6%	14.6%	14.9%	17.4%	17.9%

*FHA Financing: 90% mortgage, 30 years, 7¼% yearly interest and amortization.

costing $3 to $4 per square foot. At a characteristic density of 150 dwelling units per net acre, the land cost per unit is a little over $1,000. As of 1960, developers sometimes paid somewhat more for land per unit to build this type of structure for the same general rent level, with $1,500 per unit the upper limit.

Land for apartment houses sells for as much as $10 per square foot in the best parts of the Bronx (Riverdale) and Queens (Forest Hills, Main Street–Flushing). Column 3 illustrates how developers adjust their costs to build in these locations. Building height typically remains at six stories, but density increases slightly. The dwelling unit itself is a more expensive product, with an outdoor balcony and perhaps central air conditioning. By virtue of superior physical equipment, a location more accessible to Manhattan, and desirable neighborhood associations, the apartment can command $50 a room, or $175 per month for the unit. Under these circumstances, the developer can afford to pay more than $2,500 per unit for his land.

Within Manhattan, but away from key prestige locations, land prices of $20 per square foot require a more decided shift to high density. Typical densities here are about 350 dwelling units per acre, in buildings twelve stories high. These are fully fireproof buildings, with concrete floors, in contrast to the lighter semifireproof construction permitted in six-story structures. Unit construction costs rise substantially, but part of the increase reflects higher standards, including more expensive exterior finish and more elaborate lobbies. Service costs also rise, with a doorman and parking attendant on the payroll. In recognition of superior location and the level of physical plant and service, rents rise to $60 per room, or $210 per month for a one-bedroom apartment. Unit land costs, at $2,500, remain about the same as in the best Queens locations.

To create a suitable investment in Manhattan prestige locations, the builder improves his product still more and he raises the density. On the $60-land in column 1, developers build at densities of about 500 dwelling units per net acre, using buildings fifteen stories or higher. Rooms are larger, kitchen equipment is more elaborate, and the level of service is still higher. Rents in these luxury buildings are $85 per room, $300 per month for a one-bedroom unit. Land cost per unit is over $5,000 at this location; Manhattan developers often pay $6,000 or $7,000 per unit for luxury apartment sites.

At the other extreme of the region in terms of location are suburban sites for apartment houses. Land in White Plains, more than 40 minutes from 42nd Street in Manhattan by commuter railroad, sells for $4 to $5 per square foot in locations suitable for apartment houses. These locations are generally within walking distance of the railroad station. Here the developer's response is to provide a building very similar to the basic six-story apartment house of Brooklyn and Queens, with slightly more expensive features and somewhat lower density. As of 1960, one-bedroom apartments in Westchester brought rents of $150 per month, $10 more than apartments in outer Brooklyn or the Bronx, but this small differential was enough to permit slightly higher expenditures for land and construction in Westchester. Land cost per unit in this White Plains example is $1,600.

In these case examples I have adopted the perspective of the individual builder confronted with a set of costs that he must combine in attempting to work out a satisfactory investment. From a broader perspective, the cost and rent combinations that developers achieve in different locations are not merely the way of overcoming a given level of land costs; they are also the justification for the level of land costs. Sixty dollars per square foot constitutes a market price for luxury apartment land in Manhattan only because reasonable investments *can* be worked out at this price level. If they could not, land would not sell at this price for apartments.

Apartment land in New York generally contains existing structures that must be cleared, however. To the extent that these structures produce income, they constitute an independent standard governing the value of the site in its present use. Land sales for apartment re-use are feasible only if the site has a re-use value to the developer greater than the value of land and buildings in present use. In the land markets of the various sections of New York where apartment construction is active, re-use value, supported by the investment possibilities described here, clearly exceeds present value of land and buildings on a sufficient number of sites to provide a steady supply of marketable land.

Investment Possibilities in the Declining Areas

The examples cited so far illustrate current methods of adjusting development costs to market rents in a variety of New York locations. What can be done in the declining areas? According to the analysis in Chapter 3, accessibility to the core is a potent market factor in the New York region. As a result, the locational advantages of the older areas with respect to core access should enable them to command higher rents than more outlying areas, provided that their environment is upgraded from its present condition. A reasonable first assumption is that new one-bedroom apartments approximately 20 minutes from midtown Manhattan bring in rents $10 higher per month than comparable apartments 35 minutes away in Brooklyn and the Bronx.

Under these conditions, calculations in column 6 indicate that developers can pay more than $5 per square foot for land, a price within the $3 to $7 range that is typical of land costs in the declining areas outside Manhattan. The land cost per dwelling unit in this case is $1,500, a price consistent with present practice in developing six-story apartment houses in the outer boroughs of New York City. In this calculation, density has been held to the same level of 150 dwelling units per net acre that prevails in more outlying locations. Clearly, the cost of land constitutes no significant obstacle to rebuilding the older areas outside Manhattan. Economic conditions are sufficiently favorable to permit new apartment developments comparable to those in the outlying parts of Brooklyn and the Bronx, provided that the environment is reclaimed so that it exercises no depressing influence on rent levels. Further, the rent levels assumed here are far below the luxury category.

Some sites in the older areas will involve clearance costs higher than $3 to $7 per square foot. Public housing sites in Harlem have cost about $9 per square foot, while sites elsewhere in Manhattan have cost as much as $11 per square foot for public housing and $15 per square foot for urban renewal projects. If these sites are suitable for apartments with rents of $175 or $210 per month, as in columns 2 and 3, land costs of $10 and $20 per square foot will be consistent with development opportunities, *but even at lower rents these land costs do not rule out new development.* All the examples so far assume conventional financing on conservative terms. With the type of financing available for mortgages insured by the Federal Housing Administration, which would be available in official urban renewal project areas (under the FHA Section 220 Rental Housing Program), developers could pay higher land prices even if rents remained at the moderate levels prevailing in outlying New York City locations.

Under FHA financing, mortgages cover 90 per cent of total development cost, and the mortgage term is 30 years or longer. The conventional financing assumed so far provides for loans of two thirds of development cost, with a mortgage term of 20 years. Even with a rent of only $140 per month, $9 per square foot is a feasible land price for six-story apartment buildings at a density of 150 dwelling units per acre, under the FHA financing terms used in column 7. As a result, the Harlem land price of $9 per square foot is not excessive for typical New York six-story apartment houses, within the framework of an urban renewal project that will improve the environment and make available FHA financing. If rents higher than $140 can be obtained, land prices higher than $9 per square foot and equal to those of public housing sites in Manhattan are feasible for new construction.

Rebuilding the declining areas may call for some construction at densities lower than 150 units per acre. With FHA financing, three-story walk-up buildings are feasible on land selling for $4.50 per square foot. Column 8 presents calculations for a development of this type, with one-bedroom apartments renting once again for only $140 per month. Land prices in the declining areas of Brooklyn, the Bronx, and Queens are thus compatible even with densities of 50 units per net acre, with the aid of FHA mortgages. This density would not be feasible for Manhattan, however, unless subsidies were available.

So far as typical New York developments are concerned, these calculations demonstrate clearly that the declining areas present no major economic difficulties. Outside Manhattan, new developments comparable to current construction in outer Brooklyn and the Bronx — *and with the same general rent levels* — are economically feasible with conventional financing. In Manhattan's older areas, the same types of development are economically feasible through FHA financing. The requirements for such new developments in the declining areas are that the environment must be improved so that it does not depress rent levels *below* those in more outlying locations, and development densities must approximate those now current in more outlying locations. With FHA financing, developers have sufficient leeway so that either of these requirements may be relaxed to some extent in the declining areas of the Bronx, Brooklyn, and Queens.

Los Angeles Cost Components

In Los Angeles, as in New York, the only cost components that vary significantly with location are property taxes and land costs. Construction and operating costs are constant throughout the region for comparable structures and comparable levels of service. Building codes within the region do not differ sufficiently for any community to offer large savings in construction cost by permitting cheaper structural designs. Limited savings are possible in a few cases. Beverly Hills permits frame and stucco construction to a height of four stories, while the City of Los Angeles requires heavier construction when a building exceeds three stories. Code differences of this order, while important for some locational decisions, constitute no major cost disadvantages in the centrally located declining areas.

Property taxes follow no clear-cut geographic pattern, but the central-city rate is somewhat higher than rates in a number of outlying communities that serve as alternative locations for new apartment housing. Table 4.4 presents effective tax rates for communities in Los Angeles County; these rates are a composite of county, city, school, and special taxes for 1960–1961.

Average tax rates for communities grouped according to distance from downtown Los Angeles show no consistent variation with respect to location. The average rates hover around 2 per cent, except for communities between 25 and 35 miles away from the core, where the rates are higher. On the average, property taxes are no higher in central locations than in outlying areas, but the averages conceal some important differences among individual communities. The City of Los Angeles, with its tax rate of 2.02 per cent, compares unfavorably with several outlying communities where developers have recently been building new apartments: Beverly Hills (1.27 per cent), Long Beach (1.57 per cent), Pasadena (1.65 per cent), Santa Monica (1.66 per cent), Burbank (1.68 per cent), and Glendale (1.74 per cent). For an apartment unit with a development cost of $10,000, yearly property taxes in the City of Los Angeles would exceed those in Santa Monica by $36, or $3 per month on the rent bill. In a region such as New York, where central

Table 4.4.   Property Tax Rates for Communities in Los Angeles County, 1960–1961 (Estimated percentages of full market value)

			Miles from Core:				
0–5	6–10	11–15	16–20	21–25	26–30	31–35	36–40
Vernon 1.76	Beverly Hills 1.27	Pasadena 1.65	El Segundo 1.51	Long Beach 1.57	Pomona 2.17	La Verne 2.32	Avalon 1.95
Los Angeles 2.02	Commerce 1.55	Burbank 1.68	Santa Monica 1.66	Lakewood 1.92	Glendora 2.20	Claremont 2.35	
	Glendale 1.74	Gardena 1.84	Signal Hill 1.81	San Fernando 1.93	San Dimas 2.32		
	Montebello 1.76	Arcadia 1.90	Duarte 1.99	Rolling Hills Est. 2.00			
	South Gate 1.84	Downey 1.98	Sierra Madre 2.09	Palos Verdes Est. 2.03			
	Huntington Park 1.88	Rosemead 2.00	Monrovia 2.13	La Puente 2.09			
	Maywood 1.92	San Marino 2.02	Bradbury 2.16	Rolling Hills 2.17			
	Alhambra 2.01	Temple City 2.02	Lawndale 2.25	Azusa 2.19			
	Monterey Park 2.02	Compton 2.05	Irwindale 2.29	W. Covina 2.22			
	Inglewood 2.02	So. El Monte 2.06	Hermosa Beach 2.31	Walnut 2.26			
	San Gabriel 2.03	Torrance 2.08	Dairy Valley 2.35	Redondo Beach 2.28			
	Lynwood 2.03	El Monte 2.13	Baldwin Park 2.36	Covina 2.36			
	Bell 2.06	City of Industry 2.14	Miranda Hills 2.41				
	South Pasadena 2.07	Paramount 2.25	Manhattan Beach 2.41				
	Culver City 2.11	Norwalk 2.28	Artesia				
	Pico Rivera 2.36	Hawthorne 2.29					
		Bellflower 2.32					
		Whittier 2.33					
		Santa Fe Springs 2.45					
Average: 1.89	Average: 1.92	Average: 2.08	Average: 1.99	Average 2.09	Average: 2.23	Average: 2.34	Average 1.95

Source: Los Angeles County Assessor, Listing of tax rates for different communities in Los Angeles County, S-74, 10/60. County assessments are approximately 25 per cent of full market value; tax rates shown are therefore 25 per cent of nominal tax rates.

locations have considerable value in the rental market, this difference would be negligible. In Los Angeles, where centrality apparently has little effect on rent levels, the tax difference is worth noting and will be examined to test its significance for the declining areas in the analysis of housing investment cases.

Land Costs

In New York, land costs for apartment sites are many times higher in central locations than in outlying areas, following the general pattern of rent levels. Los Angeles contrasts sharply on both counts. The lack of any clear rental pattern related to distance from the core of Los Angeles has already been noted; land costs also seem to have very little to do with distance from the center. Figure 4.3 presents the estimated range of land prices that apartment developers have paid in recent years for sites in desirable neighborhoods lying in the western sector of the region, the same sector used for the analysis of rents.[8] As in New York, these sites all involve some clearance of existing structures. The general pattern of land prices in this sector of Los Angeles is remarkably even. Except for a slight dip near the core, in a relatively low prestige area, and a marked rise around Beverly Hills and Westwood (33 to 40 minutes from the core), all prices fall within the narrow range of $3 to $5 per square foot.

These price estimates represent typical sites for new apartment construction in Los Angeles. They do not include such special sites as land on Wilshire Boulevard itself, or land with value for commercial development. Characteristically, these sites are on residen-

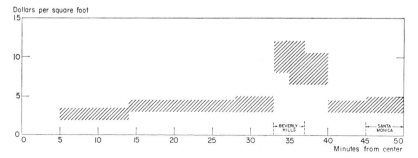

Figure 4.3. Site acquisition costs for new apartment developments, western sector of Los Angeles region, 1959–1960, and traveltimes from center.

91

tial side streets and require clearing old one- or two-family houses. Since the prices are derived from recent land sales for apartment development, they necessarily reflect land costs in areas that developers consider satisfactory for new construction. As a result, these estimates neglect areas where land has not recently been used for apartment development. Except for a few isolated sales, little information is available on land prices in the inactive older areas of Los Angeles. According to the limited information available, and in the opinion of well-informed appraisers, land costs for comparable sites in the old neighborhoods are lower than those cited in the Wilshire sector. In most cases, the old areas of Los Angeles are not encumbered with high-density structures, but only with single-family and duplex houses, so that there is little reason to expect higher prices in these areas than in the neighborhoods now being rebuilt along Wilshire Boulevard.

Two current urban renewal projects in Los Angeles furnish some insight into the cost of acquiring large tracts of land, rather than searching out small parcels at reasonable prices. The huge Bunker Hill project, covering 136 acres immediately adjacent to the central business district, was expected to cost an average of $8.78 per square foot for real estate purchases and acquisition expenses, according to appraisals in 1960. Since this land has considerable commercial value, the appropriate comparison here is with land adjacent to the central business district of another city: in New York, land costs are over $40 per square foot for renewal projects with comparable locations.

A second renewal area near downtown, but with less value for commercial development, is likely to be more representative of land costs in the declining areas. This is the Temple Project, occupying 183 acres about 5 minutes from downtown. Appraisals in 1960 indicated a probable land cost in the vicinity of $3 per square foot, a price within the range shown in Figure 4.3 for land slightly farther from the core.[9]

Cost Adjustments in Los Angeles

With land prices relatively constant for apartment developments throughout the area, the task of adjusting costs to produce satisfactory investment possibilities is much simpler in Los Angeles than it is in New York. Nevertheless, some adjustments are necessary, as the case examples in Table 4.5 indicate. Once again, information on current practice provides a basis for judging how developers can manipulate densities, construction costs, and operating costs in locations within the declining areas.[10]

Rents for new apartments are lower in Los Angeles than in New York, and the range of variation is much narrower. Typical one-bedroom units in Los Angeles generally rent for between $120 and $140 per month, while New York rents start at $140 for one-bedroom apartments and go as high as $250. Thus the range of typical cost adjustments must be smaller in Los Angeles, and the costs lower. Construction costs are markedly lower in Los Angeles, since the mild climate permits light exterior walls, and central heating facilities are unnecessary. Individual electric heaters are installed in each apartment so that each tenant pays his own heating costs. As a result, Los Angeles operating costs are also relatively low. Financing costs, on the other hand, are slightly higher in Los Angeles than in New York, with 6¼ per cent representing a typical interest rate for 20-year conventional mortgage loans in 1960.

Small variations in density constitute the main method of adjusting costs in Los Angeles. The most common type of apartment structure in Los Angeles is a two-story building of frame and stucco construction. Development densities for this type of building vary from about 40 to 70 dwelling units per net acre, depending in part upon the size distribution of apartment units, as well as upon ground coverage. Within the limits that are feasible for this type of structure, developers find it advantageous to build at the maximum densities that the public and the zoning laws will tolerate. In near-central locations, land prices alone do not require very high densities, but developers commonly build at the upper end of the normal range. Column 1 of Table 4.5 shows typical development costs near downtown, where a return above 15 per cent is feasible by building on $3-land at 65 units per acre. In locations successively farther away, as shown in columns 2 and 3, densities are slightly lower while land costs vary from $3 to $3.50, and rents vary from $125 to $130. In prime locations of West Hollywood (column 4), where rents of $140 per month can be obtained, lower densities are typical, despite land costs of $4 per square foot.

In all these cases, developers consider a return of 15 per cent

Table 4.5. Los Angeles Region: Financial Calculations for One-Bedroom Apartments

Location:	1 Los Angeles	2 Los Angeles	3 Los Angeles	4 Los Angeles W. Hollywood	5 Beverly Hills	6 West Los Angeles	7 Santa Monica	8 San Fernando Valley	9 Los Angeles Declining Area
Traveltime from Downtown	5–9 min.	10–19 min.	20–29 min.	30–34 min.	33–37 min.	40–44 min.	45–49 min.	50+ min.	5–35 min.
Land Cost per Square Foot	3.00	3.50	3.00	4.00	8.00	3.00	3.50	1.50	5.00
Building Type	2-story	2-story	2-story	2-story	3-story	2-story	2-story	2-story	2-story
Dwelling Units per Acre	65	60	55	50	65	40	50	45	50
Square Feet per Dwelling Unit	670	726	792	871	670	1,089	871	968	871
Land Cost per Dwelling Unit	2,010	2,541	2,376	3,484	5,360	3,267	3,049	1,452	4,355
Construction Cost per Dwelling Unit	7,500	7,500	7,500	7,500	10,000	7,500	7,500	7,500	7,500
Total Investment per Dwelling Unit	9,510	10,041	9,876	10,984	15,360	10,767	10,549	8,952	11,855
Equity Share (⅓)	3,170	3,347	3,292	3,661	5,120	1,077*	3,516	2,984	1,186*
Mortgage (%, 6.25%, 20 years)	6,340	6,694	6,584	7,323	10,240	9,690*	7,023	5,968	10,669*
Yearly Operating Cost	265	265	265	265	330	265	265	265	265
Tax Rate	.0202	.0202	.0202	.0202	.0127	.0202	.0166	.0202	.0202
Yearly Taxes	192	203	199	222	195	217	175	181	239
Total Yearly Cost	457	468	464	487	525	482	440	446	504
Yearly Rent	1,500	1,560	1,500	1,680	2,400	1,380	1,560	1,440	1,500
(Monthly Rent)	(125)	(130)	(125)	(140)	(200)	(115)	(130)	(120)	(125)
Cash Surplus over Cost	1,043	1,092	1,036	1,193	1,875	898	1,120	994	996
Less Yearly Interest and Amortization (8.8% of mortgage)	558	589	579	644	901	703*	618	525	774*
Net Cash Return	485	503	457	549	974	195	502	469	222
Return on Equity	15.3%	15.0%	13.9%	15.0%	19.0%	18.1%	14.3%	15.7%	18.7%

* FHA Financing: 90% mortgage, 30 years, 7¼% yearly interest and amortization.

sufficient to justify investments in new housing. Developers of luxury housing, where rents are $200 and higher for one-bedroom units, expect a higher return — about 20 per cent or more — in view of the greater risks involved in building for the relatively small Los Angeles high-rent market. In Beverly Hills, where land costs are more than twice as high as those prevailing in the rest of the region, developers can operate successfully only by providing a luxury product, with more expensive finish and interior equipment, and a swimming pool on the grounds. Thus in column 5, unit construction costs are higher, and developers choose three-story buildings to achieve high density with lower land coverage. The lower property taxes of Beverly Hills are also a factor permitting this type of development on land costing $8 per square foot.

In the Sawtelle area of West Los Angeles, developers have recently placed new units on the market at rents below the typical range by using FHA financing. Column 6 demonstrates the way this financing operates; the mortgage terms are identical with FHA terms in New York. By reducing the proportion of equity and the yearly level of interest and amortization below the terms of conventional mortgages, FHA financing permits lower rents for a given level of land costs in this case. Alternately, FHA financing would permit higher land costs for a given rent level. This type of financing requires compliance with FHA development standards, which permit maximum densities of 40 units per net acre (50 units per acre on corner lots).

Still farther from the Los Angeles core, Santa Monica presents conditions similar to those in the inner parts of the region, with comparable rent levels and land costs but a lower tax rate. The typical cost adjustment, appearing in column 7, is quite similar to those already described, but the density is lower than that in column 2, where land costs and rents are the same.

Even on vacant land, Los Angeles developers do not reduce densities much below the levels prevailing on sites that must be cleared of prior development. Vacant land zoned for apartments, with utilities available, sells for $1.50 to $2 per square foot in desirable San Fernando Valley locations. As column 8 indicates, developers produce housing at the lower end of the typical ranges of both density and rent — 45 units per acre at $120 per month — in this outlying location.

Possibilities for the Declining Areas

The calculations in Table 4.5 illustrate typical land costs that developers currently pay in Los Angeles. Costs up to $3.50 per square foot, or up to $3,000 per unit, are feasible for ordinary apartment developments. The limited information available suggests that site costs in the declining areas are not likely to exceed these levels. Where acquisition costs are higher, FHA financing can permit development at current rents and densities up to a cost of $5 per square foot. Calculations in column 9 assume a density of 50 dwelling units per net acre and a rent of $125 per month for a one-bedroom unit. At this rent, which represents the lower end of the usual range, developers can earn over 18 per cent on their equity by using FHA financing.

Rebuilding the declining areas of Los Angeles thus poses no major problems of land cost for the developer, despite the weakness of central preference in the market for new housing. As in New York, public subsidies will be needed to improve community facilities and the general environment of the older areas. *But in Los Angeles, even more clearly than in New York, land prices in the older areas are fully consistent with development costs and with market rents, provided that developers are permitted to build the type of structures that they now use elsewhere in the region, at densities that are typical of current practice.*

Hartford Cost Components

Two costs that were found to vary with location in the New York and Los Angeles regions were also found to vary in the Hartford region; they are *land costs* and *taxes.* Construction and operating costs for comparable buildings and levels of service are virtually equal throughout the Hartford region. Of the two costs that vary significantly, property tax levels are difficult to compare accurately because of the vagaries of assessment in the City of Hartford. Table 4.6 presents effective 1959 property tax rates for towns in the Hartford region for which estimates are available. The equalization ratio for the City of Hartford is uncertain, and revaluation of properties was in process at the time of this survey. The effective tax rate for Hartford in Table 4.6 follows estimates of current Hartford renewal studies in assuming assessments at two thirds of develop-

Table 4.6. Property Tax Rates for Communities in Hartford Region, 1959 (Estimated percentages of full market value)

		Miles from Core:			
0–5		6–10		11–15	
East Hartford	1.63	South Windsor	1.71	Windsor Locks	1.58
West Hartford	2.15	Bloomfield	2.27	Avon	1.62
Wethersfield	2.15	Newington	2.34	East Windsor	2.07
Hartford	3.11	Glastonbury	2.45	Simsbury	2.15
		Rocky Hill	2.52	Vernon	2.46
		Manchester	2.78		
Average:	2.48	Average:	2.35	Average:	1.98

Sources: Capitol Region Planning Agency, "1959 Tax Rates for Towns in CRPA Region." Equalization ratios from State of Connecticut, *Assessor's Report to the Tax Commissioner* (Fiscal Year ending February 1959) for all communities except the City of Hartford. Equalization ratio for Hartford estimated as two thirds of full value in Rogers, Taliaferro, and Lamb, *Renewal Program for Downtown Hartford, Connecticut,* prepared for City of Hartford (1960), pp. III-31, III-37. The above information covers 15 of the 21 cities and towns in the Hartford Standard Metropolitan Statistical Area, omitting Canton, Cromwell, Enfield, Farmington, Suffield, and Windsor.

ment cost. The effective rate of 3.11 per cent for the central city indicates a sizable disadvantage in relation to effective rates elsewhere in the region, but some developers believe the actual Hartford rate for new housing is only slightly above that of West Hartford.

If these estimated effective rates are realistic, property taxes on a $10,000 apartment unit will be almost $100 more per year in Hartford than in Wethersfield or West Hartford, two alternate locations for new apartments in the center of the region. The effects of this differential upon housing investments will be investigated by means of case examples for the Hartford region. Aside from the tax rate in the City of Hartford, however, central locations do not involve higher taxes than outlying sites. All but a few towns in the outer 5-mile rings of the region had higher effective rates in 1959 than the core cities of Wethersfield, West Hartford, and East Hartford. Property taxes are thus unlikely to create special burdens for developers of new housing in the centrally located areas outside of Hartford.

Land Costs in the Hartford Region

Acquisition costs for apartment sites in the Hartford region are clearly higher in central locations than in outlying areas, but the differences are small in comparison with those noted in New York.[11]

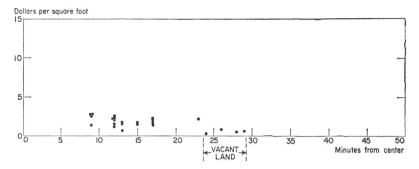

Figure 4.4.   Site acquisition costs for new apartment developments, western sector of Hartford region, 1959–1960, and traveltimes
from center.

Land in desirable locations near downtown Hartford was sold for
apartment development at about $2.50 per square foot in 1960.
Sites 10 to 20 minutes away from downtown, in Hartford and West
Hartford, were priced generally between $1.50 and $2.50 per
square foot. In these near-central locations, building sites must first
be cleared of existing structures. Farther out, vacant land zoned for
apartments sold for $.50 to $1 per square foot. Figure 4.4 presents
a compilation of sales prices for a number of apartment sites in the
sector extending westward from downtown Hartford for which
rental information was presented in Chapter 3.

The density of prior development is an important factor affecting
these prices. Apartment builders have been able to assemble good
sites in the central areas by buying spacious single-family homes on
large lots. The mansions of the late nineteenth century, built to
generous density standards, provide sites for current apartment
development. Where the old mansions have not been converted to
profitable rooming houses, a house standing on 20,000 square feet
of land may sell for $30,000, or $1.50 per square foot of land.
Close to downtown, the price is about $2.50 per square foot for a
comparable building on a large lot. These are feasible prices for
new apartment development; they represent actual recent sales to
developers. Prices are low enough for the developers, however, in
part because the once gracious homes of another generation, built
at relatively low densities, are a major source of land for new
construction.

98

The other declining sections of Hartford, in contrast, consist largely of housing built initially for a middle-income market at significantly higher development densities. In these areas, some three-family houses on lots 50 feet wide and 125 feet deep sell for $25,000 to $30,000, or approximately $4 to $5 per square foot of land. Other sites in these areas sell for $3 to $4 per square foot. In typical locations within the declining areas 10 to 15 minutes from downtown, $3 to $5 per square foot seems a reasonable land price to assume in investigating prospects for attracting new development. In less densely developed parts of the old areas, however, land prices will be lower.

Cost Adjustments in Hartford

Once again, the method for evaluating the significance of differences in property taxes and land prices is to look into the nature of current cost adjustments in areas where new construction is active and to apply adjustment techniques consistent with current practice in active locations to the declining areas.[12]

The range of rents in new apartments is relatively narrow in the Hartford region, but it reflects a central orientation in the housing market. For one-bedroom apartments in the rental sample, rents range from $125 to $147 per month in locations less than 10 minutes from the core. Comparable apartments 10 to 20 minutes from the core rent for $120 to $138 per month; the sample included no one-bedroom apartments more than 20 minutes from downtown Hartford. On the basis of this rental information, plus information on rents for two-bedroom apartments farther than 20 minutes from the core, I estimate rents for new one-bedroom apartments as $140 close to the core, $130 from 10 to 20 minutes away, and $120 more than 20 minutes away. This pattern of higher rents in more central locations helps overcome (and helps create) higher land prices in central locations, but developers must also make some adjustments in density to compensate for differences in land price.

The range of typical densities is somewhat greater in Hartford than in Los Angeles, and it exhibits a decidedly central orientation. Apartment buildings less than 10 minutes from the core are mainly four-story elevator structures with densities of about 70 units per net acre; one recent building near downtown is ten stories high, with

Table 4.7.   Size Distribution of New Apartments by Traveltime From Core, Hartford, 1950–1960

Minutes from Core:	0–9		10–19		20–29	
	Number	Per cent	Number	Per cent	Number	Per cent
Efficiency (0-bedroom) Apartments	135	49.3	46	17.5	0	0
One-bedroom	139	50.7	156	59.3	0	0
Two-bedroom	0	0	61	23.2	82	100.0
Total	274	100.0	263	100.0	82	100.0

Source: Rental inventory used in Chapter 3, Figure 3.6. Traveltime calculations described in Chapter 3, footnote 4.

a density of 225 dwelling units per acre. Most new buildings 10 to 15 minutes from the core are three-story walk-up structures, with densities of fifty to sixty units per acre. Farther out, two-story walk-ups predominate, with densities typically about 20 units to the acre. These density differences reflect not only changes in the type of structure but also in the size of apartments. As Table 4.7 indicates, efficiency and one-bedroom apartments constitute the *only* units close to the core in the sample used for this study, while two-bedroom units are the only type that appear more than 20 minutes from the core. This extreme specialization in unit types undoubtedly reflects both a desire to reduce costs in central locations and an adaptation to the nature of the market in outlying areas.

Table 4.8 presents a series of examples illustrating typical cost adjustments within the Hartford region. As in New York and Los Angeles, a return of 15 per cent on investment is generally considered the test of feasibility for new apartment development. Construction and operating costs are slightly lower than those in New York but considerably higher than those in the warm climate of Los Angeles. The vacant outlying site represented in column 3 is a convenient starting point for investigating how developers adjust unit costs as land prices and taxes rise. Total development cost per unit is $8,989 in column 3, with a land cost of $.50 per square foot, a tax rate of .0215, and a monthly rent of $120.

In column 2, 10 to 15 minutes from the core, the land price rises sharply to $1.75 per square foot and the tax rate jumps to .0311. The adjustment is a particularly favorable one, bringing both an increase in density and a lower unit construction cost. Generally, higher density implies higher unit construction cost, as in the cost

Table 4.8. Hartford Region: Financial Calculations for One-Bedroom Apartments

	1	2	3 West Hartford	4 Hartford Declining Area	5 Hartford Declining Area
Location:	Hartford	Hartford	Hartford	Area	Area
Traveltime from Downtown	5–9 min.	10–15 min.	20–29 min.	10–15 min.	10–15 min.
Land Cost per Square Foot	2.50	1.75	.50	4.00	2.00
Building Type	4-story el.	3-story	2-story	3-story	2-story
Dwelling Units per Acre	70	50	20	50	35
Square Feet per Dwelling Unit	622	871	2,178	871	1,245
Land Cost per Dwelling Unit	1,555	1,524	1,089	3,484	2,490
Construction Cost per Dwelling Unit	8,300	7,600	7,900	7,600	7,900
Total Investment per Dwelling Unit	9,855	9,124	8,989	11,084	10,390
Equity Share (⅓)	3,285	3,041	2,996	1,108*	1,039*
Mortgage (⅔, 6%, 20 years)	6,570	6,083	5,993	9,976*	9,361*
Yearly Operating Cost	330	300	300	300	300
Tax Rate	.0311	.0311	.0215	.0311	.0311
Yearly Taxes	306	284	193	345	323
Total Yearly Cost	636	584	493	645	623
Yearly Rent	1,680	1,560	1,440	1,550	1,500
(Monthly Rent)	(140)	(130)	(120)	(130)	(125)
Cash Surplus Over Cost	1,044	976	947	915	877
Less Yearly Interest and Amortization (8.5% of mortgage)	558	517	509	723*	679*
Net Cash Return	486	459	438	192	198
Return on Equity	14.8%	15.1%	14.6%	17.3%	19.1%

* FHA Financing: 90% mortgage, 30 years, 7.25% yearly interest and amortization.

adjustments typical of New York. When the structural type is limited to walk-up buildings, however, an extra story lowers rather than raises unit costs. The higher rent available in this location ($120 per year) effectively counters the increase in land cost as well as the tax increase of $91 per year, so that a return of 15 per cent is still possible.

Site costs still closer to the core rise to $2.50 per square foot (column 1), but the tax rate remains the same. Here the density adjustment succeeds in keeping land costs per unit to approximately the same level as in column 2, but construction and operating costs rise. The increase in building height to four stories marks a switch from walk-up to elevator structures, with a resulting need for extra mechanical equipment as well as a loss of interior space for elevator shafts. The rise in development costs exerts a twofold effect by also increasing the taxable value of the property; thus taxes rise slightly, even though the rate remains the same. Yearly operating costs also increase, but the rise of $120 in annual rent covers the combined cost increases, so that return on equity remains around 15 per cent.

Prospects for Declining Sections of Hartford

The problem of rebuilding the old areas of Hartford is one of coping with *higher* land costs than those in the areas where apartment developers are now operating. This is a problem not encountered in New York and Los Angeles where land costs in the declining areas were in line with costs in comparable active areas. In Hartford, land costs in many older areas are likely to exceed even those in more accessible locations where new apartments can command higher rents. Land prices in good locations less than 10 minutes from the core, where rent levels reach a peak for the Hartford area, are about $2.50 per square foot. Land costs in areas 10 to 15 minutes from the core are estimated as approximately $3 to $5 per square foot.

Column 4 presents one workable approach for developing new apartments in these locations. This solution assumes a moderate rent level consistent with the access advantages of the declining areas, using the same rent as in column 2. It assumes further that people will accept the same density that they now accept in areas of comparable accessibility. Thus the adjustment is that of column 2, utilizing three-story walk-up structures at a density of 50 units per net acre. This case, however, makes use of FHA financing, with its lower equity requirement and lower yearly carrying charges than conventional mortgages. Under these circumstances, developers can afford to pay land prices of $4 per square foot — the middle of the estimated price range — and still earn a reasonable return on investment. To the extent that these assumptions prove unworkable, land costs will have to be subsidized. If rents of $130 per month are not available, or if three-story walk-up buildings fall out of favor, $4 per square foot is too high a land cost to permit a normal return on investment. Taller elevator buildings could be substituted, using FHA financing, but the pattern of current density preferences in Hartford suggests that such buildings are marketable mainly in locations offering special site or access advantages not likely to be found in most declining areas.

If two-story buildings are used, together with FHA financing, column 5 indicates that land prices of $2 per square foot can be compatible with market opportunities in the old neighborhoods. This solution assumes a density of 35 dwelling units per acre, rather than the 20 per acre now found in more outlying locations, but the

102

increase in density appears reasonable in view of the access advantages of inner locations in Hartford. This price level for land would, of course, require a write-down from the estimated acquisition cost of $3 or more per square foot.

Conclusions

If these site acquisition costs have been estimated accurately for Hartford, FHA financing can just barely enable developers to pay the necessary price for land in the old neighborhoods. In parts of these areas, prices will undoubtedly be lower than the estimated range; here the developer will have a little leeway in adjusting his costs to market rents. Elsewhere in the declining areas, some land subsidy may be necessary to make new development feasible, but large write-downs will not be required so long as development is limited to three-story walk-up buildings. If plans for rebuilding call for lower densities than those now prevailing in central locations, land prices will be out of line with re-use possibilities. This last condition, however, would impose a strain on the economics of development in the old neighborhoods of the other regions as well: if developers cannot build the type of structures in the declining areas that they now use in comparable locations at densities typical of current practice, they will have difficulty earning a normal return.

Where public policy aims at facilitating the same type of new development within the declining areas that now takes place elsewhere in the region, the main task is to raise environmental standards to the level of presently desirable locations. If the environment is improved to this extent and FHA financing is made available, land prices in the declining areas are roughly compatible with current types of development and current rents in comparable locations within all three study areas.

This exploration of development costs and their adjustment in the light of varying market circumstances has helped identify a number of critical factors affecting the first precondition for rebuilding: a balance between site costs and re-use values. Chapter 5 will test each study area for the second precondition, a sufficient *scale* of demand to permit the replacement of deteriorated housing within a reasonable number of years.

CHAPTER FIVE

THE REGIONAL FRAMEWORK

New York, Los Angeles, and Hartford meet the first pre-condition for rebuilding their declining areas: potential re-use values of land for new housing are roughly in line with site acquisition costs in all three cities, although Hartford is a borderline case. So far, this study has said nothing about the quantity of new development that may be feasible or the rate at which cleared sites can be put to new uses. These additional considerations enter into the second precondition for a rebuilding program: that the demand for new housing sites must be great enough to utilize all cleared land not needed for environmental improvements (schools, community facilities), within a reasonable number of years.

This chapter will indicate that New York and Los Angeles pass the second test, but Hartford does not. Why is Hartford weak on both counts? How do such dissimilar cities as New York and Los Angeles both meet the full set of conditions for rebuilding? Which factors seem to exert the strongest influence upon the feasibility of attracting new housing into the old areas? By combining an analysis of possible rebuilding rates with the earlier analysis of land costs and re-use values, this chapter will draw into focus some of the most important factors governing the feasibility of rebuilding programs.

Under present conditions, three factors are of outstanding importance: the degree of central preference in the housing market, the relationship between the density of previous development on the site and the density of new development, and the size of the market for new apartments. Future shifts in metropolitan structure are likely to alter both land costs and demand characteristics, but the key issue ahead is whether large migrations of poor people will continue to populate the aging neighborhoods. A continuing flow

104

of disadvantaged newcomers would give weight to arguments for the retention of old housing on social grounds and at the same time would give continued economic value to this housing.

Land Utilization Rates for New Construction in New York

The rate at which new housing can absorb cleared sites in the old neighborhoods depends upon how much apartment housing can be attracted into such areas in the future and the development density of this housing. Chapter 4 demonstrated the economic feasibility of building typical nonluxury apartment houses without major public subsidy in the declining areas of all three cities. For New York, it is reasonable to assume that the type of new apartment construction now predominating in Manhattan requires special sites close to the central business district or in areas of particularly high prestige. This Manhattan luxury housing, with its high rents, seems an unlikely candidate for the old neighborhoods in upper Manhattan and in the inlying parts of the Bronx, Brooklyn, and Queens.

The market from which these declining areas can draw is the medium-rent apartment sector, which is currently locating in various parts of the Bronx, Brooklyn, and Queens. For this market, the older areas can offer the attraction of a location closer to the center of the region — a factor of great importance in New York rental housing. If cleared sites could offer good surrounding environments, new housing there could probably earn rents above prevailing levels farther away where new apartment houses are currently being developed. But calculations in Chapter 4 assumed only that new housing in areas to be rebuilt would command *the same rents* as those in the cheapest new apartments in the region, or $40 per room per month. With FHA mortgage aids, developers can pay full land costs for these inner sites and offer locational advantages at attractive rents.

Thus the logical basis for estimating New York land utilization rates is the amount of new private construction in the Bronx, Brooklyn, and Queens — the new housing that can conceivably be attracted to the inner areas. (I shall exclude new apartments in the suburbs on the assumption that suburban location is a necessary feature of such housing.) In the past decade, these boroughs had a varying volume of new housing construction. The early part of the decade was not a time of great development, owing in part to material shortages during the Korean War. By the end of this period, construction rose to boom levels. I shall exclude the boom of the late 1950's by counting only housing completions from 1951 through 1960, thus omitting the many starts in 1959 and 1960. In the first part of this decade, Queens still had considerable vacant land available, with a resulting high rate of new construction despite the Korean War; to discount the vacant land factor, I shall take note only of the slower 1956–1960 rate of completions.

The 10-year total completions, including those in Queens projected from the 1956–1960 volume, were 108,524 new units in private apartment structures.[1] At current development densities, this housing would require 724 acres of net residential land for the 10-year period, or 72 acres per year. If development were at the somewhat lower densities now prevailing in urban renewal project areas — densities that would be feasible without subsidies in the many older areas where land costs are $7 or less per square foot — the land utilization rate would be 109 acres per year.

New York also has a large public housing program to consider. In the case of public housing, new Manhattan developments are likely candidates for utilizing sites cleared in the older neighborhoods; and of course public housing now built in various parts of the Bronx, Brooklyn, and Queens could also go into such areas. The 1951–1960 volume of public housing construction was 70,306 units, occupying 865 acres of land at current public housing densities, or 87 acres per year. New York City Housing Authority plans call for an accelerated rate of construction in the coming years,[2] but I shall assume that construction in excess of the 1951–1960 rate will go to vacant outlying sites. Thus the combined rate of land utilization of private housing and public housing at current densities is 159 acres per year. If private housing were developed at typical urban renewal densities, the rate would be 196 acres per year (see Appendix B).

Are these rates likely to continue? I have attempted to project reasonable rates by excluding such clearly temporary phenomena as the 1959–1960 boom and the 1951–1955 Queens construction wave on vacant land. Further, I have totally excluded the boom in Manhattan luxury housing. The market for private moderate-rent apartments consists primarily of small families; it has been noted

106

previously that only 25 to 30 per cent of the new private units in the outer boroughs have more than one bedroom (Table 4.2). Population projections for the region foresee a continued increase in the age categories likely to constitute single people, young married couples with no children or one preschool child, and older couples whose children have left home.[3]

These population projections suggest a continuing long-term demand for new moderate-rent apartments in New York City, similar to the housing now being developed in the outer boroughs. There is little reason to expect a sharp decline in this type of apartment construction, except for temporary market fluctuations.

Aside from a recession, the major factor that could cause a reversal of recent trends would be a further shift of preferences to favor single-family homes, but such a shift would be likely to work gradual rather than sudden changes. And the 1951–1960 rates of construction used in this study reflect the period of greatest suburbanization that the United States has ever experienced.

Time Required for Rebuilding in New York

Within the declining areas, many kinds of housing will be found. Which buildings should be replaced and which rehabilitated will depend upon local standards, policies, and rebuilding plans. The city-wide total of substandard housing units, however, can serve as a useful approximation of the total amount of housing replacement that might conceivably be contemplated within the near future in presently declining neighborhoods and in those where population losses are imminent.

In New York, old housing is so heavily utilized at present that a program to replace *all* deteriorated housing would create a serious housing shortage. The 1960 Housing Census reported only 53,000 nonseasonal nondilapidated units vacant and available for rent or sale. In contrast, 147,000 housing units were classified as either dilapidated or deteriorating and lacking plumbing facilities — in either case, unlikely to be suitable for rehabilitation, and a prime target for clearance. Additional vacancies in the region outside New York City add another 78,000 units to the reserve of sound units for relocation; but the combined reserve is still smaller than the stock of deteriorated housing in the City alone, and there are many more deteriorated units in the rest of the region.

107

New construction will replace deteriorated units with housing priced too high for low-income groups. If replacement units caused other housing to filter down to lower cost levels, rebuilding might not create hardship even in the absence of a large vacancy reserve. But as the housing market has operated until now, new housing barely keeps pace with an expanding demand resulting from new household formation. Since the projected volume of new housing is consistent with recent experience, new development is likely to create only a small surplus for lower cost levels. Thus the lack of a suitable vacancy reserve should exercise a powerful constraint upon any effort to remove worn-out housing from the scene.

If the old housing were to become increasingly vacant, the ability to rebuild cleared sites with new housing need not exercise such a serious constraint. My estimate of the land area occupied by deteriorated housing is 1,145 acres. At the combined land utilization rate for private and public housing that could conceivably be attracted to cleared sites in the old areas, 7.2 years would be required to rebuild these 1,145 acres at current development densities (see Appendix B). If the private housing were built at typical densities for urban renewal projects, less than 6 years would be required.

An alternate objective for New York might be the replacement of all old-law tenement houses. These are structures built before 1901, with physical characteristics that make successful rehabilitation extremely difficult. I estimate that old-law tenements occupy 1,552 acres of land. Absorption of these sites would require 9.8 years at current building densities, or 7.9 years if private housing were to follow urban renewal densities.

If rebuilding is also to take account of the current rate of deterioration of old housing, an additional 27 acres of land would require clearance during each year of a program designed to eliminate all deteriorated structures. Calculations in Appendix B indicate that replacement at current densities would require an extension of the rebuilding program from 7.2 to 8.5 years.

How realistic are these time estimates? It is clear that drastic measures would be necessary to divert *all* new private apartment housing from the outer boroughs of the City to designated clearance sites. In addition to such incentives as FHA financing aids and environmental improvements, measures would have to be taken to restrict or prohibit new apartment construction outside the declining neighborhoods. Not the least of the problems would be persuading developers of moderate-rent apartments to build in Negro and Puerto Rican enclaves. Realistically, only a portion of this new building could be attracted to the sites that had just been cleared of deteriorated housing.

In addition, the scale of clearance would have to extend beyond land occupied solely by substandard housing. To carve out suitable building sites might require demolishing some adjoining structures. On the other hand, new residential development would not be expected to utilize all land that had been cleared. Some areas would be better suited to nonresidential development — industry, commerce, institutions. Even in residential areas, a good deal of land would be needed for new schools and other community facilities.

Several points are clear from this discussion:

1. The present occupancy of old housing in New York is a far more serious constraint for a rebuilding program than the ability to utilize cleared sites.
2. A large potential demand for cleared land exists in the volume of current moderate-rent private housing as well as the volume of public housing.
3. An energetic program to rebuild cleared sites need not require an astronomical time span to complete the job.
4. Even a partially successful program could initiate a policy of rebuilding through gradual replacement in those sections of the City where environmental deficiencies are least serious.

Land Utilization Rate in Los Angeles

With a larger vacancy reserve, Los Angeles is probably better equipped to begin rebuilding its deteriorated housing in the near future. Although information has not been gathered on the cost levels of vacant housing, some 46,000 nondilapidated permanent units were vacant and available in the City of Los Angeles in 1960 and another 66,000 in the rest of the region. Substandard units — dilapidated, or deteriorating and lacking plumbing facilities — totaled 24,800 in the City of Los Angeles. I estimate the land occupied by these units as 2,755 acres (Appendix B).

These substandard units are located primarily in the central sections of Los Angeles. Most are within 5 miles of the core, some are 5 to 10 miles away, and a sprinkling are farther removed. The potential market for housing sites in these locations is a limited one. In contrast to New York, centrality plays only a minor role in the Los Angeles housing market, registering chiefly in the form of lower vacancy rates in more central locations. Even with environmental improvements, I assume that the inner areas would have only average advantages for new residential development and could not attract very much housing that now goes to prestige areas farther away. My assumption is that the potential market consists of new apartment housing now locating elsewhere in the central areas, within a radius of 10 miles from the downtown core. In terms of land costs and likely returns, this type of development is economically feasible without public subsidies on land in the declining areas.

From 1950 to 1960, apartment units increased by 98,000 within this zone. The volume of *new* construction was probably somewhat higher, since some housing was demolished for freeway construction and other public works. But I have conservatively assumed a new construction volume of 98,000. At typical Los Angeles density, the land utilization rate would be 196 acres per year. All substandard units could be replaced at this rate in 14.0 years. If new construction followed the slightly lower densities prescribed by the Federal Housing Administration, rebuilding would require 11.2 years. In the past decade, the amount of substandard housing in Los Angeles declined. A moderate allowance for clearing newly deteriorated housing would not lengthen these time spans materially.

The extent of *future demand* for apartments in Los Angeles is difficult to project without a detailed housing market study. Yet several factors suggest a continuation of the present high volume. The market for this housing, as in New York, consists mainly of single people, young married couples, and older people—three groups likely to continue increasing in the Los Angeles population. Rents for these units are moderate, so no volatile luxury market is involved. Further, the rents calculated for this housing in Chapter 4 are at the low end of the typical Los Angeles scale, where the market is likely to have greatest staying power.

The time required for a rebuilding program in Los Angeles is longer than the estimate for New York, in part because Los Angeles has no public housing program. Still, the time span is finite in Los Angeles, as in New York. With due allowance for unrealistic elements in the assumptions, it is clear that Los Angeles also has a sizable potential market for cleared sites.

Rebuilding Capacity in Hartford

The very limited demand for new apartment housing sets a low ceiling on the potential ability of new development to absorb cleared sites in Hartford. Only 13 per cent of the new housing units in the metropolitan region from 1958 to 1960 were in apartment buildings, compared with 48 per cent in New York and 46 per cent in Los Angeles at about the same time.[4] Further, the City of Hartford can attract only part of this small regional total, for the advantages of central location are not decisive in the Hartford housing market.

A careful study of the rental market conducted in 1959 projected an annual average of 3,500 new dwelling units of all types for the Hartford region through 1970.[5] If we assume that the apartment market will continue to constitute only about 15 per cent of total housing production, new construction will provide some 5,000 apartment units in the 1960–1970 decade. On the basis of past performance, the City of Hartford seems unlikely to attract much more than half the regional total of new apartments, or 2,500 units in 10 years. The housing market study estimated approximately this range of activity, consisting of 1,800 moderate-rental units in and near downtown Hartford, plus some luxury housing that might compete with high-priced single-family homes. These estimates assume that public action will create new housing sites in a desirable residential environment.

At current central-city densities, the land absorption rate for 2,500 new multifamily units in 10 years would be only 5 acres of net residential land per year. If construction were at a slightly lower density of 35 units per acre, which would require some land subsidy, 7.1 acres per year could be utilized.

How does this rate compare with the land that could be cleared through a program to eliminate all deteriorated housing? I estimate that some 185 acres of land in the City of Hartford are currently occupied by dilapidated housing and deteriorating housing lacking plumbing facilities (Appendix B). At the projected absorption rate of 5 acres per year, 37 years would be required to rebuild cleared

111

areas. Even at the higher rate of 7.1 acres per year, 26 years would be required.

At current rates of housing obsolescence for Hartford, land utilization for new apartments could barely keep up with the clearance of newly deteriorated areas. From 1950 to 1960, I estimate a yearly *increase* of 6.6 acres of land occupied by substandard housing. Thus the present capacity to rebuild housing sites could be utilized entirely to keep pace with growing obsolescence, without making any inroads on the backlog of substandard areas.

Hartford also lacks a suitable vacancy reserve for undertaking a rapid program of replacing deteriorated housing in the old residential neighborhoods. But even if the rate of abandonment were to accelerate, it is clear that the potential for rebuilding clearance sites with new housing is severely limited in Hartford.

Factors Conditioning the Feasibility of Rebuilding

All three study areas meet the first precondition for rebuilding— a balance between site costs and re-use values—but only New York and Los Angeles have a sufficient potential capacity to rebuild cleared sites in a reasonable period of time. Three sets of characteristics best explain these findings:

1. Metropolitan structural features that condition the degree of central preference in the housing market.
2. The relationship between the density of previous development on clearance sites and the density of new development.
3. The size of the market for new apartments.

Metropolitan Structure

The economic requirements for attracting new housing to the declining areas do not call for any particular type of regional structure. *Some* new housing is economically feasible in the declining areas of such contrasting regions as New York, Los Angeles, and Hartford. Although certain metropolitan elements are powerful organizers of locational demand within the housing market, no particular element is a *sine qua non* for attracting new housing to the old areas. As the case of Los Angeles demonstrates clearly, housing preferences need not even favor central locations in order to generate sufficient re-use value for rebuilding the inner areas.

112

The sole general requirement that must be met if any new housing is to be feasible as a private investment is that development and operating costs must be commensurate with market advantages.

Thus the problem of feasibility must be approached from the dual perspective of both costs and returns. Metropolitan structure clearly affects the returns. A strong downtown core, and a lack of inlying vacant land, promote rental demand for central locations. Taken alone, a strong downtown core appears to exercise the stronger influence. In Hartford, with a moderately strong central business district, inlying housing brings a rent premium despite the availability of large tracts of vacant land within a short drive of the center. In Los Angeles, where vacant land is far removed from the center but the core is relatively weak, the only noticeable sign of central orientation appears in residential vacancy rates, which are lower in central than in outlying locations.

Densities Before and After Rebuilding

The major variables in costs within each region are tax rates and land prices. The influence of tax differentials in retarding new housing development in central areas has probably been exaggerated; this study has found present central-city tax rates generally compatible with the economic requirements of new housing. *Land costs are by far the more significant variable.* The question of prior density is important because of its relation to land costs.

Current land costs depend very much upon the density of previous development. Where past development has been at high density, as in Manhattan, land costs are high enough so that some special market compensations must be available if developers are to be attracted. In Los Angeles, the low density of prior development facilitates site acquisition at prices that are fully compatible with normal rental returns, even though rents are no higher in central areas than in more outlying locations. In Hartford, differences in prior densities between the old neighborhoods and areas where rebuilding is now active largely account for land cost differentials that will make renewal of the declining areas difficult, unless some subsidies are available.

Although the density of previous development is a critical factor influencing land acquisition costs, high densities and high land prices can be overcome in several ways. One typical cost adjustment is to build new housing at high densities where land costs are high. This type of adjustment has its limitations, since unit construction costs rise as densities increase, but it contributes significantly to the private developer's ability to build in high-cost locations. The feasibility of high-density construction as a development tactic is also limited by the degree of public acceptance of multistory living — a factor to be considered in connection with the size of the apartment market.

High land costs can also be overcome by reducing other costs. Thus, FHA mortgage financing, with generous loan commitments at interest rates below those prevailing for conventional mortgages, can provide an economic basis for new housing in some high-cost locations in New York and Hartford. Other measures to reduce development and operating costs — tax reductions, easing of building code requirements — could conceivably help developers work out an acceptable investment package in locations where land costs are high.

Densities of the past thus influence new development densities, but with some room for modification. This influence takes the practical form of setting minimum density ranges for new development, which developers cannot easily undercut without some form of subsidy. To the extent that low density itself has a market value, the developer can use a generous amount of high-cost land and recoup his investment through high rents. But the demand thins out when prices become very high. If land selling at $3 per square foot is used for single-family homes on small lots, a single lot would cost the purchaser some $15,000, pricing the finished house well beyond the mass market.

Under present cost conditions, land cleared of housing built at apartment densities must generally be re-used for apartments, but moderate density reductions may be possible. With FHA financing, but without further subsidy, new development in New York can bring densities down from 200 to 150 units per acre in some areas, and from 80 to 50 per acre in others.

Density increases, on the other hand, greatly facilitate the economics of rebuilding. New development is easy in most of Los Angeles because densities of 50 or more units per acre replace old housing at 8 to 10 units per acre.

Only a sharp downward break with densities of the past creates severe economic problems. When the declining areas of cities are vacated to a greater extent than they are now, land costs may well fall to levels that will permit drastic density reductions. In the meantime, programs to replace old housing will have to confront the powerful influence of the past, working through high land costs.

Demand for New Apartments

This chapter has already taken note of the strong connection between the size of the market for new apartments and the rate at which cleared sites can be utilized. In the last few years, multifamily housing has accounted for 48 per cent of all new private housing in the New York metropolitan region, 46 per cent in Los Angeles, and only 13 per cent in Hartford, with the consequences that I have identified for the potential rate of rebuilding.

Nationally, apartment units have been accounting for about 20 per cent of total private housing starts in recent years. From 1958 through 1960, the multifamily proportion ranged from 18 to 21 per cent; in the first seven months of 1961, this proportion went up to 25 per cent.[6] Apartment demand is by no means constant, however. In the early 1950's, the multifamily share ranged from 9 to 15 per cent nationally.

Future volumes of apartment construction are likely to depend upon many factors that are national rather than local in character. The most significant recent analysis of the national market for rental housing calls particular attention to the high price of renting an apartment compared to the cost of owning a house, and to opportunities for broadening the rental market through changing this price relationship.[7] Many measures would have to be applied at the national level to be effective, such as equalizing tax treatment for renters and homeowners and making FHA financing as attractive for apartment developments as it is for single-family houses.

Yet even if the national apartment construction rate is at a high level, one can easily imagine regions in which the demand for apartments will be far below the national proportion. Small metropolitan areas with vacant land readily accessible to downtown and with employment centers distributed throughout the region may be weak both in central preference and in apartment demand. If such regions have declining areas consisting of old housing developed at moderate or high densities sometime in the past, acquisition costs may represent a serious obstacle to rebuilding. Land prices of $2 to $5 per square foot are far too high for most single-family housing; yet areas of old multifamily buildings are currently unlikely to be available at lower prices. If single-family housing is the only feasible housing in such a region, two alternatives are open. Land prices would have to be heavily subsidized, or rebuilding could be postponed until the old structures are practically worthless.

In regions with considerable apartment activity, the situation is different. It was noted in Chapter 1 that many regions besides New York and Los Angeles have had sizable volumes of apartment construction recently, particularly Chicago, Philadelphia, Washington, San Francisco, San Diego, Miami, Minneapolis, Atlanta, and Seattle. Here the rebuilding of central areas will depend upon whether or not a sufficient portion of the total construction can be attracted into areas slated for rebuilding. Metropolitan structure is important in this connection, for the degree of central preference for new housing will have much to do with the location of new developments.

Regional Characteristics in the Future

The analyses in this study place heavy emphasis on current conditions. What can be expected in the future? Metropolitan regions have been changing rapidly in the last few decades, and public preferences have also been shifting. Future changes will undoubtedly influence the economic conditions that have been described, but the direction of influence depends upon the particular patterns of change that may emerge.

It is possible to foresee several changes that would affect locational preferences. Further decentralization of jobs and services is likely to reduce preferences for inlying locations. If new housing is to be feasible, development and operating costs will have to fall correspondingly. Job decentralization will probably also encourage the abandonment of old inlying housing. To the extent that it does, acquisition costs are likely to drop, but it is uncertain whether they will fall sufficiently to remain in line with a slipping demand for new housing in central locations.

Changes in metropolitan transportation may trigger large shifts in central preferences. The abandonment of commuter railroad lines serving the suburbs is likely to increase preferences for central locations, provided that in-town transportation does not deteriorate and that the volume of in-town employment remains relatively stable. Curtailment of public transportation service to the older areas is likely to produce an opposite effect by depriving these areas of current access advantages to the core. Highway programs that provide relatively greater access benefits for outlying land than for the aging central areas are also likely to shift consumer preferences *away* from inner locations. Once again, the net effect is difficult to forecast, since this type of shift may also speed the abandonment of existing housing.

Changes in density preference may also have a dual result, affecting both old housing and new housing. If people insist on increasingly lower densities for new housing, building and operating costs in the declining areas must fall to levels that will enable developers to build at lower densities. But if people reject high densities in the market for old housing as well as new, clearance sites may come on the market at prices below current levels.

In the consideration of costs, the key question for the future is whether old housing will decline in value soon enough to match any decrease in central preference or any increasing rejection of high densities. Here the basic factors are the extent of demand for low-cost housing and the supply that becomes available. A drop in the migration of low-income groups to the cities would curtail demand and thus accelerate the process of abandonment as earlier occupants raise their incomes and move to better housing.

A continuing high level of demand for low-cost housing is likely in most large cities for the next decade or two. If this expectation is correct, the cost of clearance sites will depend upon whether the housing market can expand the amount of satisfactory housing available to residents of the old areas. The rate at which suburban housing filters down to lower-income groups is crucial in this respect. In a broader sense, this question revolves around the ability of the housing industry — or of public housing alternatives — to offer acceptable housing possibilities to people now living in substandard conditions. If the housing industry and public measures fail this test, the old housing will remain an economic asset, and rebuilding will be difficult.

Other cost factors can also impede rebuilding. Tax differentials within a metropolitan region may widen in the future. Property taxes in the central cities of the three study regions are currently close enough to those in outlying locations so that they do not deter new construction in centrally located areas. If the central cities lose a major part of their property tax base through decentralization of business and industry, and if alternate taxes are not devised, tax levels may take on greater significance. If, on the other hand, suburban tax levels rise quickly as a result of increasing costs for schools and public services, the differentials may not widen greatly. Much will depend upon changes in local tax structure and upon whether political and legal mechanisms operate to equalize tax burdens.

Clearly, the effects of future changes in metropolitan regions cannot be predicated by partial analysis. Decisions to build new housing will reflect the total structure of costs and returns in the old neighborhoods and elsewhere in the region. Careful observation of the housing market will be necessary to determine the effects of changing conditions as they unfold. The most predictable effects are those that might arise from an expansion of the housing supply, particularly the supply of units at price levels that low-income groups can afford. Change in this direction is likely to mean an accelerated abandonment of old housing and a lowering of its acquisition cost. Changes that affect preferences for apartments and central locations will have more complex results, since they may have an impact on the demand for old housing as well as new.

Income Levels and Housing Choices

The complexity of these last effects — the differing impact of shifting preferences upon new and old housing — is at the root of the rebuilding problem. If preferences that dominate the market for new housing were reflected in the demand for old housing, widespread changes in taste would result in the abandonment of old units that failed to meet contemporary standards. But the problem of rebuilding is that the old units are not abandoned quickly, and they retain enough value so that clearance is expensive. The economic difficulties of replacing old housing thus reflect a

118

split in the housing market between the demand for new and old housing.

Most large cities have a dual housing market. A large part of the population can choose from a wide range of housing possibilities. If prevailing taste among this group shifts from apartments to single-family houses, as it has recently, large numbers of people can leave their apartments and find split-level and ranch homes, whether new or purchased from earlier occupants.

Another sizable part of the population does not have the income that would allow so wide a choice. Low-income groups, regardless of their preferences, must occupy the cheapest units on the market. There are many reasons to suppose that the poor now occupying the discarded housing of the old neighborhoods actually share many of the preference patterns of middle-income people living in better housing in superior surroundings. Because they do not have the means to satisfy these preferences, large numbers of them continue to live in housing that neither they nor other groups want any longer. But their occupancy gives value to this housing, so that clearance and replacement are difficult. At the same time, a strong community life often develops in these areas, so that their premature clearance creates genuine hardships and social dislocations for people forced to move.

This split in the housing market could be reduced by a continuing rise in the incomes of lower economic groups relative to the cost of housing or by an expansion of the supply and variety of low-cost housing. The elimination of many low-skill jobs through automation and the persistence of high unemployment among disadvantaged urban groups, however, may well foreshadow a slowing of economic progress for people now in the old neighborhoods. As long as poverty remains, publicly subsidized housing will be needed. To the extent that public programs fail to meet total needs and large numbers of people continue to live in substandard conditions, rebuilding the old neighborhoods will be difficult economically — though possible in many cases — and unadvisable socially, except on a limited and gradual basis.

CHAPTER SIX

POLICIES FOR REBUILDING

PART 1: ALTERNATIVES FOR PUBLIC ACTION

The rebuilding of cities is now a matter of general public concern. Both the federal government and the cities are heavily involved in problems of housing and the future of declining neighborhoods, but the development of public policies that link housing concerns with rebuilding programs is a difficult task. Results of this study provide a sharp definition of some major issues involved in the choice of objectives for public policy and a number of guidelines for achieving housing goals while rebuilding the city.

If public policies are to serve broad social goals, there can be little justification for clearing away houses as long as they have a useful function. Big-city experience in the 1950's has demonstrated that the term "gray areas"—with its implications of abandonment and disuse—is a misnomer for the old neighborhoods. These areas serve rather as *zones of passage* for low-income groups new to urban life, and for other residents unable to afford higher rents or not yet prepared to leave the social surroundings of the old communities. Under present conditions, the large-scale clearance of aging neighborhoods deprives people of valuable housing resources and in many cases brings on further hardship by uprooting people who have strong ties to a local community.

Despite the evident need for old housing, many cities have already cleared large residential areas for urban redevelopment projects. The search for additional real estate taxes, the political value of physical symbols of progress, aesthetic objections to decaying neighborhoods, and the application of current housing standards to structures built 50 or more years ago are rationales for such clearance programs. But the adverse social and political consequences of harnessing rebuilding policies to these approaches

120

have become increasingly evident, and policy changes are clearly in order.

If the objective of public policy is to clear only *surplus* housing, what can be done with the declining neighborhoods? Major alternatives are:

1. Leave these areas untouched until they are virtually abandoned, then acquire the properties at reduced prices, clear them, and rebuild the cleared sites for new purposes.
2. Rebuild these areas gradually, replacing the old housing in small parcels as vacancy rates rise.

The first alternative raises serious problems of maintaining public services during the lengthy period of abandonment and dislocating remaining residents after population falls to a low level. The second is more difficult to achieve, but avoids these problems. Although neither alternative would force occupants of the old housing to leave in the near future, the first would eventually displace those that remained, and past experience suggests that a large number will remain even after occupancy has declined for many years. In addition, a gradual rebuilding will offer some people a chance to find new housing without leaving the community, and will widen the choices available to nonresidents who are in the market for new housing.

If these are the objectives — to limit clearance to structures that are no longer useful, and to promote a high degree of residential choice for the city's people — gradual rebuilding is a suitable technique. But how can public policies start this process? Public action can help create the preconditions for a gradual rebuilding, and public action is vital to establish necessary environmental conditions for rebuilding the older areas. This chapter will take a closer look at both types of action.

The three cities included in this study have all initiated programs to rebuild some of their older areas. In New York, new and interesting policies have been developed to bring about a planned rebuilding. In Los Angeles, certain basic policies are still being formulated for dealing with the old neighborhoods. In Hartford, where the preconditions for rebuilding are lacking, policymakers face particularly difficult obstacles. I shall review the current situa-

121

tions in all three cities to see how they relate to the findings of this study.

Urban Renewal and Low-Cost Housing

Public policy for rebuilding old areas of the city must recognize a large and continuing demand for low-cost housing. In the past decade, huge migrations of low-income groups from rural areas to the cities have kept steady pressure behind this demand. The greatest of these migrations, the movement of Negroes from the rural South to the urban North, reached near-peak levels in the 1950's. Yet the Negro population remaining in the South, an obvious source of future migrants, also grew to record levels by 1960. With large migrations likely to continue, and with high birth rates among recent arrivals, the pressure for low-priced housing is not likely to subside quickly.

It is obvious to observers of urban renewal practice in the United States that public officials have often been insensitive to this continuing need. Projects to clear old housing and develop high-cost apartments provide tangible symbols of civic progress, augment the property tax base, and enhance the appearance of formerly rundown sections. Policymakers justify such projects by pointing out the poor physical condition of the old housing and by urging the social objective of bringing "middle-class leadership" back to central areas. These approaches to urban renewal fail to take account of total housing needs in the community.

A recent study of capital requirements for urban renewal illustrates this fault in renewal policy in its review of the program of a representative medium-sized city. The renewal program for Case City (New Haven, apparently), based on an application of architectural standards to various parts of the city, calls for the redevelopment or rehabilitation of areas where two thirds of the population now live. The low-income groups now occupying these areas cannot afford the costs of new or rehabilitated housing and would have to be relocated elsewhere. Without a substantial low-income housing program, "Case City would be faced with the prospect of replacing the population of those areas where two thirds of the city's people now live with a market drawn from the stable areas where one fifth of the city's population lives, plus some suburban returnees."[1] The authors note that such a program is possible only if incomes rise for a large part of the population and if a substantial proportion of disposable income goes for housing expenditures.

Renewal programs of this kind would have highly destructive effects if they were put into effect in the near future. Fortunately, such programs have moved slowly in the past, so that they have not destroyed enough low-cost housing to affect the general improvement from 1950 to 1960, although they have certainly retarded improvement in New York. Despite the limited progress of most renewal programs to date, however, they have had many unfortunate effects. The very act of clearing an area and scattering its occupants often destroys valuable and unique social ties that have developed over the years.

As early as 1937, George Orwell found disturbing evidence that slum clearance in English cities disrupted many cherished features of personal and communal life. "When you walk through the smoke-dim slums of Manchester," he noted, "you think that nothing is needed except to tear down these abominations and build decent housing in their place. But the trouble is that in destroying the slum you destroy other things as well."[2]

Current renewal policies have barely caught up with Orwell's insights. A 1959 advisory report to the Mayor of New York examined City renewal practices of the 1950's and characterized relocation experience in very much the same way:

> Forcing people to leave their old neighborhoods is probably the major source of bitterness and opposition to slum clearance. Slums, after all, are neighborhoods and communities. They teem with people who like the place in which they live for simple but deep-rooted reasons.[3]

Many careful studies have documented and detailed the intricate network of personal and social relationships that are often found in the old and declining communities.[4] If anything is to be learned from the bitter experience of large-scale clearance projects (some of which are chronicled in these studies), it is that any necessary rebuilding of such neighborhoods should be carried out slowly and displaced people should be offered relocation housing within remaining portions of the same community.

Recent experience with clearance projects argues for a policy that will enhance the individual's opportunity to choose his community, his housing, and the time when he wishes to move. Cities with active renewal and public works programs have disrupted the lives of many thousands of their residents in the last decade. Urban renewal projects from 1949 to 1961 encompassed areas containing 230,000 families, almost all with low incomes; and the majority were Negroes with particularly difficult problems in finding good housing.[5] In the face of this massive use of governmental coercion to disrupt residential neighborhoods, the reaction of an elderly woman in New York to a proposal to change the name of Third Avenue illustrates a growing public attitude: "They should leave this city alone! They should keep their cotton-pickin' fingers off!"[6]

Effects of Population Decline

Two guidelines for the scale of rebuilding programs are clear so far:

1. Recent migration and housing trends indicate the desirability of limiting the total scope of rebuilding to the number of *surplus* low-cost dwelling units, in order to avoid removing needed housing from the market.
2. Numerous sociological analyses indicate the desirability of avoiding a forced displacement of low-income people from communities where they have strong ties. Where community life is strong, the scale of rebuilding should ideally be limited according to the amount of *locally* available relocation housing for people who wish to stay in the area. As the occupants gradually abandon the old housing in such an area, rebuilding should proceed in a series of stages.

These guidelines allow a first approximation to rebuilding policies — suggesting a slow rate of rebuilding under present conditions in most big cities — but the major policy alternatives for the old neighborhoods involve more complex considerations. These alternatives are (a) to postpone rebuilding until the areas are virtually abandoned, or (b) to maintain a steady rebuilding process, replacing the old structures as they deteriorate or become vacant.

The first of these alternatives, waiting for abandonment, is sure to be a process drawn out over several decades, with a great likelihood that much of the housing will still be occupied as long as

124

it is available. Gradual abandonment has been the fate of many neighborhoods that once served as reception areas for the great waves of European immigrants at the turn of the century. The West End of Boston reached its population peak around 1910, when over 32,000 people lived there. The area declined steadily afterward, as the foreign-born population and their children moved on to newer locations. By 1950, population had fallen below 17,000, but the housing vacancy rate was only 5 per cent. In 1950, a large part of this area was earmarked for an urban redevelopment project. Official project designation came in 1952, and the impending clearance of the area was publicized repeatedly until the actual takeover in April 1958. Large-scale abandonment began, but the majority of units were still occupied at the time of land acquisition when the vacancy rate reached a peak of 38 per cent.[7]

The Lower East Side of Manhattan had a similar process of decline, but without the threat of clearance. The area filled with immigrant Jews and Italians, reaching a population peak of 541,000 in 1910. As these occupants moved on to better housing, no further immigrant waves replaced them, with the exception of a small influx of Puerto Ricans. Population reached a low of 205,000 in 1940, and held at about the same level in 1950. During this long period of abandonment, the number of dwelling units shrank from a high of 108,000 to a low of 71,000 — a proportionately smaller reduction for housing than for population — and the vacancy rate never exceeded 30 per cent.[8]

After the process of abandonment is well advanced, the people who remain have special reasons to do so. Leo Grebler describes the Jews who stayed on the Lower East Side as "the poor, the orthodox, the servers of cultural needs, some of those having businesses in the area, and the aged."[9] Walter Firey, in his study of the North End of Boston, maintains that long-term residents of this area were those who wished to identify with Italian culture and the Italian community.[10] An analysis of occupants in a redevelopment area in Indianapolis characterizes the most persistent residents as the "indolent," the "adjusted poor," and the "social outcasts."[11] A long process of self-selection is at work here. When a majority of the population leaves an area, people who remain clearly have some special attachment to the place. Having chosen deliberately to remain, they are likely to be most severely affected by forced

125

relocation. Thus, even at the end of a long waiting period, rebuilding an old neighborhood by large-scale clearance will still involve a considerable amount of forced uprooting and the destruction of remaining community life among a particularly vulnerable group of people.

This pattern of decline would also entail serious problems during the long process of abandonment. When population is thinning out while the physical equipment of the area remains intact, service costs would be high in relation to the number of people deriving any benefit from local facilities. As Raymond Vernon has pointed out (Appendix C), streets and utilities would have to be maintained at previous levels for a dwindling population; police and fire protection could not be cut back; school structures would have to be maintained for small enrollments. Capital investments in modern facilities or environmental improvements would be difficult to justify against other claims for public funds, since the life of these facilities would be geared to the uncertain life expectancy of the old housing. Declining areas would probably receive minimum service and no new investment, despite the needs of the people who remain.

Gradual Rebuilding

The alternate approach is a process of continuous rebuilding, keeping pace with the gradual abandonment of old housing. Such a program would be difficult to manage, but the potential gains are significant. The pattern of change is evolutionary: new residents enter in small numbers each time a handful of new buildings is completed. This influx would prevent any problem of underutilization. Services and new facilities would be related to new housing as well as old. At no stage would it be necessary to force large numbers of residents out of the area. Rebuilding would proceed by small increments, with each stage depending first upon the voluntary abandonment of some old housing.

At each stage, some poor people would be displaced, even though clearance would be limited to deteriorated and predominantly vacant structures. But those displaced from their homes would have an opportunity to relocate within the same area, since an adequate *local* vacancy reserve would be one cornerstone of the gradual rebuilding policy. The availability of some new housing within the community would widen residential choices for people

126

in the area with rising incomes who might want better housing in the same locale and for outside people who would have an additional area in which to find some new housing. A possible fringe benefit is that gradual rebuilding would promote diversity in an area, rather than the homogeneity of a large-scale clearance project rebuilt all at once.

If new housing is to be attracted into the declining residential areas, their physical setting will have to be improved significantly, with new community facilities and a high level of public services. These environmental changes would also benefit' occupants of the old housing. By making the area more desirable generally, environmental upgrading might slow the process of abandonment and might encourage more widespread rehabilitation of old housing. From a social point of view, these are desirable side effects, providing an improved environment for low-income people and prolonging the useful life of existing buildings. Such benefits may not please the municipal tax assessor if they slow the process of new development, but his perspective should not be decisive.

Environmental improvements, coupled with a steady process of rebuilding, may also raise the cost of site acquisition in the older areas. To the extent that a rise in price reflects increased utilization of the old structures, no conflicts with public objectives will arise, since rebuilding is not to be attempted while areas are still heavily utilized.

But site prices may rise because of speculative rebuilding values in an area where new development is active. If price increases threaten to block new development or to force up new densities to undesirable levels, the municipality may be able to forestall price inflation by a policy of advance property acquisition before rebuilding and environmental improvement are well under way. Early property acquisition need not influence the timing of clearance: buildings could be leased for operation or could be operated by the city until they are ready for replacement. Alternately, the city might obtain long-term options to buy properties at current prices before making major public investments in an area. Less directly, prompt reassessment to keep pace with rising values would discourage the holding of property on speculation.

In some circumstances, gradual rebuilding may be inconsistent with desired directions of change. Some old residential neighbor-

127

hoods may be better suited for nonresidential functions in the future. Such transitions from residence to industry or large institutions, for example, may involve a general realignment of the street pattern, different utility systems, and a radically different land pattern. In such cases, rebuilding in small stages may be virtually impossible because of the sheer magnitude of physical change and reorganization. Some types of new development — heavy industry, truck terminals — may have a deteriorating effect on the environment for remaining residents rather than a positive effect on the quality of residential services.

These severe constraints on gradual rebuilding are not likely to be typical. Where residential areas are to remain residential in the future, slow rebuilding will indeed create more complex physical planning problems than complete clearance. But the advantages of gradual rebuilding are considerable in bypassing the problems of slow decline and eventual dislocation of the remaining community.

Creating the Conditions for Gradual Rebuilding

Policies to achieve a gradual rebuilding of the old residential areas consist of two separate phases: creating the preconditions for rebuilding, and establishing a setting that will attract new development. This study has focused considerable attention on the preconditions and the critical points at which public action can influence them. Less information is available about the final conditions for rebuilding; but the general nature of the problem is clear, and some useful conclusions can be drawn from those current renewal plans that aim at a gradual rebuilding process.

Two basic lines of attack are open for public action designed to strengthen the preconditions for attracting new development into the old residential areas: increase public preferences for these locations and reduce development and operating costs for the developer. The relationships that have been noted between metropolitan structure and locational preferences for new housing point the way for the first approach. To raise consumer demand, public action can be taken to *strengthen the downtown core* in terms of employment, service and recreational facilities; *increase the access advantages of the old areas* to downtown or to other activity centers; *remove competitive vacant land from the market;* and, of course, *improve the local environment in declining areas.*

Specific action to accomplish these objectives could take many different forms, depending upon local constraints and resources. Downtown renewal programs, improvements in the transportation system, the acquisition or regulation of vacant land—all offer opportunities to influence locational choices by manipulating the functional structure of the region. Such actions will produce complex effects, and none are likely to be undertaken solely to promote rebuilding of the declining areas. But these are illustrations of some ways in which public programs can conceivably increase demand for housing sites in the areas to be rebuilt.

Where costs and returns for new housing are out of line in the declining areas, the other approach is to lower costs. Direct financial subsidies are an obvious method: tax abatements and low-interest loans, for example. Less direct methods involve devaluing substandard properties by enforcing building and occupancy code requirements to reduce the profits of illegally operated housing, or formulating tax policies for the same purpose. All these methods are highly complex and generate many side effects; they cannot be undertaken without careful study of the housing market and analysis of the likely results of contemplated action. In a housing market where low-rent units are scarce, code enforcement measures may result in a transfer of maintenance costs from owners to tenants through rent increases. Where low-cost units are in large supply and vacancies are growing, prudent policy may simply involve waiting for vacancy rates to rise high enough to turn prices downward. Measures to expand the supply of sound low-cost housing, such as well-conceived public housing programs, are also likely to help devalue deteriorated structures in the declining areas.

An aspect of the abandonment of declining areas that appeared very clearly in the three regional analyses was the slowness of minority group dispersal from central locations. Where continued occupancy of the old housing represents the free choice of individuals who wish to remain in their communities, such decisions should be respected. To a certain extent, however, decisions to remain in the old areas result from discrimination in the private housing market or from fear of discrimination. The elimination of such barriers is an objective that needs no further justification. Fair housing legislation and other steps to open the suburban market to all groups in the population will widen the range of

129

choice for minority families and will probably also speed the process of vacating substandard housing in the old areas.

The total demand for new apartments in a region is a critical factor in meeting the prerequisites for a gradual rebuilding of old neighborhoods. The importance of action at the national level in broadening the apartment market has already been noted. In addition, local actions that promote demand for inlying areas are likely to promote an acceptance of apartment densities as one condition of living near the center of the region. Local programs to reduce development and operating costs in rebuilding areas may also make possible a reduction in rents to levels competitive with the cost of owning a single-family house. Finally, local experiments with design innovations in multifamily structures may stimulate increased interest in this type of housing.

Local governments exert considerable power over the pattern of new apartment construction through the regulation of maximum densities in zoning legislation. Density regulations for areas to be rebuilt must steer a course between two conflicting objectives. In order to make new buildings feasible on expensive cleared sites, density regulations should permit fairly intensive development. But in order to use the limited apartment market as an effective force for rebuilding many old areas, maximum densities should not go so high as to exhaust the total potential for new apartments in just a few locations. Both criteria must enter into the choice of appropriate densities, for zoning itself is a tool for rebuilding and may reduce current land prices by controlling maximum development densities. The choice of densities should therefore reflect a careful consideration of the general demand for space for apartment housing in a region and the supply of feasible sites, as well as the economics of new development and the preferences of people who will live in the new housing.

Improving the Environment

In areas that meet the preconditions for rebuilding, attracting new development will require still further public action. Developers of new housing usually avoid the declining areas where deteriorated old housing is concentrated, although this is not inevitably the case. A major task for public programs is to correct whatever environmental factors keep new development out of the old neighborhoods.

130

Most current efforts in this direction emphasize the selective clearance of run-down properties, the provision of new community facilities (schools, parks, playgrounds), traffic improvements, redesigning of streets to enhance their appearance, and occasionally the development of a modern shopping plaza. An important feature in all these current plans is the rehabilitation of much of the older housing. Although most of these programs are too new to permit an evaluation of results, several general considerations are already clear:

1. Old residential areas differ markedly in their ability to attract new private housing, with important consequences for public programs. Some areas have special advantages for new housing: good accessibility to a center of activity, proximity to prestige locations, attractive views, or other special site characteristics. In such areas, little public action may be necessary to spur private rebuilding of cleared sites. In an area in Los Angeles, which will be described later in this chapter, the sole public expenditure required to set off a wave of rehabilitation and rebuilding was the administrative overhead for a series of building inspections and code enforcement orders.

   In contrast, some areas are so lacking in attractions that private building seems unlikely, even with environmental improvements. In such areas, private developers may have to receive special financial incentives, or perhaps some form of public housing is the only feasible type of new development. A successful rebuilding program is likely to encompass both extremes among old neighborhoods, as well as many in between. To cope with such a broad range of conditions will require more than mere reliance on private development: special inducements will have to be offered in some areas, and varying degrees and types of subsidy may be required in others.

2. One way to regard these differences is in terms of the differing multiplier effect of public investment in generating private expenditure in different areas. From the point of view of municipal finance, this relationship will be an important one, but a socially responsible rebuilding program will seek goals

131

other than maximizing this multiplier effect. Investments in public facilities and the community environment are more than techniques to attract new development; they are also means for providing good services and surroundings for people in the old neighborhoods.

3. Residential areas will also differ with respect to the amount of clearance and rehabilitation that is justified at any stage of a rebuilding program. Although the rate of rebuilding would be geared to the availability of vacant units within the area, the physical characteristics of existing structures will affect the types of treatment used in the rebuilding program. Certain types of structures, such as the brownstones in New York, are particularly suited to rehabilitation. Others may be of a structural type unsuitable for modern needs (old-law tenements), or may be uneconomical to renovate.

4. The use of renovation may have to be sharply limited in low-income areas unless subsidies are granted, for rehabilitated rental units are likely to be too expensive for many poor families. Under these circumstances, where rehabilitation would mean removing low-cost units from the market, government-induced renovation should move no faster than the growth of vacant relocation units in the area or the rise of incomes in the community. Present rebuilding programs generally call for extensive rehabilitation of older units, but these programs often envision a substantial amount of relocation out of the area. In some areas, however, moderate rehabilitation may be within the means of present occupants.

5. The public cost of gradually rebuilding old residential areas is sometimes lower than the cost of urban renewal clearance projects and sometimes in the same general range, but public investments are largely for community facilities rather than for land subsidies. Information has been compiled for eleven renewal projects that emphasize the conservation and rehabilitation of existing housing rather than large-scale clearance; all are located in cities over 100,000 in population (Table 6.1). Net project costs per net acre of land (excluding streets) range from $19,000 for the Mack-Concord Conservation Area No. 1 in Detroit to $268,000 for the Harlem Park Project No. 2 in Baltimore.

132

Table 6.1. Selected Characteristics of Conservation-Rehabilitation Projects

City and Project	Net Project Cost (Thousands of dollars)	Size of Project (Acres excluding streets)	Net Project Cost per Net Acre (Thousands of dollars)	Net Project Cost per Net Acre for Clearance Projects (Thousands of dollars)	
				Average cost	Number of projects
Atlanta:					
University Center	7,806	101.4	77.0	24.8	4
Baltimore:					
Harlem Park No. 2	5,871	21.9	268.1	269.8	11
Chicago:					
Illinois Institute of Technology	2,961	27.9	106.1	202.4	22
Columbus:					
Market Mohawk	7,384	67.0	110.2	77.9	1
Denver:					
Whittier School	1,101	7.8	141.2	49.1	2
Detroit:					
Mack-Concord Conservation No. 1	3,895	205.0	19.0	110.1	8
Nashville:					
East Nashville	20,270	359.5	56.4	212.3	1
New Haven:					
Dixwell	11,285	187.1	60.3	297.0	2
Wooster Square	23,052	169.5	136.0		
Oakland:					
West Oakland General Neighborhood Renewal Plan	26,400	671.0	39.3	Not available	
Philadelphia:					
East Poplar Numbers 1, 4, 5, 6	1,651	8.1	203.8	211.6	16

Source: U.S. Housing and Home Finance Agency, Urban Renewal Administration, *Urban Renewal Project Characteristics* (June 30, 1961), Characteristics Directory of Projects as of June 30, 1961; Detroit information in part from Maurice Frank Parkins, *Neighborhood Conservation: A Pilot Study* (Detroit: Detroit City Plan Commission in Cooperation with Housing and Home Finance Agency, 1958); New Haven information from New Haven Redevelopment Agency; Oakland information from Redevelopment Agency of the City of Oakland, *Information Bulletin No. 3*, "A General Neighborhood Renewal Plan for West Oakland" (no date).

Clearance projects exclude projects in areas classified as predominantly open before renewal; averages are weighted according to area of project.

In many cities, costs for these projects are considerably lower than the average costs per acre for clearance projects, but costs for the two types of programs show no consistent relationship. There are important differences, however, in the composition of the local government share of project costs. Cities tend to have greater expenditures on site improvements and supporting facilities for nonclearance projects and to have greater cash outlays for land acquisition and write-down in clearance projects.[12]

Thus the cost of gradually rebuilding old residential areas should not be regarded as separate from local expenditures on public works and community facilities. Rebuilding these areas within the framework of the federal urban renewal program will mean federal subsidies of two thirds (or three fourths) of the cost of public works benefiting project areas. The capacity of cities to spend on the order of $30,000 to $70,000 per acre (typical local shares of the cost range shown in Table 6.1) will have to be determined individually, but considerable sums may be available out of normal public works allocations.

PART 2: NEW YORK, LOS ANGELES, AND HARTFORD

Renewal Policies in New York

Of the three study areas, New York has made the most use of urban renewal programs in recent years and offers the richest case material for an evaluation of public policy. The discussion here will be limited to renewal in the City of New York, where the bulk of the declining residential areas is concentrated, and where the most interesting programs in the region have developed. At first, government-sponsored renewal projects based on the Housing Act of 1949 were concentrated in and around central Manhattan, but the sphere of operations was soon extended to upper Manhattan (the upper West Side, Harlem), areas of Brooklyn close to Manhattan, and a scattering of projects in outer Queens and the Bronx. The Housing and Redevelopment Board, which now administers urban renewal programs in New York, has already undertaken new developments in typical older residential locations of Manhattan, the Bronx, and Brooklyn, and has begun to plan still further incursions into such areas.

New York is no model of enlightened public policy working toward broad social objectives. The severe shortage of low-cost housing in New York has already been noted. Despite this shortage, redevelopment projects started between 1950 and 1960 demolished 22,000 low-cost dwelling units. Even this volume of destruction is only a small part of the total clearance resulting from all forms of

134

public action including highway construction. Total public demolition displaced 15,000 families per year by 1960, and City projections assume no easing of this pace in the next few years.[13]

New York has continued to press on with the largest urban renewal effort in the country, but the program has provoked tremendous public opposition. It has already brought about two Congressional investigations and has stirred many pressures for change within the body politic. One indication of desperate citizen reaction to the untimely clearance of old housing is a recent proposal to forbid the demolition of all rent-controlled housing in sound condition. As a result of these pressures, the program is now being modified to give more emphasis to conservation and rehabilitation, to eliminate renewal projects intended solely for luxury housing, and to build more small public housing developments in neighborhoods that are being renewed.[14] Despite these concessions, much clearance is still contemplated.

Until recently, New York has been largely insensitive to the continued need for old housing, but it has pioneered boldly in using public programs to promote a rebuilding of old residential areas. Little governmental effort is needed to raise demand for inlying sites or to lower acquisition costs. These factors are currently in a favorable relationship with one another, and the large current volume of apartment construction provides a potential basis for re-using cleared sites. The current office-building boom in Manhattan seems to assure the maintenance of a strong core — an important factor promoting central housing preferences — without requiring direct governmental action. Improvements in the subway system — some of which are currently under way in Manhattan, such as the lengthening of stations and the acquisition of new equipment — will also help maintain the central orientation of New York's housing market. Other government action is likely to promote the voluntary abandonment of deteriorated housing: the City Housing Authority has announced plans to build 57,000 new public housing units during the next few years, while City and State anti-bias legislation continues to widen the private housing market for minority groups now concentrated in the old neighborhoods.

With economic preconditions already favorable, New York is currently working to improve the social and physical environment of the declining areas. In areas where existing buildings still have a useful life ahead, City efforts have involved code enforcement, tax abatements to induce private rehabilitation, improvements in streets and street lighting, new community facilities, and a host of social services: English classes for adults, nursery schools, public health programs, and casework guidance.[15] But where plans call for rebuilding with some new private construction, the problem is one of attracting middle-income families into neighborhoods surrounded by poor people living in old housing. This problem may ease once an initial middle-income development helps diversify the character of the neighborhood, but the current task is to trigger the initial population change. New housing and new community facilities can accomplish physical change in the immediate environment, but run-down surroundings jeopardize the chances of attracting middle-income occupants to the new housing.

A policy emerging in New York seeks to overcome the reluctance of middle-income families to move to new apartments in the old areas by offering privately built housing at "bargain" rents.[16] The mechanism for this policy is a series of financial incentives to developers of rental or cooperative housing, authorized by the New York State Mitchell-Lama law. State or City loans are available to developers for terms up to 50 years at 4 to 4½ per cent interest, covering up to 90 per cent of development cost. In addition, the City grants abatements up to 50 per cent in real estate taxes. (This program may also be combined with land write-downs in federally aided renewal areas.) The result is a substantial reduction in yearly financing and operating costs and a smaller equity share in new development in comparison with conventional financing and normal assessments. Rents are established by prior agreement between the sponsor and the City or State supervising agency. Under this program, rental units have come on the market for $25 to $30 per room; new apartments in conventionally financed private buildings rent for $40 per room or more. Mitchell-Lama cooperatives also offer advantageous prices to the public: down payments are generally $400 to $600 per room, with monthly carrying charges of $18 to $25 per room.

The Mitchell-Lama program has been in operation since 1946, but only recently has it become a tool used specifically to induce new construction for a middle-income market in the old and declining areas. The policy switch has taken the form of turning down applications of sponsors who propose new developments in areas where unsubsidized private construction is active. The rationale on the part of New York City officials is to avoid a situation in which new middle-income apartments in choice locations undercut the market for comparably priced units in the neglected areas. An additional objective of this policy is to safeguard the tax base of the City by avoiding subsidized building in areas where fully taxpaying property would otherwise develop.

Results of this policy are not yet evident. Two different phases of the program will be interesting to watch. First is the question of whether the low rents of Mitchell-Lama developments will succeed in attracting an initial contingent of middle-income residents to a few bright islands set among a sea of obsolescent housing. The first new developments are sizable islands, however. An early venture in the Williamsburg section of Brooklyn will occupy 24 acres; another development is expected to use some 38 acres of land in the Brownsville area of Brooklyn.

If the scale of these initial developments is suitable for attracting the desired rental market, the second phase of the strategy must still be tested. Will the introduction of middle-income people into the old areas trigger later unsubsidized private development, or will rents have to be held below normal levels in order to continue rebuilding these areas? The problem at this stage will be to devise further changes in the environment that will allow the old areas to command rents consistent with their locational advantages, if the objective is to attract conventional private housing.

Gradual Rebuilding in New York

The large scale of these particular Mitchell-Lama developments is not really appropriate for the gradual rebuilding of old neighborhoods in accordance with objectives of avoiding forced relocation and clearing only surplus housing. Assembling land for a site of 25 or 30 acres will inevitably mean displacing many people and sweeping away a considerable amount of housing, including some that is neither surplus nor deteriorated. A gradual approach would require clearing smaller plots on a highly selective basis and introducing new buildings among old ones on the same street. An urban renewal project currently in progress on the West Side of Manhattan is closer to this model of gradual rebuilding and involves a number of interesting implementation techniques.

The West Side renewal area, however, does not conform to the general goal of replacing surplus, substandard housing in declining areas, for the area is not a declining one and its housing is over-utilized.[17] From 1950 to 1956, the population climbed from 33,000 to 39,000, with a large influx of people from Puerto Rico and a smaller exodus of white non-Puerto Rican residents. By 1956, 20 per cent of all living quarters were overcrowded (more than 1.5 persons per room); and with the conversion of many furnished rooms into family housing units, a third of all units lacked adequate bathroom facilities. The West Side program is nevertheless useful as an illustration of how gradual rebuilding might be accomplished in a more suitable area.

In this renewal area, sites cleared for new buildings are small, ranging from 7,200 square feet to 40,000 square feet. Over the four stages of the program, some entire street fronts are to be rebuilt, but at any one stage the new buildings are mainly noncontiguous. In the early stages, new development thus adjoins old buildings, some of which are in poor condition. Part of the program for attracting new development into this area is the eventual rehabilitation of most of the older structures that are to be retained. For some time, however, new buildings will have old and even substandard neighbors. Despite this potential drawback, developer interest in the project has been high, and both rehabilitation and new construction are already under way.

Another feature of the strategy for attracting new development is the addition of new community facilities. These include a new elementary school and playground, a new playground for an existing school, and various walkways and small open spaces.

In addition to physical improvements in the neighborhood, New York has an impressive set of tools in its varied programs for stimulating new building. As of 1960, plans for the West Side anticipated either conventional financing or FHA Section 220 mortgages for some new buildings and Mitchell-Lama financing for others. Rehabilitation can be undertaken through conventional or FHA financing. In addition, some low-income public housing is to be built in the area. At the end of the second stage, the ratio of new private housing units to new public units was expected to be

2.5 to 1, with private housing rising to a higher proportion in the remaining stages.

New York has still other programs for new private housing, in-. volving various degrees of tax abatement and financing assistance and dependent upon a profit limitation of 6 per cent. In the field of public housing, there are City programs for low- and middle-income projects, as well as state and federal low-income programs.[18] Other cities that wish to sponsor extensive rebuilding programs will have to develop similarly diversified tools to fit the highly individual character of different neighborhoods and different people.

Although many of these programs involve some public subsidy, the relationship of land cost to land value is basically satisfactory for new private housing in the West Side renewal area. No federally aided land write-downs are contemplated, and a considerable amount of new housing is expected under conventional or FHA financing, with no tax abatement or other City subsidy. Despite anticipated land costs as high as $16 per square foot, new apartments to rent at only $45 per room are considered feasible through FHA financing. One reason why actual site costs are not excessive for new development is that the densities follow normal levels for new construction in New York rather than the somewhat lower levels prevailing in large-scale urban renewal projects. Density for the total project area will remain about the same before and after rebuilding.

If the timing of various stages follows the suggested schedule of two and one-half years per stage, the rebuilding of this area will be far from gradual. Nevertheless, with more time allotted per stage, this plan could serve as a model for the gradual approach. Only the first two stages are worked out in detail. At the end of the second stage, about one third of all the living quarters in the area will be replaced with either new or rehabilitated housing.

Both rehabilitation and clearance will require the relocation of some former residents, but new public housing will be included within the area, and a number of families are expected to have incomes high enough for renovated or new units. Of 2,600 families expected to be relocated, about 1,300 are likely to be in the low-income category. With only 500 new public housing units in the area, at least 800 families will have to be relocated elsewhere.

With some modifications, this type of plan would be suitable for the gradual rebuilding of an old residential area. The most important change would be to postpone any clearance or rehabilitation until more vacancies are available in the area. Then, with slower staging and more public housing, the community could start a steady rebuilding process.

The Double Standard in Urban Renewal

Urban renewal in New York has also raised serious questions about the purposes of public aid used for channeling private development into otherwise inactive parts of the City. Is the sole purpose to stimulate the rebuilding of old areas, or is there an additional objective of promoting higher quality housing developments than private builders provide elsewhere in the City? Economic analyses in Chapter 4 assumed that the rebuilding of declining neighborhoods would generally involve structural types and development densities similar to those currently in use elsewhere in the region. So far as densities are concerned, urban renewal in New York has departed considerably from normal development practice. Private housing developments in and near central Manhattan are usually built at densities of 300 to 500 dwelling units per net acre. Densities in large-scale Manhattan urban renewal projects have been less than half as high, ranging from 100 to 150 dwelling units per net acre. In the other boroughs of New York, where typical densities of private development are about 150 units per acre, urban renewal densities vary mainly between 50 and 100 units per net acre.[19]

From the point of view of public policy, a double standard is clearly involved here. Maximum densities of private development are controlled by zoning regulations. Thus the developer who builds at densities of 500 units per acre has governmental approval to do so. Yet when public subsidies are made available for urban renewal projects, maximum densities are set at levels far below usual practice. This is a costly procedure, requiring substantial subsidies to permit a normal profit when expensive land is to be developed according to exceptional density standards. The costliness of this approach results in large part from the inconsistency between zoning and renewal standards. Normal development densities, as regulated by zoning, strongly influence the value of land in areas where rebuilding is active or anticipated. Values resulting from

140

expectations of normal development potential will almost certainly exceed values for re-use at lower densities. Subsidies are necessary if the gap is to be bridged at all.

A large part of New York's expenditures on urban renewal have gone to purchase nothing more than reduced development densities in renewal areas. The Washington Square Southeast project is a particularly striking example. Located on the fringe of Greenwich Village, where private construction has accounted for a great deal of rebuilding in recent years, the project involved a land acquisition cost of $33 per square foot.[20] Typical land costs for privately developed housing nearby were between $30 and $40 per square foot. While unsubsidized developments nearby were built at densities exceeding 300 units per net acre, the Washington Square project has a density of 138 units per acre. Rent levels are about the same as those in new buildings nearby. Net project costs were 15.4 million dollars for a site of 14.5 acres, or over 1 million dollars per acre. Without public site assembly, new construction might not have been possible at this location, but the site could conceivably have been assembled and sold at cost for development at typical densities. Instead, the area was subsidized to the extent of 1 million dollars per acre to achieve a lower density. Some observers of renewal in New York point to an additional cause for high subsidies; they maintain that in the absence of competitive bids, the gap between project costs and resale prices has been unnecessarily high in many project areas, even after allowance for density restrictions.

Subsidies for lower densities may also serve other objectives. Most New York City projects differ from Washington Square Southeast in that they are not located in areas where private development has been active. Thus they initiate new construction in otherwise stagnant areas, and they may generate later unsubsidized building. A project currently contemplated for the Brownsville area of Brooklyn would have densities below those of private development as one means of attracting middle-income people into what is now a low-prestige neighborhood.

But the difficult question of double standards remains. If one objective of public policy is to change the standards of private development in the direction of lower densities, urban renewal is a costly tool and perhaps not a very effective one. Zoning can be a much more powerful way of changing development standards. New York has made an effort to reduce private development densities through its new zoning law, but the maximum permitted densities of 400 or more units per acre are still twice as high as those in renewal projects.

As long as this difference persists, the City is in effect attempting to reach high standards through renewal but willing to settle for lower standards in its more influential zoning regulations. This situation suggests a need for both clarifying the objectives of re-building and coordinating the various means of achieving these objectives. Reducing the density of new construction may be a highly desirable goal. Calculations in Chapter 4 indicated that with FHA financing, new housing can be built in the older parts of the Bronx, Brooklyn, and Queens at densities as low as 50 units per acre. Under present cost conditions, land write-downs are not necessary to permit moderate density construction in the old resi-dential areas. But if zoning regulations allow higher densities, special incentives will probably be necessary to attract new housing at densities below the prevailing level.

Zoning measures should be tied more closely to rebuilding ob-jectives in still another respect — to help divert new apartment construction from outlying parts of New York into the declining residential areas. A rapid rebuilding rate would be possible if new development could be drawn into the old neighborhoods. To do so on a broad scale would surely require the use of zoning restric-tions to limit outlying apartment building, as well as the use of environmental improvements to make the old areas more attractive.

Zoning is but one example of public measures that should be coordinated with rebuilding programs. Tax policies and capital in-vestment programs are other obvious spheres of public activity that can aid or hinder the rebuilding of declining areas. New York is far advanced in the measures it has devised to promote the re-building of its older sections, but many loose ends of public policy must still be tied together if this rebuilding is to succeed.

My major quarrel with New York's programs, however, is not with techniques but with basic policies. Despite some attempt at gradual rebuilding on the upper West Side and in a few other areas now in the planning stage, the City still appears committed to a large-scale project approach, even while the housing shortage persists. This policy is bound to create serious problems for dislocated low-income families, while it continues taking needed low-cost housing off the market.

The Setting for Renewal in Los Angeles

Los Angeles is in a favorable position for starting a rebuilding program. Vacancy reserves in the City of Los Angeles are at an ample level generally, with an estimated vacancy rate of 4.7 per cent in the declining areas. Although the timeliness of large-scale clearance in Los Angeles is far from certain, the vacancy reserve exceeds the supply of deteriorated housing by a sizable margin in both the City and the region, so that a careful replacement of surplus housing could probably begin.

Economic conditions are highly favorable for rebuilding the older areas of Los Angeles. Although the demand for new housing gives few market advantages to central locations, development and operating costs in central areas are entirely consistent with current rent levels so long as the environment is satisfactory. Site acquisition costs are low; blighted areas in the Los Angeles region consist primarily of single-family houses, with only a handful of row houses or tenements. Even land assembly is no problem. Typical lot dimensions are 50 to 60 feet of street frontage and a depth of 120 or 125 feet. Apartment developers ordinarily require no more than a single lot of this size for a new structure with 8 to 10 units. Where the surrounding environment is unfavorable, however, each developer would probably need some assurance that others would rehabilitate or rebuild nearby property. Finally, the size of the rental market is no obstacle, with multifamily buildings accounting for almost half the new dwelling units in the region since 1957.

Under these circumstances, public action to create a favorable economic setting for rebuilding seems hardly necessary. Nevertheless, government programs presently contemplated for other purposes are likely to have the incidental effect of promoting greater demand for housing in central areas. These programs include a number of measures designed to strengthen the central business district through more intensive commercial development and a proposed mass transit rail system.[21] The mass transit system would start with a twelve-mile route from downtown Los Angeles along Wilshire Boulevard to the new Century City development in the west, and an eleven-mile route to El Monte in the east. Improved accessibility to downtown along these two corridors is likely to strengthen demand for housing sites in inner areas adjacent to the transit routes, particularly if plans for expanding downtown activity are successful.

The first renewal projects in Los Angeles have been close to downtown, but even the limited experience in these prime locations illustrates the favorable economic conditions for urban renewal in this region. By 1961, land acquisition was under way for the Bunker Hill project, an area of 136 acres adjacent to the central business district and slated to be cleared primarily for business expansion. Advance appraisals indicated an average cost of $8.78 per square foot for land purchases and acquisition expenses.[22] Estimated returns from the resale of land average $7.23 per square foot, so that the anticipated land subsidy will amount to only $1.55 per square foot, or about $68,000 per acre. Other project expenses — relocation, site improvements, overhead — will constitute additional subsidies, but the combined net project cost or total subsidy is expected to be only $164,000 per acre. This is not an obscure declining neighborhood but choice commercial land. Comparable renewal projects near the commercial area of Manhattan (Columbus Circle, Lincoln Square, Pennsylvania Station South) have required total subsidies in the vicinity of 1 million dollars per acre.

Another Los Angeles project in the planning stage in 1961 was the Temple area about 5 minutes northwest of the central business district, intended for clearance and residential re-use. With an anticipated gross project cost — including land acquisition, site improvements, and all other expenditures — of only $4.45 per square foot, or $189,000 per acre, subsidies were expected to be still smaller than in the Bunker Hill project. According to resale estimates, the net project cost was expected to be $63,000 per acre. Again, New York clearance projects with comparable locations have required subsidies many times as great. The West Park, New York University–Bellevue, Cooper Square, and Washington Square Southeast projects are all residential areas quite close to the business center of Manhattan; subsidies for these projects ranged from $600,000 to 1 million dollars per acre.

One small renewal project in Los Angeles has already been completed without any subsidy: the Ann project, formerly a residential area near downtown, has been cleared and put to industiral re-use without benefit of land write-down.

Although none of these initial projects have penetrated the old residential sections away from downtown, other areas officially designated for renewal study are scattered throughout the City of Los Angeles; and several outlying communities in the region have also started renewal programs. The first project in Santa Monica also presents an economic picture highly favorable for renewal, but it is by no means in a typical declining area. The Ocean Park project will use a choice site near the business center of Santa Monica, with an excellent view of the Pacific Ocean. As of 1961, real estate purchases and acquisition expenses for this site were expected to average $6.32 per square foot; and land resale value was appraised at $4.97 per square foot, for a mixture of new residential and commercial development.[23] Thus the expected land subsidy amounts to only $1.35 per square foot, or $59,000 per acre.

Official renewal efforts have not yet begun to cope with rebuilding typical old residential neighborhoods. As a result, policies have not yet been devised to take account of the special problems in such areas. The limited renewal experience in this region suggests, however, that public rebuilding programs will not require major subsidies for reducing land costs. The role of government in Los Angeles renewal is now largely that of assembling tracts of land on a scale suitable for rebuilding, investing in public improvements for renewal areas, and taking charge of relocation. The favorable economic setting for renewal in Los Angeles suggests that this role need not change when public programs begin to operate in the declining residential areas.

Mixing New and Old Housing in Residential Rebuilding

Rebuilding an area in small stages requires mixing new and old housing in a fine-grained pattern. To some observers of real estate practice, this pattern seems impossible to achieve when the old housing is in poor condition. Yet the upper West Side of New York is well on the way to achieving such a mixture, even before many of the old buildings are rehabilitated. Los Angeles also has an area where public action has induced new development side by side with substandard old housing. In Los Angeles, developers of new housing had assurances that building and occupancy codes

145

would be enforced to bring the neighboring old structures at least up to code standards.

Los Angeles has had an active code enforcement program operating largely outside the official urban renewal project areas.[24] One of the areas recently chosen for intensive code enforcement was the Sawtelle section of West Los Angeles located near several high-prestige areas of recent growth: Brentwood, Beverly Hills, and Santa Monica. Before the code enforcement program started, housing in the Sawtelle area consisted primarily of deteriorating single-family houses built in the late nineteenth century. Each property owner was given a list of repairs that would be necessary to bring his building up to code standards, with a thirty-day time limit to start work. Property owners were confronted with the alternatives of making repairs, having the City make repairs and assess their cost against the property, or selling the property. If rehabilitation costs were expected to exceed 50 per cent of the replacement cost of the building, the City was to start demolition proceedings in the event of noncompliance.

The Federal Housing Administration in Los Angeles agreed to insure loans for new development in the Sawtelle area, and would-be developers soon appeared on the scene with offers to buy many of the properties. The net result of this code enforcement program was a wave of new apartment construction, as well as the rehabilitation of many original structures. The number of buildings demolished, however, almost equaled the number repaired: 386 were demolished and 397 repaired.[25]

This project differed from normal urban renewal approaches in a number of important respects. The City made no physical improvements in the area and gave no relocation assistance. Land subsidies were not involved; total costs to the City were the administrative expenses necessary to carry out code enforcement procedures. What was accomplished? Social gains were dubious, with a large number of former residents leaving the area to make way for new construction. The physical change of the area alone is impressive. Experience in the Sawtelle neighborhood illustrates the favorable economic conditions for rebuilding in Los Angeles, as well as the possibility of mixing new and old housing even in an area that has long been bypassed by new development.

146

Other neglected areas in Los Angeles may not respond quite as easily to code enforcement programs. In less favorable locations, developers may be unwilling to bid for properties even when the owners are under some duress. In minority areas, the demand for new apartments may be less certain. When the surrounding neighborhoods are deteriorating, a larger scale of action may be necessary in order to attract new housing, and major public investments in local facilities may be a prerequisite for new private housing. In short, later attempts to rebuild blighted areas may have to incorporate approaches similar to those in New York, but the basic economic conditions are likely to be highly favorable in any case.

Old Housing and Minority Groups

Recent policy discussions within the federal housing agencies in Los Angeles have touched on another aspect of the declining areas that has been mentioned many times before: the extent to which old housing is an asset for disadvantaged groups in the City. Minorities in Los Angeles — Negroes, people of Mexican and Japanese background — cannot enter freely into the housing market despite the fact that many minority families have adequate incomes to buy new houses.[26] The nonwhite population (primarily Negroes and Orientals) constitutes about 9 per cent of total population in the region; yet according to estimates of the Federal Housing Administration, only 1.9 per cent of all new dwelling units constructed in the region between 1950 and 1956 were occupied by nonwhites. In the San Fernando Valley, a major boom area for new single-family developments since World War II, population soared from 155,000 in 1940 to 840,000 in 1960; yet aside from one segregated district in Pacoima with a Negro population of about 4,000, no more than a few dozen Negro families lived in the Valley in 1960.

Minority groups are now heavily concentrated in central areas of the region, and efforts to break down barriers of prejudice in the housing market are unlikely to produce sudden changes. The rate of decentralization among Negroes and, to a lesser extent, Mexicans and Japanese is likely to be slow for some time to come. In view of these unfortunate social characteristics of the suburban housing market, the Federal Housing Administration and Housing and Home Finance Agency offices in Los Angeles have been recon-

147

sidering their policies toward central areas where minority groups live.[27] Financing for home repairs has generally been difficult to obtain in these areas, and FHA assistance has only recently become available in a few of them. A position that has been advanced in these policy discussions is that many people would be eager to rehabilitate housing in the inner areas if financing were available on terms comparable to those for new housing. A reshaping of government policies to stimulate the flow of mortgage funds into these areas would, according to this view, represent a highly effective means of enabling minority groups to improve their housing conditions long before the suburbs are open to them.

The old housing is a strong social asset. Whether renovated or in its present condition, it provides living accommodations for groups unable to compete freely in the market for new housing. Economic calculations alone would reveal nothing of this special value that old housing has for minority groups. In Los Angeles, site acquisition costs are moderate and re-use values are high, but much of the old housing has a far greater social value than its acquisition cost would suggest. The Los Angeles situation calls attention once again to the danger of establishing public policy solely on economic terms. Declining areas are generally ambiguous in terms of their economic value, but public policy decisions should reflect an appraisal of the extent to which these areas are social as well as economic assets.

So far as Los Angeles is concerned, implementing policies for rebuilding the older areas — with new as well as rehabilitated housing — will call for approaches broader than those now in use in the region. To stimulate rehabilitation, public action will probably have to provide the same background conditions that are necessary to attract new housing. These conditions include public investment to provide facilities and services for upgrading the environment. Operations to improve declining Los Angeles neighborhoods will almost certainly have to combine elements of three separate programs: urban renewal, code enforcement, and favorable terms for financing home improvements. The main tasks of public policy in the region are to formulate clear objectives for the old areas and to weave together these separate techniques into an appropriate program for each area.

Renewal Policies in Hartford

Vacancy rates in Hartford have risen to the point where limited rebuilding could probably be started without depleting the supply of low-cost housing, but Hartford has problems of economic feasibility. A look at the choices confronting policymakers in Hartford will illustrate some of the difficulties in cities that do not meet the preconditions for rebuilding. The previous analysis of Hartford indicated a somewhat ambiguous situation with respect to the balance between land cost and land value in old residential areas. Although the apartment market displays some central preference in terms of rents as well as densities, land costs in the declining areas are slightly high in relation to likely rental returns. In many cases the gap can be bridged by FHA financing, but slight land subsidies may be required under some circumstances. The second precondition — a sufficient demand for housing sites in the older areas — is more clearly lacking since the total market for new apartments is small in Hartford.

Recent renewal activities in Hartford will probably strengthen central preferences in the housing market. In the mid-1950's, the decision of a major insurance company (Connecticut General) to move its headquarters from downtown Hartford to suburban Bloomfield gave an air of instability to downtown. Since then, an active renewal program has helped to safeguard the existing situation and to stimulate expansion in the central business district. Two renewal projects were in execution by 1960: one will provide a site for the new Phoenix Mutual headquarters building as well as other offices while the other is expected to be used for a mixture of business and light industry. Four more projects were in the planning stage by 1960, all in or near downtown. One will clear land for a convention hall, another will aim for retail expansion, a third for a combination of luxury apartments and offices, and the remaining project for new moderate-rental apartments overlooking the Connecticut River near downtown.

This program is likely to enhance the pulling power of downtown materially, both in a functional sense and in terms of improved appearance. The four projects within the central business district will rebuild more than 25 acres of downtown land with modern structures; two nearby projects will convert 100 acres to new uses.

Central activity will increase, and the mixture of new uses will add variety to the core.

While these developments are likely to increase the attraction of downtown, other government action may divert housing demand from the inner areas to outlying vacant land. Concurrently with the downtown renewal projects, a major highway program has been under way in the Hartford region. Several new expressways now under construction or planned for the near future will improve access from many outlying locations to downtown Hartford. Since abundant vacant land is available only 7 or 8 miles from the core, much of the demand for housing sites readily accessible to downtown may be filled by new developments on open land rather than in the declining areas. Zoning restrictions in suburban communities will play a key role here, for a shortage of land zoned for apartments may shift development to alternate sites in the inner areas. Nevertheless, the availability of open sites within short driving times from central Hartford is likely to make single-family houses a most attractive alternative to in-town apartments, even when access to downtown is a prime consideration.

In contrast to Los Angeles, urban renewal in Hartford involves high land costs and substantial subsidies. As of 1961, site acquisition costs for three downtown clearance projects planned for the near future were expected to range from $17 to $24 per square foot, with total subsidies at levels comparable to those in New York: $780,000 to $946,000 per acre.[28] These are not sites in typical old residential areas, however. Typical site costs in the old neighborhoods of Hartford range for $3 to $5 per square foot. Two clearance projects in areas near the core fall roughly within this range, with expected land acquisition costs between $3 and $4 per square foot.

In my analysis of Hartford, I noted that land costs of $3 to $5 per square foot are slightly higher than site costs in locations where private rebuilding is currently in progress. Developers of new housing in the old-mansion territory of Asylum Hill rarely pay more than $2.50 per square foot for apartment sites. Resale value of land in the Riverview project, intended for moderate rental (nonluxury) apartment buildings, was estimated as $2 per square foot. The anticipated Riverview project re-use value is not a result of lowering normal densities; it simply reflects current market prices for

150

apartment land elsewhere in the City of Hartford. Although the advantages of FHA financing can help close the gap between acquisition costs and re-use values in urban renewal areas, some subsidies will probably be necessary. In New York, land subsidies are likely to be needed in the older areas only if developers are required to build housing at densities lower than normal. In Los Angeles, land subsidies are likely to be unimportant. But in Hartford, present land costs are out of line with re-use values.

At current levels, the land subsidy in Hartford need not be very high. The expected gap between cost and resale price in Riverview was about $3 per square foot, or some $130,000 per acre. The net project cost anticipated for Riverview was $204,000 per acre, but 8 of the 24 acres in the project area are to be turned into a public park rather than sold as part of the apartment development. With some land subsidy needed in addition to expenditures for relocation and public improvements, rebuilding the old residential areas will be more expensive in Hartford than in Los Angeles, but much less expensive than in New York.

Size of the Apartment Market in Hartford

In addition to the imbalance between site costs and re-use values, Hartford faces a serious obstacle to rebuilding in the limited size of the market for new apartments. I have estimated the land utilization rate for new multifamily development as 5 to 7 acres per year in the City of Hartford. The Windsor Street renewal area in Hartford alone provides more than 70 acres of cleared land just outside the central business district. This project was originally intended for apartment development, but difficulties in finding apartment developers led to a change in plans in favor of new business and industrial development. According to the housing market study and my rough estimate, some 10 years of accumulated new apartment housing would be required to take over this 70-acre central site.

What can Hartford do to rebuild its declining areas, given the limitations of high acquisition costs and small demand for new apartments? Several general strategies seem worth considering. One is to spread the new construction rather than concentrate it in a few large clearance areas — a policy which has social merit in any case. New development can be parceled out to various areas, injecting some new life into each one. Even so, the potential rebuilding rate is so slow that 37 years would be required just to absorb sites cleared of housing now deteriorated.

An alternate strategy would be to broaden the demand for apartments. This could be done by providing types of multifamily housing that are new to the region. The housing market study cited previously suggests luxury apartments as one type of new housing that may extend the market by competing with upper levels of the single-family market. This is the strategy of the proposed Bushnell Plaza renewal project, which will offer expensive apartments on a highly desirable site overlooking Bushnell Park close to the heart of downtown. Other possibilities are to experiment with row houses, town houses, or other forms of new housing that can be built at moderately high densities. Still another approach would be to broaden the market by producing apartments at rents below current levels. Counterparts of the New York Mitchell-Lama program might be devised for this purpose if subsidies are to be provided; or construction and financing methods might be manipulated to minimize production costs.

Another strategy would work at reducing acquisition costs of land in the declining areas, using measures already mentioned in this chapter, such as building subsidized housing to speed the depopulation of the old areas and enforcing housing codes or altering tax policies to chip away at operating profits in deteriorated housing.

Hartford may well represent a common situation among relatively small cities with vacant land available for development nearby. The inner parts of the city were developed at moderately high densities in the past, but tastes in the housing market have now changed. As the older parts wear out, private development cannot absorb the sites at current acquisition costs. Apartment developers can afford to pay almost as much for the land as present property is worth, but the total demand for apartments is too small to permit rebuilding more than a few acres a year, even if subsidies are available to close the gap between site costs and re-use values. The major housing demand is for new single-family homes, but developers cannot pay anything close to current land prices in the old residential areas for single-family sites.

Rebuilding with single-family houses would require large subsidies. With acquisition prices of $3 to $5 per square foot, clearing an acre will cost between $130,000 and $270,000 for land purchases alone, in addition to relocation and demolition expenses and environmental improvements. Resale value for single-family development would probabaly not exceed $10,000 per acre. Clearance for single-family re-use is not financially impossible: net project costs per acre for converting a Hartford neighborhood to single-family use would be far lower than typical net project costs per acre for the many New York City projects located near the business area of Manhattan. But where the demand for building sites is limited, as in Hartford, rebuilding programs must be weighed against inevitable land subsidies, as well as against other social and economic considerations.

General Policy Implications

This review of renewal experience in New York, Los Angeles, and Hartford raises a number of major issues involved in formulating public policies. First are the questions of when to replace existing housing and how much to replace. Decisions of this kind should depend upon the extent to which old housing is a social or economic asset. Economic value is likely to enter into rebuilding decisions through the influence of acquisition cost, but social value is not so readily apparent. Thus in Los Angeles, although site acquisition costs are reasonable for new apartment development, much of the old housing represents a scarce resource for minority groups. Elsewhere, the vacancy rate may be a good indicator of the need for retaining low-cost housing.

To govern the timing of new development, I propose that vacancy rates be determined on a local basis and that rebuilding should not begin in a neighborhood until the occupancy of the dwelling units falls off sufficiently to create a surplus. Each increment of new construction would depend upon the prior abandonment of other housing in the area.

Is a policy of gradual rebuilding feasible? Cities will find themselves confronting very different sets of policy choices, depending upon whether or not they meet the preconditions for rebuilding. If the prerequisites are weak or missing, public strategy can proceed along the lines that have been suggested to increase demand for housing sites in the old areas or to reduce their acquisition cost. A major vehicle for increasing demand is the physical planning program of the metropolitan region, particularly plans for the downtown core, the transportation system, and competitive vacant sites. Reducing acquisition costs implies devaluing the old housing through building alternative and superior low-cost housing, strictly enforcing building and occupancy codes, or instituting tax policies designed to reduce the profitability of deteriorated housing. Alternately, land costs may be reduced through subsidies or rebuilding may be attempted for nonresidential purposes.

If the economic background is favorable for rebuilding — as it is in New York and Los Angeles — the task of public policy is quite different. In this case, strategies must be devised to initiate and stage the actual rebuilding of declining areas, and public action must be shaped to attract new development into the old areas. Much experimentation will be necessary, but the techniques now in use for the upper West Side area in New York are probably a reasonable model. Components of this model are the improvement of the physical setting through public works and housing rehabilitation, the staging of limited clearance, and the implementation of a battery of housing programs to fit different situations. Housing alternatives should encompass different methods of financing, different degrees of public assistance, and public as well as private construction — all of which are represented in New York programs.

A successful program also involves coordinating rebuilding objectives with other spheres of public action, particularly with zoning and other regulation of private building outside renewal areas. Coordination is also necessary between rebuilding activities and the general apparatus of physical planning, including public works programming, highway construction, and over-all regional development. Even when the preconditions for rebuilding are present, regional growth must be guided so that the older areas become logical locations for new development.

The distinction between an economic situation favorable for rebuilding and one that is unfavorable is not sufficiently appreciated in recent discussions of urban renewal. Where the old areas of a city are stagnant, observers generally assume that economic costs and benefits are out of line for new development or that the demand for housing sites is very limited. Hence the frequent view that the root of the "gray areas" problem lies in acquisition costs that are too high for the level of demand. Clearly, this is not always the case. Even when costs and returns are in line, however, the old residential areas may remain inactive. Difficulties of site assembly, problems with the scale of operations, the effects of the surrounding environment, insufficient governmental commitments to improve old areas, and lack of entrepreneurial imagination may block rebuilding even when the economic situation is favorable.

For many cities with characteristics similar to either New York or Los Angeles, the problems of rebuilding declining areas may result much more from failure to capitalize upon favorable economic situations than from disparities in the economics of new development. Strategies for rebuilding these cities will have to focus on specific techniques for attracting new development into the old neighborhoods.

How difficult this job will be is far from clear. Some neighborhoods, such as the Sawtelle area of West Los Angeles, are located so favorably that a policing of minimum code standards in the old housing, together with the availability of FHA financing, is sufficient to attract large numbers of apartment builders. Most areas that are ripe for rebuilding, however, will show signs of long neglect and deterioration, both public and private. To attract new housing, considerable public investment in streets, landscaping, parks, schools, and other community facilities would be required — as in the West Side renewal area of New York.

Further improvements in the setting for new housing will be tied closely to the replacement of old housing. Public action will probably include the selective clearance of deteriorated buildings and either incentives or aid for the rehabilitation of usable old housing. Several reinforcing effects are likely to operate in such areas: environmental improvements provide an inducement to conserve and renovate the old structures, and as these structures acquire a new lease on life, the rebuilding process is held to a gradual pace.

Rising site acquisition costs may be part of this pattern, but they seem unlikely to pose a serious danger for a policy of gradual rebuilding. High prices for sound structures that are well utilized are of little consequence since such housing would not be scheduled for clearance. Prices for houses with high vacancy rates are likely to reflect re-use value of the land rather than the current earning power of the buildings, but the rebuilding program itself will establish re-use values. Housing that is deteriorated but still fully occupied — and therefore has high current earnings — may pose a problem, but not an insoluble one. Rebuilding should in any case be postponed until an expanded supply of low-cost housing creates local vacancies in deteriorated housing. In addition, code enforcement and tax policies could be employed to limit the earning power of substandard housing, or the city could acquire such property before undertaking environmental improvements in the area. The major threat to land prices in areas slated for gradual rebuilding will be a tendency of some property owners to hold out for speculative land values; but this inflationary force could also be checked by early acquisition, strict code enforcement for buildings on the property, and assessment increases to keep pace with rising values.

Social Obstacles to Rebuilding

The economics of rebuilding are probably more amenable to the influence of public programs than are the deeper social problems that underlie the reluctance of housing developers to build in old neighborhoods. The differences between people who can afford to live in new housing and those who live in the old buildings in declining neighborhoods are more than differences in income. They are often differences of social class, personal values, and ways of life. Various social welfare programs operating in the old neighborhoods — social casework, vocational training, adult education, youth guidance — may tend to level these distinctions in the long run, or at least to curb some of their outward signs. But for many years, they will play an important role in determining the chances of rebuilding old areas slowly, with new and old residents living near each other in the process.

If the driving force in the market for new housing today is a desire for social, economic, and racial segregation — as some critics of the suburban movement maintain — prospects are dim indeed for a gradual rebuilding of old neighborhoods, or for any socially oriented renewal policy. If the poor must always be kept out of sight, there are few alternatives to either abandoning the old neighborhoods to a long period of neglect or rebuilding them by clearance large enough to push out any unwanted neighbors.

But in fact very little is known of the extent or influence of social prejudice in the market for new housing. There are many examples of neighborhoods with mixed social composition, and these should be studied before hasty conclusions are put forth about the impact of social and racial prejudice upon housing choices.[29] New Yorkers, for example, have long been accustomed to the juxtaposition of luxury apartment houses with run-down brownstones in neighborhoods with locational advantages. Interracial areas are becoming more common as Negroes break out of their old ghettoes. Even when prejudices are strong, the complex operations of the housing market may nevertheless produce mixed social patterns. Not all groups who can afford new housing share the same social values: families without children may well regard many questions of neighborhood composition with indifference. And of those who hold strong social prejudices, not all have the resources to satisfy them, and not all will wish to sacrifice other values in order to do so.

These are the issues that will really determine the future of declining neighborhoods. This study has disagreed with recent interpretations that see the rebuilding problem as a product of powerful economic forces pushing land prices out of line with land values for renewal. As a minimum, this economic argument must be qualified carefully. In many cases, it is clearly wrong. Analyses of land costs and values in this study suggest that the fundamental problems are not economic but environmental and social. The ability of public programs to meet social objectives in the rebuilding of cities will depend to a large extent on learning more about these social and environmental constraints. Hopefully, future research in this area of public policy will move away from economic arguments that have clouded the basic issues and will approach more directly questions of how Americans want to live in cities, how they select neighborhood locations, and how determined they are to live apart from people who are different.

POPULATION AND HOUSING STATISTICS FOR NEW YORK, LOS ANGELES, AND HARTFORD REGIONS

Table A.1. New York Metropolitan Region

1. Population Change, 1950–1960

	Population 1950	Population 1960	Per Cent Change 1950–1960
New York–Northeastern New Jersey Standard Consolidated Area	12,911,994	14,759,429	+14.3
Central Cities: New York, Newark, Jersey City	8,629,750	8,463,305	−1.9
Remainder of Standard Consolidated Area	4,282,244	6,296,124	+47.0

Sources: See Table A.1.2

2. Racial Components of Change in Central-City Areas of Population Loss, 1950–1960

	Change in White Population, 1950–1960		Change in Nonwhite Population, 1950–1960	
	Number	Per cent	Number	Per cent
Manhattan	−284,777	−18.3	+22,957	+5.7
Bronx	−26,462	−1.8	+68,916	+69.2
Brooklyn	−110,856	−4.0	+168,403	+79.0
Newark	−97,260	−26.8	+63,704	+84.2
Jersey City	−39,224	−16.4	+16,308	+77.8
Total	−558,579	−9.2	+340,288	+41.9

Sources: Calculated from *U.S. Census of Population: 1950*, Vol. 2, *Characteristics of the Population*, Part 32, *New York*, Tables 33, 41; and Part 30, *New Jersey*, Table 33; *U.S. Census of Population: 1960*, General Population Characteristics, *New York*, Final Report PC(1)–34B, Tables 20, 27; and *New Jersey*, Final Report PC(1)–32B, Table 20.

3. Distribution of Negro Population, 1950 and 1960

	Total Population 1950	1960	Negro Population 1950	1960	Per Cent of Total Regional Negro Population 1950	1960
New York–Northeastern New Jersey Standard Consolidated Area	12,911,994	14,759,429	1,013,424	1,557,069	100.0	100.0
Manhattan	1,960,101	1,698,281	384,482	397,101	37.9	25.5
New York City outside Manhattan	5,931,856	6,083,703	363,126	690,830	35.8	44.4
Newark	438,776	405,220	74,965	138,035	7.4	8.9
Jersey City	299,017	276,101	20,758	36,692	2.0	2.4
Total Central Cities: New York, Newark, Jersey City	8,629,750	8,463,305	843,331	1,262,658	83.2	81.1

Sources: U.S. Census of Population: 1950, Vol. 2, Characteristics of the Population, Part 32, New York, Tables 33, 34, 42, and Part 30, New Jersey, Tables 33, 34; U.S. Census of Population: 1960, General Population Characteristics, New York, Final Report PC(1)–34B, Tables 21, 28; and New Jersey, Final Report PC(1)–32B, Table 21.

4. Distribution of Puerto Rican Students in Public Schools, by Boroughs of New York City, 1956 and 1960

	Number of Students 1956	1960	Per Cent of Total 1956	1960
Manhattan	48,952	56,154	43.4	36.9
Bronx	30,417	43,943	27.0	28.9
Brooklyn	30,078	47,457	26.7	31.2
Queens	2,846	3,932	2.5	2.6
Richmond	448	525	0.4	0.3

Sources: J. Cayce Morrison, The Puerto Rican Study: 1953–1957 (New York: City of New York Board of Education, 1958), p. 171; City of New York Board of Education, Bureau of Educational Program Research and Statistics, "Special Census of School Population, October 31, 1960," (Publication No. 167, March 1961), Table 2. Puerto Rican students defined as born in Puerto Rico, or born on mainland with one or both parents born in Puerto Rico. Special schools excluded from above tabulation.

5. Age Characteristics and Race, 1950 and 1960

	1950 Per Cent of Population Under 18 White	Non-white	1960 Per Cent of Population Under 18 White	Non-white	1950 Per Cent of Population 65 and over White	Non-white	1960 Per Cent of Population 65 and over White	Non-white
New York–Northeastern New Jersey Standard Consolidated Area	25.1	27.5	30.4	34.9	8.0	3.8	10.1	4.7
Manhattan	18.4	23.6	20.6	29.1	10.0	4.0	14.2	6.4
Bronx	25.0	31.0	27.3	36.7	7.6	3.0	11.6	4.0
Brooklyn	25.7	31.1	28.5	38.1	7.8	3.1	10.9	3.5
Newark	25.0	30.2	27.6	39.1	7.9	3.3	11.8	3.7
Jersey City	25.9	33.4	29.2	41.7	7.6	3.7	10.9	3.8

Sources: Calculated from U.S. Census of Population: 1950, Vol. 2, Characteristics of the Population, Part 32, New York, Tables 33, 41; and Part 30, New Jersey, Table 33; U.S. Census of Population: 1960, General Population Characteristics, New York, Final Report PC(1)–34B, Tables 20, 27; and New Jersey, Final Report PC(1)–32B, Table 20.

6. Occupancy Characteristics and Race in Central Cities, 1960

| | White Population | | Nonwhite Population | |
	Occupied housing units	Population per housing unit	Occupied housing units	Population per housing unit
New York City	2,301,891	2.88	352,554	3.24
Newark	88,612	3.00	39,160	3.56
Jersey City	78,339	3.05	10,213	3.65

Sources: Calculated from *U.S. Census of Housing: 1960, Advance Reports, Housing Characteristics: States,* HC(A1)–33, *New York,* Table 1, and HC(A1)–31, *New Jersey,* Table 1; *U.S. Census of Population: 1960, General Population Characteristics, New York,* Final Report PC(1)–34B, Table 20, and *New Jersey,* Final Report PC(1)–32B, Table 20.

7. Population and Dwelling Units in New York City Areas of Population Loss, 1950–1960

| | Noninstitutional Population | | Total Dwelling Units | | Non-institutional Population per Dwelling Unit | |
	1950	1960	1950	1960	1950	1960
Manhattan	1,945,466	1,694,644	635,944	645,393	3.06	2.63
Bronx	1,442,907	1,420,989	432,259	474,030	3.34	3.00
Brooklyn	2,728,814	2,625,068	814,134	878,815	3.35	2.99

Sources: U.S. Census of Population: 1950, Vol. 2, *Characteristics of the Population,* Part 32, *New York,* Table 34. *U.S. Census of Population: 1960, General Population Characteristics, New York,* Final Report PC(1)–34B, Table 28; *U.S. Census of Housing: 1950,* Vol 1, *General Characteristics,* Part 4: *Michigan–New York, New York,* Table 1; J. Anthony Panuch, *Building a Better New York: Final Report to Mayor Robert F. Wagner* (March 1, 1960), "Changes in the Housing Supply of New York City by Borough," p. 36 (compiled by New York City Department of City Planning from Department of Buildings data).

8. Housing Vacancies in Central Cities and Metropolitan Area, 1960

	Total Nonseasonal Housing Units	Per Cent Vacant
Total of New York, Jersey City, Newark, Paterson-Clifton-Passaic Standard Metropolitan Statistical Areas	4,671,740	3.3
New York City	2,735,272	3.0
Newark	134,727	5.2
Jersey City	91,802	3.5
Remainder of 4 Combined Standard Metropolitan Statistical Areas	1,709,939	3.7

Sources: Calculated from *U.S. Census of Housing: 1960,* Advance Reports, *Housing Characteristics: States,* HC(A1)–31, *New Jersey,* Table 1, and HC(A1)–33, *New York,* Table 1. The New York–Northeastern New Jersey Standard Consolidated Area consists of the Standard Metropolitan Statistical Areas of New York, Jersey City, Newark, and Paterson-Clifton-Passaic, plus Middlesex County, New Jersey and Somerset County, New Jersey. Middlesex and Somerset Counties are omitted from this table.

9. Central-City Housing Utilization, 1950 and 1960

| | Per Cent of (Nonseasonal) Units Vacant and Available in Sound Condition | | Number and Per Cent of (Nonseasonal) Units with 1.01 or More Occupants per Room | | | |
| | 1950 | 1960 | 1950 | | 1960 | |
			Number	Per cent	Number	Per cent
Manhattan	0.8	2.5	99,846	16.5	92,386	13.3
Bronx	1.0	1.5	90,811	21.6	70,926	15.3
Brooklyn	1.0	1.7	138,369	17.6	110,053	12.9
Newark	0.7	4.1	18,216	15.1	16,600	13.0
Jersey City	0.5	2.5	12,418	14.8	10,077	11.4

Sources: Calculated from *U.S. Census of Housing: 1950,* Vol. 1, *General Characteristics,* Part 1, *U.S. Summary,* Tables 27, 29, and Part 4, *Michigan–New York,* New York Tables 17, 19; *U.S. Census of Housing: 1960,* Advance Reports, *Housing Characteristics: States,* HC(A1)–31, *New Jersey,* Table 1; *U.S. Census of Housing: 1960,* Vol. 3, *City Blocks,* Series HC(3), Numbers 96, 249, 252, Table 1; New York Department of City Planning *Newsletter,* December 1961, p. 2. Information for Manhattan, Brooklyn, and the Bronx for 1960 covers all housing units, including seasonal. Vacant units are those classified as year-round, nondilapidated, available for rent or sale.

10. New Dwelling Units Authorized by Building Permits in Central-City Declining Areas, 1951–1960

| | Number of Dwelling Units | |
	Private Housing	Public Housing
Manhattan	52,219	23,009
Bronx	33,419	16,913
Brooklyn	50,081	19,821
Newark	4,513	7,754
Jersey City	2,091	1,396
Total	142,323	68,893

Sources: U.S. Department of Labor, Bureau of Labor Statistics, "New Dwelling Units Authorized by Local Building Permits," Annual Summaries, 1951–1957; U.S. Bureau of the Census, *Construction Reports: Building Permits,* C40–8, "New Dwelling Units Authorized by Local Building Permits," Annual Summaries, 1958–1960.

Table A.2.   Los Angeles Metropolitan Region

1. Population Change, 1950–1960

	Population 1950	Population 1960	Per Cent Change 1950–1960
Los Angeles–Long Beach Standard Metropolitan Statistical Area	4,367,911	6,742,696	+54.4
City of Los Angeles	1,970,358	2,479,015	+25.8
Remainder of Standard Metropolitan Statistical Area	2,397,553	4,263,681	+77.8

Sources: See Table A.2.2.

2.   Racial Components of Change in Central-City Population, 1950–1960

	Change in White Population 1950–1960		Change in Nonwhite Population 1950–1960	
	Number	Per cent	Number	Per cent
City of Los Angeles	+303,035	+17.2	+205,622	+97.2

Sources: Calculated from *U.S. Census of Population: 1950,* Vol. 2, *Characteristics of the Population,* Part 5, *California,* Table 33; *U.S. Census of Population: 1960, General Population Characteristics, California,* Final Report PC(1)–6B, Table 20.

3.   Distribution of Negro Population, 1950 and 1960

	Total Population		Negro Population		Per Cent of Total Regional Negro Population	
	1950	1960	1950	1960	1950	1960
Los Angeles–Long Beach Standard Metropolitan Statistical Area	4,367,911	6,742,696	218,770	464,717	100.0	100.0
City of Los Angeles	1,970,358	2,479,015	171,209	334,916	78.3	72.1

Sources: U.S. Census of Population: 1950, Vol. 2, *Characteristics of the Population,* Part 5, *California,* Table 34; *U.S. Census of Population: 1960, General Population Characteristics, California,* Final Report PC(1)–6B, Table 21.

4.   Distribution of Japanese Population, 1950 and 1960

	Total Population		Japanese Population		Per Cent of Total Regional Japanese Population	
	1950	1960	1950	1960	1950	1960
Los Angeles–Long Beach Standard Metropolitan Statistical Area	4,367,911	6,742,696	37,947	81,204	100.0	100.0
City of Los Angeles	1,970,358	2,479,015	25,502	51,468	67.2	63.4

Sources: U.S. Census of Population: 1950, Vol. 2, *Characteristics of the Population,* Part 5, *California,* Table 47; *U.S. Census of Population: 1960, General Population Characteristics, California,* Final Report PC(1)–6B, Table 21.

5.   Age Characteristics and Race, 1950 and 1960

	1950 Per Cent of Population Under 18		1960 Per Cent of Population Under 18		1950 Per Cent of Population 65 and over		1960 Per Cent of Population 65 and over	
	White	Non-white	White	Non-white	White	Non-white	White	Non-white
Los Angeles–Long Beach Standard Metropolitan Statistical Area	26.1	27.6	33.4	37.9	9.4	4.7	9.3	4.6
City of Los Angeles	23.1	26.3	29.5	35.8	10.2	4.6	11.3	4.9

Sources: Calculated from *U.S. Census of Population: 1950,* Vol. 2, *Characteristics of the Population,* Part 5, *California,* Table 33; *U.S. Census of Population: 1960, General Population Characteristics, California,* Final Report PC(1)–6B, Table 20.

6. Occupancy Characteristics and Race in Central City, 1960

	White Population		Nonwhite Population	
	Occupied housing units	Population per housing unit	Occupied housing units	Population per housing unit
City of Los Angeles	746,065	2.76	129,945	3.21

Sources: Calculated from *U.S. Census of Housing: 1960, Advance Reports, Housing Characteristics: States,* HC(A1)–5, *California,* Table 1; *U.S. Census of Population: 1960 General Population Characteristics, California,* Final Report PC(1)–6B, Table 20.

7. Population and Dwelling Units in Areas of Population Loss, 1950–1960

	Population		Total Dwelling Units		Population per Dwelling Unit	
	1950	1960	1950	1960	1950	1960
Central Area	129,578	92,656	56,896	45,760	2.28	2.02
East Area	238,653	213,341	66,641	62,944	3.58	3.39
North East Area	162,654	159,044	57,285	58,070	2.84	2.74
Total	530,885	465,041	180,822	166,774	2.93	2.79

Sources: Los Angeles County Regional Planning Commission, based on data from U.S. Censuses of 1950 and 1960. 1950 dwelling units from *U.S. Census of Housing: 1950;* 1960 dwelling units derived from 1950 data, adding new construction and conversions, subtracting demolitions and mergers through April 1960. Central statistical area includes the Downtown, University, and Westlake sections of the City of Los Angeles. East statistical area includes the Boyle Heights, Central, and Wholesale Industry sections of the City of Los Angeles, and the unincorporated areas of Belvedere, City Terrace, and East Los Angeles in Los Angeles County. North East statistical area includes the El Sereno, Elysian Park, Highland Park, Lincoln Heights and Silver Lake (southern part) sections of the City of Los Angeles.

8. Housing Vacancies in Central City and Metropolitan Area, 1960

	Total Nonseasonal Housing Units	Per Cent Vacant
Los Angeles–Long Beach Standard Metropolitan Statistical Area	2,358,405	6.1
City of Los Angeles	933,354	6.1
Remainder of SMSA	1,425,051	6.1

Source: Calculated from *U.S. Census of Housing: 1960, Advance Reports, Housing Characteristics: States,* HC(A1)–5, *California,* Table 1.

9. Central City Housing Utilization, 1950 and 1960

| | Per Cent of Nonseasonal Units Vacant and Available in Sound Condition | | Number and Per Cent of Nonseasonal Units With 1.01 or More Occupants per Room | | | |
| | 1950 | 1960 | 1950 | | 1960 | |
			Number	Per cent	Number	Per cent
City of Los Angeles	2.7	4.9	68,822	10.0	72,007	8.2

Sources: Calculated from *U.S. Census of Housing: 1950,* Vol. 1, *General Characteristics,* Part 1, *U.S. Summary,* Tables 27, 29; *U.S. Census of Housing: 1960,* Advance Reports, *Housing Characteristics: States,* HC(A1)–5, *California,* Table 1; *U.S. Census of Housing: 1960,* Vol. 3, *City Blocks,* Series HC(3), Number 178, Table 1. Vacant units are those classified as year-round, nondilapidated, available for rent or sale.

Table A.3. Hartford Metropolitan Region

1. Population Change, 1950–1960

	Population 1950	Population 1960	Per Cent Change 1950–1960
Hartford Standard Metropolitan Statistical Area	406,534	525,207	+29.2
City of Hartford	177,397	162,178	−8.6
Remainder of Standard Metropolitan Statistical Area	229,137	363,029	+58.4

Sources: See Table A.3.2.

2. Racial Components of Change in Central City Population, 1950–1960

| | Change in White Population, 1950–1960 | | Change in Nonwhite Population, 1950–1960 | |
	Number	Per cent	Number	Per cent
City of Hartford	−27,580	−16.8	+12,361	+96.6

Sources: Calculated from *U.S. Census of Population: 1950,* Vol. 2, *Characteristics of the Population,* Part 7, *Connecticut,* Table 33, and *U.S. Census of Population: 1960, General Population Characteristics, Connecticut,* Final Report PC(1)–8B, Table 20.

164

3. Distribution of Negro Population, 1950 and 1960

	Total Population 1950	Total Population 1960	Negro Population 1950	Negro Population 1960	Per Cent of Total Regional Negro Population 1950	1960
Hartford Standard Metropolitan Statistical Area	406,534	525,207	14,233	28,689	100.0	100.0
City of Hartford	177,397	162,178	12,654	24,855	88.9	86.6

Sources: U.S. Census of Population: 1950, Vol. 2, Characteristics of the Population, Part 7, Connecticut, Table 34; U.S. Census of Population: 1960, General Population Characteristics, Connecticut, Final Report PC(1)–8B, Tables 20, 21. Negro population of Standard Metropolitan Statistical Area unavailable for 1950; Negro population shown is that of 1950 Standard Metropolitan Area, which covers all significant centers of Negro population in the region.

4. Age Characteristics and Race, 1950 and 1960

	1950 Per Cent of Population Under 18 White	Non-white	1960 Per Cent of Population Under 18 White	Non-white	1950 Per Cent of Population 65 and over White	Non-white	1960 Per Cent of Population 65 and over White	Non-white
Hartford Standard Metropolitan Statistical Area	26.5	32.2	34.9	40.3	8.5	4.4	9.8	3.9
City of Hartford	23.9	32.6	26.6	42.3	8.8	4.2	12.3	3.7

Sources: Calculated from U.S. Census of Population: 1950, Vol. 2, Characteristics of the Population, Part 7, Connecticut, Table 33; U.S. Census of Population: 1960, General Population Characteristics, Connecticut, Final Report PC(1)–8B, Table 20. 1950 information is for Hartford Standard Metropolitan Area; 1960 information for Hartford Standard Metropolitan Statistical Area, which covers 1950 Standard Metropolitan Area plus towns of Canton, Cromwell, East Windsor, Enfield, Suffield, Vernon, and Windsor Locks.

5. Occupancy Characteristics and Race in Central City, 1960

	White Population Occupied housing units	White Population Population per housing unit	Nonwhite Population Occupied housing units	Nonwhite Population Population per housing unit
City of Hartford	47,783	2.87	6,852	3.67

Sources: Calculated from U.S. Census of Housing: 1960, Advance Reports, Housing Characteristics: States, HC(A1)–7, Connecticut, Table 1; U.S. Census of Population: 1960, General Population Characteristics, Connecticut, Final Report PC (1)–8B, Table 20.

6. Housing Vacancies in Central City and Metropolitan Area, 1960

	Total Nonseasonal Housing Units	Per Cent Vacant
Hartford Standard Metropolitan Statistical Area	163,454	3.9
City of Hartford	57,545	5.1
Remainder of SMSA	105,909	3.3

Source: Calculated from *U.S. Census of Housing: 1960, Advance Reports, Housing Characteristics: States*, HC(A1)–7, *Connecticut*, Table 1.

7. Central-City Housing Utilization, 1950 and 1960

	Per Cent of Nonseasonal Units Vacant and Available in Sound Condition		Number and Per Cent of Nonseasonal Units with 1.01 or More Occupants per Room			
	1950	1960	1950		1960	
			Number	Per cent	Number	Per cent
City of Hartford	1.4	4.1	6,852	13.4	5,053	9.2

Sources: Calculated from *U.S. Census of Housing: 1950*, Vol. 1, *General Characteristics*, Part 1, *U.S. Summary*, Tables 27, 29; *U.S. Census of Housing: 1960*, Advance Reports, *Housing Characteristics: States*, HC(A1)–7, *Connecticut*, Table 1; *U.S. Census of Housing: 1960*, Vol. 3, *City Blocks*, Series HC(3), Number 96, Table 1. Vacant units are those classified as year-round, nondilapidated, available for rent or sale.

RATES OF LAND UTILIZATION FOR NEW APARTMENT HOUSING IN NEW YORK, LOS ANGELES, AND HARTFORD

NEW YORK

This study assumes that moderate-priced apartment housing currently built in the Bronx, Brooklyn, and Queens constitutes the potential supply of new private construction that might be attracted into the central declining areas. The 1951–1960 construction rates in these boroughs provide a basis for estimating land consumption rates. In Queens, however, the 1951–1955 rate was unusually high because considerable vacant land was still available at that time. I have therefore projected the 1956–1960 rate for Queens to a 10-year period in order to use data reflecting more typical construction volumes in built-up areas.

New dwelling units completed in private multifamily structures, 1951–1960, number:

Bronx	16,650
Brooklyn	32,534
Queens	
(1956–1960 rate)	59,340
Total	108,524 units[1]

At a typical new-development density of 150 dwelling units per net acre, the 1951–1960 private construction volume in these boroughs would cover 723.5 acres in 10 years, or 72 acres per year. If developments in the declining areas follow the somewhat lower densities of urban renewal projects, they will be built at about 100 units per acre. At this density, the 1951–1960 construction volume would use 1,085.3 acres in 10 years, or 109 acres per year.

167

Public housing built anywhere in the City can conceivably be channeled into the declining areas as part of a rebuilding program. I shall take account of public housing construction in Manhattan, the Bronx, Brooklyn, and Queens from 1951 to 1960, on the assumption that a similar volume can be located in declining sections of these boroughs in future 10-year periods. The City Housing Authority has announced plans for an accelerated rate of construction, but I shall assume that the surplus over the 1951–1960 rate will be located in other parts of the City.

Public housing completions from 1951–1960 were 21,623 units in Manhattan and 48,683 units in the Bronx, Brooklyn, and Queens.[2] Typical densities for public housing are about 100 units per acre in Manhattan and 75 units per acre in the other boroughs. At these densities, the 10-year volume for Manhattan would utilize 216 acres, and the volume in the other boroughs would use a total of 649 acres. In all, public housing would thus require 865 acres, or 87 acres per year.

Private housing at typical densities, plus public housing, would thus utilize 159 acres per year. Private housing at urban renewal densities plus public housing would use 196 acres per year.

If New York were to clear all the deteriorated housing in its declining areas, how much land would be available for rebuilding? Deteriorated housing, as I define it, is not suitable for rehabilitation. In terms of 1960 census definitions, I have counted units classified as dilapidated and units classified as deteriorating but lacking plumbing facilities. I thus assume that deteriorating units with all plumbing facilities can be rehabilitated. On this basis, Manhattan had 80,358 deteriorated units in 1960, while the Bronx, Brooklyn, and Queens had 66,901.

I estimate average densities of deteriorated housing as 200 units per acre in Manhattan and 90 per acre in the other boroughs.[3] At these densities, deteriorated housing would occupy 402 acres in Manhattan and 743 acres in the other boroughs, for a total of 1,145 acres.

Private housing at current densities, plus public housing, would utilize this land at a rate of 159 acres per year. The time required for absorbing 1,145 acres would thus be 7.2 years.

Private housing at urban renewal densities, plus public housing,

168

would consume land at a rate of 196 acres per year. In this case, 5.5 years would be required to absorb the 1,145 acres.

It is also necessary to take into account the rate at which additional existing housing will become deteriorated. Changes in enumeration from the 1950 census to the 1960 census create some complications in estimating the rate of deterioration for the 1950's. In 1950, housing condition was classified as either nondilapidated or dilapidated. In 1960, a three-way classification was used: sound, deteriorating, or dilapidated. Although the definition of dilapidated condition did not change, enumerators seem to have classified many doubtful cases as deteriorating in 1960. Consequently, the 1960 deteriorating category includes some housing that was classified as either dilapidated or nondilapidated in 1950.

To approximate constant definitions of condition, I shall equate dilapidated housing of 1950 with dilapidated housing of 1960 *plus* that portion of 1960 deteriorating housing that is lacking one or more plumbing facilities. On this basis, the number of units suitable for clearance grew by 25,521 in Manhattan from 1950 to 1960 and by 12,740 in the Bronx, Brooklyn, and Queens. At densities of 200 per acre in Manhattan and 90 per acre in the other boroughs, the amount of land occupied by deteriorated housing grew by 269.2 acres in 10 years, or 27 acres per year.

The statistical comparison used here for New York — as well as for Los Angeles and Hartford — is only a rough approximation, however, and overstates the increase in substandard housing. A major problem of comparability has been mentioned in Chapter 2: as a result of changes in the kinds of housing covered by the census, many substandard single-room dwellings were counted in 1960 but not in 1950. An unofficial study conducted by the staff of one New York public agency found that if adjustments are made for these single-room dwellings, the amount of substandard housing in the city actually *decreased* from 1950 to 1960. It is nevertheless instructive to consider the results of my own crude comparison, with its exaggeration of the current increase in deterioration.

If newly deteriorated housing is replaced by private development at current densities, plus public housing, the over-all land utilization rate of 159 acres per year must be reduced by 27 acres per year to take account of continuing deterioration. The residual rate of 132 acres per year would absorb the 1,145 acres of land occupied by deteriorated housing in 1960 in 8.5 years.

The higher rate of land utilization resulting from private housing developed at urban renewal densities, plus public housing, would have to be reduced from 196 acres per year to 169. At this rate, the 1,145 acres of clearance land in 1960 would be absorbed in 6.2 years.

An alternate objective for New York might be to replace all old-law tenements. These structures were all built prior to 1901, and have many obsolete physical features that make rehabilitation impractical. As of 1958, Manhattan and the other three boroughs with which this study is concerned had 387,954 old-law tenements.[4] I estimate the average density of these structures as 250 units per net acre. At this density, old-law tenements occupied 1,552 acres in 1958.

At the low rate of rebuilding — 159 acres per year — the time required to absorb these 1,552 acres would be 9.8 years. At the high rate — 196 acres per year — 7.9 years would be required.

The following table summarizes the time necessary to rebuild cleared sites in New York, if *all* new private apartment housing is diverted from the outer boroughs into clearance areas, and if public housing construction at 1951–1960 rates is also located in these areas:

	Time to Rebuild All Deteriorated Housing, Including Future Deterioration	Time to Rebuild All Old-law Tenements
Low Rate of Land Utilization: (Private plus public housing, private at current densities)	8.5 years	9.8 years
High Rate of Land Utilization: (Private plus public housing, private at urban renewal densities)	6.2 years	7.9 years

LOS ANGELES

This study assumes that new private housing currently built in the older areas within 10 miles of downtown Los Angeles constitutes the development that could conceivably be attracted into

170

the declining areas, which also lie within this 10-mile band. From 1950 to 1960, the net increase within this zone was 98,042 multi-family dwelling units.[5] Total new construction was probably greater, since some units were lost to demolition for highways, but this figure will be used as a basis for calculation.

At the typical construction density of 50 units per acre for this part of the City, new building would absorb 1,961 acres in 10 years, or 196 acres per year.

According to the 1960 Housing Census, the City of Los Angeles had 24,800 housing units that were either dilapidated or deteriorating and lacking plumbing facilities. The extent of deterioration decreased slightly from 1950 to 1960 in terms of the basis for comparison already explained for New York. For the near future, at least, attention may be limited to the housing that is already deteriorated. At typical densities of 8 to 10 units per acre for old housing, the 24,800 deteriorated units occupied approximately 2,755 acres in 1960.

With new private housing utilizing 196 acres per year, and with no public housing construction program under way, the total time required for rebuilding 2,755 acres of cleared land would be 14.0 years.

HARTFORD

On the basis of a housing market study of Hartford[6] and my own projections, I estimate the potential demand for multifamily housing within the central Hartford area as 2,500 units in 10 years. At the typical current density of 50 units per acre in central locations, this volume of new development would utilize 50 acres in 10 years, or 5 acres per year. If the density is reduced to 35 units per acre, the land consumption rate will be 71.4 acres in 10 years, or 7.1 acres per year.

According to the 1960 Housing Census, the City of Hartford had 3,235 housing units that were either dilapidated or deteriorating and lacking plumbing facilities. I estimate the average density of this old housing as 15 to 20 units per acre. Thus the deteriorated units occupy about 185 acres.

At the low rate of land consumption (5 acres per year), 36

ycars would be required to rebuild these 185 acres; at the higher rate of 7.1 acres per year, 26.1 years would be required.

From 1950 to 1960, the amount of deteriorated housing in Hartford increased by 1,126 units. At a density of 15 to 20 units per acre, this increase would represent an increment of 66 acres in 10 years, or 6.6 acres per year.

If this rate of deterioration continues, the low land utilization rate of 5 acres per year would not even permit rebuilding to keep pace with the spread of deterioration. At the high rate of 7.1 acres per year, all but one-half acre per year would have to be devoted to coping with the increase in deterioration.

URBAN STRUCTURE AND THE LOCATION OF NEW HOUSING: A REVIEW OF THEORETICAL WORKS

Studies of urban economics and city form have advanced many theoretical statements seeking to explain the location of urban activities. Theoretical approaches have long recognized accessibility as a factor influencing both the location of new housing and the land rent of different sites for residential use. In this section, I shall examine several theories based primarily on accessibility, as well as two comprehensive models of the urban land market that relate accessibility to other factors shaping the residential pattern. The section will also review studies that have identified changing urban patterns and dynamic characteristics of urban structure, with particular emphasis on the shifting residential patterns that have created areas of residential decline in the centers of growing regions. The purpose of this survey is to identify the major structural features underpinning the pattern of housing locations and to observe their role in forming the areas of decline.

Accessibility and the Location of New Housing

The growth patterns of nineteenth-century cities show clearly the effects of accessibility on housing locations. Successive changes in transportation systems, from the horsecar to the electric transit line, extended the area within commuting range of the center by a series of finite jumps. Homer Hoyt analyzed the significance of these transportation changes for the development of Chicago:

> The time and expense required to go from the center of the city outward or upward, and not physical extension, determines the effective supply of urban land.

. . . Accessible building space in Chicago in 1833 was the ground and the layer of air above the ground to a height of about 50 feet, within walking distance over dirt roads to the main channel of the Chicago River. Outward extension began with plank roads and street railway lines. Omnibuses and horse cars which traveled at a rate of 6 miles an hour instead of a walking pace of 3 miles an hour doubled the radius of settlement. Cable cars in the eighties, with a speed of 12 miles an hour, doubled the radius again along trunk lines. Suburban steam railroads and elevated electric lines, traveling at from 25 to 30 miles an hour, again doubled the radius of settlement along their routes.[1]

Transportation improvements had observable effects on both the configuration of the city and the density of settlement at different distances from the center. As Hoyt noted in a subsequent study of American urban growth, most cities had a compact circular form before 1880, when stagecoaches and horsecar lines were the chief means of internal transportation.[2] Central preferences were strong during this period, and the housing market was confined to a small area surrounding the core. With the coming of cable cars, elevated steam railways, and electric surface transit, axial growth extended out from the previously developed area in bands along the new transit lines. Before 1880, urban growth meant substantial increases in density in the central area, with only limited growth at the periphery. Subsequently, densities rose more slowly near the core (in part because business development replaced residences) and at an accelerated rate farther away, while the limits of settlement pushed out to new locations. Figure C.1 illustrates population densities by 1-mile zones from the center of Chicago for 1860, 1880, and 1900.

Hoyt's analyses focus on the center of the city as the destination most influential in shaping the housing pattern. Economic activity was of course highly centralized in the nineteenth-century city, but even at that time the core was not the sole location of jobs or of retail activity. Hoyt assumes the dominance of downtown as an employment center: "The practical limit to the supply of urban land is set . . . by the amount which is accessible to people working at a certain strategic spot."[3] The center has become increasingly less strategic in most American cities. Hoyt's view of accessibility as a factor shaping the housing market is widely accepted, but the

174

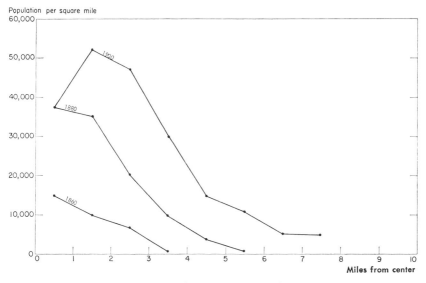

Figure C.1. Population density by distance from center of Chicago, 1860–1900.

Source: Data taken from Homer Hoyt, *One Hundred Years of Land Values in Chicago* (Chicago: University of Chicago Press, 1933), p. 484. Population increase 1860–1880: 394,092; 1880–1900: 1,195,277.

extent to which recent trends have diluted the significance of *access to the center* is largely unknown. Recent analyses of density as a function of distance from the core confirm that the center is still a powerful organizing force in the housing market, but its potency varies significantly in different cities.[4]

Accessibility and Land Value

Theories of land rent also recognize the significance of accessibility to the center. Richard M. Hurd adapted the agricultural theories of Ricardo to urban land, attributing land values to differences in accessibility between sites at the margin of settlement and those more favorably located:

> The dependence of value in land on economic rent is clearly seen in the origin of any city, utility in land arising when the first buildings are erected, but not value in land, as is evidenced by the fact that the first settlers are commonly allowed to build their houses wherever they please and enclose whatever land they need, as occurred in New York and many other cities. As a city grows, more remote and hence

175

inferior locations must be utilized and the difference in desirability between the two grades produces economic rent in locations of the first grade, but not in those of the second. As land of a still more remote and inferior grade comes into use, ground rent is forced still higher in land of the first grade, rises in land of the second grade, but not in the third grade, and so on.[5]

In Hurd's formulation, accessibility affects rents only in so far as different sites offer different degrees of access to the center, with the most remote settled areas constituting the base for his scheme of land values. Thus, to determine the value of a site with some particular degree of accessibility, one must know how it compares in accessibility with other sites in the same urban area. Access advantages rather than access characteristics per se are the basis of land values, according to this hypothesis. While empirical testing is difficult, some confirmation is available in Hoyt's description of the early rise in central land values when Chicago's peripheral growth began in the 1830's.[6]

Later theories of land value incorporate Hurd's insights into the significance of access differences for the land market, while refining the concept of accessibility. In the work of R. M. Haig, land values reflect savings in transportation costs:

> The term accessibility . . . really means ease of contact—contact with relatively little friction. The friction of space may be overcome by means of transportation; but transportation involves costs. Rent appears as the charge which the owner of a relatively accessible site can impose because of the saving in transportation costs which the use of his site makes possible. The activities which can "stand" high rents are those in which large savings in transportation costs may be realized by locating on central sites where accessibility is great. The complementary character of these two things—site rents and transportation costs—is imperfectly recognized. . . .
>
> . . . Site rents and transportation costs are vitally connected through their relationship to the friction of space. Transportation is the means of reducing that friction, at the cost of time and money. Site rentals are charges which can be made for sites where accessibility may be had with comparatively low transportation costs. While transportation overcomes friction, site rentals plus transportation costs represent the social cost of what friction remains.[7]

Here, too, *relative* accessibility is the key to rent levels. Site rents reflect cost savings in comparison with alternate locations.

176

In evaluating the desirability of central locations for new housing, Haig would take account of other possible sites and their access characteristics. A location 15 minutes from the core of a large metropolitan region may offer time savings of 30 minutes in comparison with alternate sites on open land at the fringe of the developed area. In a smaller region, sites 15 minutes from the core may be in competition with open land only 5 or 10 minutes farther away. If Hurd and Haig are correct, the size of the region, or the distance (or traveltime) from the core to the nearest large supply of vacant land, will have great significance in determining the attractiveness of inner sites for new housing.

Subjective Evaluation of Accessibility

In Haig's writings, the costs of overcoming friction are largely an objective matter of the time and expense necessary to go from one place to another. Thus improvements in the transportation system reduce the costs of overcoming friction by shortening traveltime and reducing financial expenses for the consumer. But subjective elements also enter into the costs of friction, as Haig points out in his discussion of accessibility as a factor in the housing market:

> If the economic activity seeking a site happens to be housing, is not the problem worked out in this fashion? In choosing a residence purely as a consumption proposition, one buys accessibility precisely as one buys clothes or food. He considers how much he wants the contacts furnished by the central location, weighing the "costs of friction" involved — the various possible combinations of site rent, time value, and transportation costs: he compares this want with his other desires and resources, and he fits it into his scale of consumption, and buys.[8]

Haig's intellectual successors in the literature of urban location theory have developed the subjective element still more explicitly. Richard U. Ratcliff points out the element of personal evaluation that determines the significance of objective access characteristics in shaping a structure of land values:

> Space costs are inherent in our physical world. This disutility of distance is the joint product of the activities involved, the distance, the available means of overcoming the distance, and the importance of

177

the contact to the persons or activity concerned. No matter why people want to be near something or somebody, their preference is expressed in terms of value and becomes an economic force.[9]

Walter Firey has interpreted land-use patterns in Boston by referring the evaluation of accessibility not merely to personal preferences but to social systems and their cultural origin. In Firey's interpretation, "the very impeditiveness of space itself does not reside in it as a physical phenomenon but rather in the cost-fulness which it imposes upon social systems that have to deal with it." Since social systems reflect cultural values, Firey sees the cultural component as central to locational processes. In terms of this cultural component, "land gains its impeditive character, by which particular social systems cannot function unless they find suitable locations."[10]

Access Requirements as Part of a Movement System

In the work of Robert B. Mitchell and Chester Rapkin,[11] communication requirements between different activities form the basis of locational patterns within urban regions, but their requirements are more complex than a need for access to a single destination. Each activity has a "packet of movement systems" associated with it. If the activity is a residence, it serves as the base for many trips. To understand the choice of a residential location, one must know the destinations of all these trips. If they are scattered, accessibility cannot be achieved by spatial proximity but must result from a location offering good transportation to many dispersed places. Trips to shopping, to entertainment, to schools, and to jobs are all part of the movement system for a family. Housing locations thus reflect a need for access to a variety of destinations rather than access to the downtown core alone.

This viewpoint provides an approach to analysis rather than a theoretical model that would explain how a particular location is chosen when the objective is to have access to many activities. One useful part of the approach, the concept of linkage, offers some insight into the resolution of varying access needs. For certain types of movements, physical proximity is required. A linkage is a relationship between activities characterized by frequent inter-action requiring proximity in space. Mitchell and Rapkin illustrate linkages between business establishments, but the concept would be applicable to a home-school relationship for young children. Where such linkages exist, the locational choice will be near linked activities, but need not be near other activities where access requirements can be met without proximity.

Mitchell and Rapkin go beyond a static approach to consider the role of movement in changing the locational pattern of activities. Here again they offer only a framework for investigation, but several points are useful for understanding changing residential patterns. Changes in the internal structure of an establishment alter its movement requirements. In the case of a family, movement requirements that correspond to the ages of its members will presumably have much to do with changes in location over time.

Still other ways in which movement requirements bring about new locational choices are through shifts in the location of trip destinations and changes in the street system and other movement channels. The dispersal of employment from the core and the development of new highways are obvious illustrations of the ways in which these factors have altered movement requirements and have contributed to the outward spread of housing in recent years.

Mitchell and Rapkin treat the subject of access requirements in considerable depth; and they go far beyond earlier analysts in suggesting approaches to the dynamics of locational change. Nevertheless, they continue to focus on accessibility needs as the major consideration influencing locational choices.

Density and Access in Locational Models

Two recent works, in contrast, view the process of locational choice as a balancing of access requirements and the demand for space. These works present comprehensive (though static) theoretical models of locational forces in the urban land market, drawing elements from earlier writings but combining them more systematically.

William Alonso has devised a model covering both business and residential locations.[12] The driving force in his residential theory is the individual consumer's weighing of commuting costs against the advantages of cheaper land. By assumption, all employment is located in the center of the city, where land costs are highest. When a person considers different locations, he realizes that

179

commuting costs (in time and money) increase as he moves away from the center. To prepare a series of alternatives that will each yield him equal satisfaction, he decides by how much the price of land must be reduced as he moves away from the center in order to compensate him for the extra commuting cost. In making this decision, he considers commuting costs in subjective terms and decides on appropriate land price reductions in terms of how much satisfaction he derives from buying a larger site to redress the increased commuting cost.

By means of this evaluation of alternate satisfactions, the consumer develops a schedule of prices that he will bid for land at different distances from the center to maintain the same level of satisfaction at all locations. An individual will have a series of these "bid rent curves" corresponding to different levels of satisfaction. For any given price level of land, the consumer will choose the location that places him on his curve of highest satisfaction. Individual points of equilibrium are found by a method adapted from the standard solution of consumer equilibrium in economics; market equilibrium involves the simultaneous determination of locations, densities, and land prices by a process of iteration starting with an assumed land price at the center.

Assumptions underlying the determination of bid rent curves are significant. Land and accessibility are both positive goods in the housing market; consumers are assumed to want both central locations and large lots, although individuals each make their own evaluation of these two goods and may want them in different proportions. Empirical evidence in the New York Metropolitan Region Study is consistent with these assumptions in suggesting that accessibility and land area per dwelling unit are substitutes, with reductions in one balanced by gains in the other. Hoover and Vernon have analyzed net residential density, median income, and access time to central Manhattan for a group of communities in the rapidly growing suburban area around New York City. For any given level of median income, communities with better access have higher residential densities (that is, less residential land per dwelling unit). For any given degree of access, communities with higher median incomes have lower densities. And for any given level of density, communities with higher median incomes tend to have better access. Higher incomes thus appear to buy more

180

land per dwelling unit and better access, but they buy each at a sacrifice of the other.[13]

Transportation Advantage and Position Rent

The recent work of Lowdon Wingo, Jr.[14] resembles Alonso's model in many ways, but calls attention to several other structural features that are assumed to influence the location of new housing. Wingo's model involves only residential land and relies on the journey to work as the basic organizing force. Commuting costs depend upon the organization and technology of transportation, as modified by the individual's own valuation of leisure time lost while traveling to work. These costs of transportation establish a structure of "position rents," which reflect savings in traveltime and cost:

> Position rent is simply the economic advantage in transportation costs of any location with respect to the most disadvantaged position occupied, that is, the maximum amount that a user would be willing to pay rather than occupy the marginal location.[15]

Different levels of position rent imply different amounts of land area per dwelling unit. Assuming that ground space has diminishing marginal utility for the individual, Wingo postulates that the greater the position rent, the less space will be used. Each household has its own valuation of residential land space, as in Alonso's model, although in this case the demand schedule for space is independent of location. The household chooses its optimum location as follows:

> As it moves toward the employment site, position rent increases and transportation costs decrease until it finds a position in which the marginal saving in transportation costs is just equal to the marginal value of the residential space given up. Through this process of substituting transportation costs for space costs, locational equilibrium is achieved.[16]

The mechanism for finding optimal locations is similar to Alonso's, and Wingo also assumes a substitution effect between accessibility and land area.

Wingo's model recognizes the significance of two metropolitan characteristics that have been taken as variables in this study. Following Hurd, he uses the location of the outer margin of settlement as a determinant of access advantages and of rental values based on these advantages, at more central locations. Wingo is careful to stipulate that access advantages and rent structures are modified by the consumer's subjective evaluation of the costs of travel.

In the simplest version of Wingo's model, all employment is located at the center. This simplifying assumption is later relaxed, and Wingo demonstrates a method for taking noncentral employment locations into account. The effects of a secondary employment node are a reduction of densities and land values near the center of the region, a rise near the new employment node, and an outward shift of the margin of settlement.

Scope of This Study

Both these models, and indeed almost all the works reviewed, focus on employment location and the journey to work as basic organizers of the housing pattern. The more advanced theories recognize subjective and social factors as they affect consumers' evaluations of travel costs and land-area requirements. These factors are incorporated into the theory by means of individual preference schedules; the models assume little about the nature of these preference schedules other than that access and land area are substitutes for one another, and that both follow the principle of diminishing marginal utility.

Although the journey to work is unquestionably an important market factor, other forces also have a significant effect on the housing pattern. Wingo acknowledges the likely importance of prestige and culture group associations, variations in the quality of local services, and other considerations. He suggests that complex substitution effects may take place among these factors: households may sacrifice nearness to employment for prestige locations, or may pay higher rent to be near a good school. Firey's work and several other studies consider these influences, but most of the theoretical literature excludes them, concentrating instead on variables related to the journey to work and the demand for ground space. Wingo notes that patterns which emerge from the operations of these few variables would be optimal only if other features were either generally distributed or had little influence in individual decisions.

182

To what extent should analyses of locational preferences recognize such considerations as neighborhood prestige and the quality of local service? The objective of this study has been to gauge the feasibility of developing new housing as part of a program to rebuild older neighborhoods. Where rebuilding programs are contemplated, many physical characteristics of a neighborhood, and its level of services, are subject to extensive manipulation. It has appeared useful, therefore, to treat these aspects of the local environment as elements that a renewal program can direct satisfactorily so that social and cultural considerations will not obstruct rebuilding. The location of employment, the access characteristics of an area, and its relationship to the outer margin of settlement cannot be controlled as directly, although they can be affected by public policy over a period of time. I have chosen to regard these structural factors as exogeneous "givens." The question is then one of determining the degree to which these structural characteristics promote or hinder the rebuilding of the declining areas in view of the tastes and preferences of the existing population of the region, with the government assumed to have adequate power for reshaping the local environment satisfactorily.

Changing Urban Patterns and the Problem of Declining Areas

Recent patterns of urban growth have called increasing attention to problems of decline in the older parts of cities. In the nineteenth century, urban growth typically meant an increase in population and density throughout the region, with old central areas converted to more intensive uses partly through rebuilding at higher densities. More recently, new construction has bypassed inlying sites in favor of peripheral locations, leaving the older areas to decline in population and density. A number of studies have given special attention to the increasing abandonment of these older areas and to the factors that inhibit their rebuilding as modern residential neighborhoods.

Homer Hoyt observed the shifting patterns of population and land value that marked the decline of Chicago's oldest areas before 1930. Population in the zone within 2 miles of the center grew, but at a decreasing rate, until 1910; from 1910 to 1930, it declined. Population in the zone 2 to 4 miles from the center rose until

1910, held steady until 1920, and then declined.[17] These changes were reflected in population density:

> The population of Chicago was at first concentrated near the center of the city and the density curve resembled a cone with the sides sloping sharply downward. As population increased and transportation facilities improved, the base of this cone widened and the rate of most rapid population increase passed to successive belts of land, each one in turn farther from the main business district. After 1870 the height of the population pyramid rose only slowly but the base widened rapidly. In the twentieth century the number of people living within the areas that once contained the entire city stopped advancing and began to decline. . . . A large crater has appeared near the heart of the city. . . .[18]

Land values followed the density pattern; Hoyt takes note of "a valley in the land-value curve between the Loop and the outer residential areas."[19] The Loop itself is not part of this picture of decline, however. New construction added a significant amount of floor space to the central business district in the 1920's, and land values rose steadily, although at a lower rate than the rise in total Chicago land values. Thus Chicago in 1933 consisted of live areas in the core and at the fringe, with a declining intermediate area:

> The heart wood of the organic Chicago is constantly replacing old tissues with new ones, in marked contrast with the static condition of the belt of dead wood around the Loop known as the "blighted area" which has ceased to grow.[20]

Studies of other regions have documented similar shifts in population distribution. Hans Blumenfeld has described the phenomenon that Hoyt noted—that the zone of most rapid population increase moves steadily outward from the core—as "the tidal wave of metropolitan expansion."[21] Blumenfeld's historical analysis of Philadelphia illustrates not only the tidal wave effect but also the static or declining condition of areas between the core and the wave of expansion. Contrast the growth pattern of nineteenth-century Chicago (Figure C.1) with the pattern of twentieth-century Philadelphia in Figure C.2. Even after the transit improvements of the 1880's enabled Chicago to burst its earlier commuting-time boundaries, densities continued to increase substantially in all central areas except the core itself (0–1 mile zone), where business

184

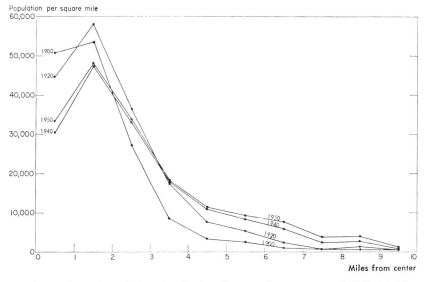

Figure C.2. Population density by distance from center of Philadelphia, 1900–1950.

Source: Data taken from Hans Blumenfeld, "The Tidal Wave of Metropolitan Expansion," *Journal of the American Institute of Planners,* Vol. 20 (Winter 1954), Table 6, p. 14.

expansion helped push out residences. Except for this innermost zone, the Chicago density gradient sloped steeply upward toward the core in 1900, much as in 1880.

In Philadelphia, growth from 1900 to 1920 followed the earlier Chicago pattern, with density decreasing only in the innermost zone and increasing substantially in other zones near the center. From 1920 to 1940, a new pattern emerged, producing sharp cutbacks in density through the 2–3 mile zone, a point of stability in the 3–4 mile zone, and large increases in density spread over the suburban rings starting 4 to 5 miles from the center. The wartime period of 1940–1950 saw density gains throughout the region, but their magnitude was negligible in most inner zones, and the most noticeable upward shifts were once again in the areas more than 5 miles from the core. During this 50-year period, the zone with the greatest percentage increase in population shifted from the 4–5 mile zone from 1900–1910 to the 7–8 mile zone in 1940–1950, moving outward at an average speed of 1 mile per decade.

The New York Metropolitan Region Study also confirms both the tidal wave pattern and the static or declining character of zones

185

close to the core of the region. Hoover and Vernon modify the growth wave concept to take account of two different and widely separated rings of growth, one marked by single-family construction in the suburbs and the other by apartment development closer to the center.[22] Although the wave of apartment construction has injected new life into older parts of the New York region, density trends approximate those of modern Chicago and Philadelphia. Figure C.3 depicts population densities in 1920, 1940, and 1955, for the suburban New York region (excluding New York City and Nassau County). This plotting of density against traveltime to the core via commuter railroad constitutes a good base for historical comparison, since the traveltimes have remained relatively constant since 1920. Nevertheless, the pull of the center has evidently weakened, particularly since 1940. From 1940 to 1955, population dropped slightly in the nearest time zone, increased slightly in the next zones, and registered greatest gains in zones far removed from the center. Thus the density curve flattened noticeably from 1940 to 1955. If New York City had been included in this sample, the density curve would have flattened still more strikingly, since the City lost population after 1950.

Other analyses of population distribution within metropolitan regions furnish additional evidence that growth now takes place mainly in outlying locations, while central areas remain static or actually decline.[23] What does this new growth pattern mean? Clearly, the tidal wave effect does not reflect merely the filling of inner areas to some standard capacity and the overflow of excess population into successively more distant rings. Some central locations have relatively low densities. The first time zone in the New York suburban sample shown in Figure C.3 had a density of about 1,500 persons per square mile in 1940, and yet failed to grow in the next 15 years. In contrast, parts of Chicago with densities of 20,000 per square mile in 1880 filled to a density of more than 40,000 per square mile in 1900. Since 1950, central areas have not merely been bypassed by new growth: eleven of the twelve largest cities in 1950 lost population from 1950 to 1960, while their metropolitan areas expanded.[24]

This evidence points consistently in one direction: central locations are less preferred for housing now than they were 50 years ago. The distribution of population within a region reflects a com-

186

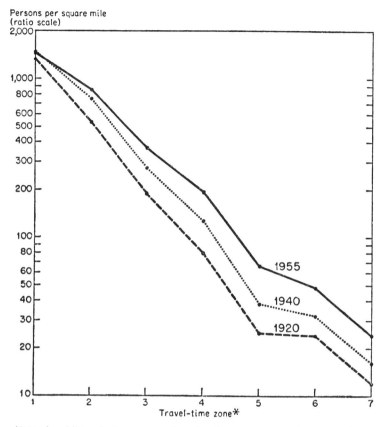

Persons per square mile
(ratio scale)

Travel-time zone*

* Each additional time zone after the first represents about 15 minutes additional travel time.

Figure C.3.   Relation between population density and approximate travel-time to Manhattan, New York metropolitan region, 1920, 1940, 1955 (New York City and Nassau County excluded).

Source: Edgar M. Hoover and Raymond Vernon, *Anatomy of a Metropolis* (Cambridge, Massachusetts: Harvard University Press, 1959), Chart 14, p. 186.

plex interaction of many factors; but the desire for central location, which is one of these factors, has evidently become less important in relation to other considerations.

Reasons for the Population Shift

What are some of these other considerations? Studies of housing patterns take several different approaches. Hoyt explains the abandonment of central Chicago as a combination of objectionable social

187

and physical conditions in the center and the pull of new housing and new facilities in outlying areas. The old housing of central Chicago became a magnet for socially marginal occupants: racial and ethnic minorities, criminal elements. The presence of these groups stimulated old American residents nearby to look elsewhere for housing. Improved transportation facilities made new neighborhoods practical on the outer edge of the city, and the new developments had pulling power of their own:

> The attractions of modern buildings and of motion-picture places, banks, and chain stores in these newly settled communities were the centrifugal forces that whirled people from their old abodes into the new bright-light areas. In their wake, between the Loop and the new sections were left the "blighted areas."[25]

At the same time, new immigration from Europe dropped sharply, and few newcomers appeared in the city to take up vacancies in the center. As of 1933, Hoyt saw little demand for the blighted areas for any purpose.

The literature describing recent urban change is filled with plausible explanations for the rapid suburban growth since World War II.[26] Widespread automobile ownership and the construction of modern highway networks are often singled out for special emphasis. Auto transportation for workers and truck transport for freight freed many industries from central locations and enabled them to build expansive horizontal plants on outlying sites. As work places decentralized, suburban homes were able to offer increasingly good access to jobs. With the general shift to the automobile, proximity to public transportation has become less important even for residents who require access to downtown. New highways have opened up huge areas of accessible and inexpensive land for housing development. Retail outlets have followed residences out to the suburbs; the large new suburban market has been able to support impressive shopping concentrations within short driving times of residential areas. All these developments, plus easy financing for home purchases, have made suburban living feasible for large numbers of families. The low-density suburban environment in itself has been a great attraction to families with increasing leisure time and with young children.

On the basis of a study of current housing patterns in Philadelphia, Chester Rapkin and William Grigsby suggest that the attraction of low-density living is a particularly strong factor influencing the housing choices of families with children, and that the attraction is to single-family houses specifically rather than merely to a suburban environment. Surveys of households in outlying elevator apartment houses, located near excellent school facilities, revealed as low a proportion of families with children as in new apartment houses in central Philadelphia.[27] A different survey of 300 households living in high-rent units in the centers of New York, Philadelphia, and Chicago corroborates the rejection of apartment living by families with children: only one fifth of the households consisted of husband and wife with minor children, although close to half of all nonfarm households in the United States are in this category.[28]

The limited appeal of apartment living for families with children has several implications for the declining areas. To the extent that the rejection of apartment units is a new development, it constitutes one force promoting population decline in central locations. But families with children carry particularly heavy weight in population totals. If departing families with children are replaced by childless couples or single adults, total population will decline even though the stock of housing may be fully utilized.

The Alternatives: Peripheral Growth or Redevelopment

The preceding discussion adopts the viewpoint of the housing consumer in an attempt to understand how the declining areas have reached their present condition. Another useful perspective is that of the housing producer and the market within which he operates. At all stages in the growth of a metropolitan area, developers can build new housing on vacant fringe land or in already built-up areas. In the latter case, they may be able to build on remaining vacant lots or, more typically, they will have to assemble building sites by demolishing existing structures. Peripheral growth, rather than redevelopment, has accounted for most of the expansion of the housing supply of metropolitan areas in the last few decades. If the declining areas are to be rebuilt for residential use, the task of the next decades is to divert a larger proportion of new housing construction from peripheral growth to redevelopment.

Studies of urban housing patterns contain a number of interesting views on the prospects of redevelopment as an alternative to peripheral growth. Hoyt's works in the 1930's view redevelopment in terms of the private developer operating without special government assistance. Within this framework the greatest obstacles to redevelopment arise from the small scale at which the individual developer operates and his difficulties in assembling large sites. Hoyt maintains that obsolete surroundings and diversified ownership of land in the blighted areas together keep out new housing. Only high-grade apartment developments generate rental returns sufficient to pay the cost of acquiring existing buildings, but potential occupants who can afford the necessary rents will object to living among obsolete surroundings. If the developer could clear a sufficiently large area, he could provide a totally new environment, but diversified land ownership makes the assembly of large tracts difficult and costly. Hoyt notes that redevelopment is occasionally feasible, if existing structures are flimsy or scattered, and if land is cheap and easily assembled. In rare circumstances, developers can build apartment houses in obsolete surroundings:

> Such apartments can rise even in the midst of a poor area because the tall building itself, rising from humble surroundings like a feudal castle above the mud huts of the villeins, is a barrier against intrusion.[29]

Since the 1930's, the idea of government participation in redevelopment has become increasingly accepted. With the exercise of eminent domain to condemn blighted areas, sites can be assembled in spite of diversified ownership, and the economic effect of holdouts can be minimized. At first, several state programs authorized public acquisition of land for rebuilding; since the Housing Act of 1949, federal subsidies have been available to bring site acquisition costs down to feasible resale prices for new housing.

This growing appreciation of the role of government participation is evident in Walter Firey's 1947 analysis of land-use changes in central Boston. One of Firey's main purposes is to demonstrate the significance of noneconomic factors in shaping urban development. The history of Boston includes one successful case of renewing an old area that had begun to decline. The revival of Beacon Hill involved primarily the remodeling of old structures rather than clearance and redevelopment, but Firey considers the method of renewing Beacon Hill applicable to areas requiring redevelopment, as well. This method relied heavily on governmental measures to block commercial and apartment construction from filtering into the neighborhood. Protective zoning, consisting of a low height limit and restriction to exclusively residential use, preserved the existing structures and enabled private developers to buy them at reasonable prices for rehabilitation.

Firey's contribution to this discussion is his recognition of the role of public measures in promoting the rebuilding of older areas. Unlike Hoyt, he sees good future prospects for redevelopment through official promotion of redevelopment corporations and through aid in the form of assessment and tax adjustments as well as zoning regulations. The most promising basis for stimulating housing demand in central Boston, according to Firey, is the symbolic value of its historic buildings and monuments. Firey holds that, with government assistance, developers can capitalize on the symbolic associations of sites in the older areas of Boston by locating new housing there.

Limits of Peripheral Growth

Subsequent analyses generally accept the idea of government assistance in redevelopment, but few regard historic sites as a significant basis for renewing older areas, largely because the supply of historic sites falls far short of the supply of deteriorated districts in American cities. Two recent works suggest that the outward push of peripheral growth will set up pressures for redevelopment in central areas and thus act as an equilibrating mechanism. Hoyt points out in a 1958 article that the spread of single-family home-building has created a situation in which home buyers must travel farther and farther out each year to find a new house. Despite the construction of new highways, traveltimes between vacant land and the core lengthen as vacant land becomes more remote. In Hoyt's view, traveltime to the core has once again become a significant factor promoting central redevelopment rather than peripheral growth. Many families, particularly those without children or with preschool children, are willing to live in apartment houses in order to save traveltime between home and work. Apartment rentals generate sufficient income so that the builder can afford to pay from $2 to $5 per square foot for his site, a price that enables him to clear old one-family structures.[30]

191

The authors of *Housing Choices and Housing Constraints* also regard peripheral growth as a self-correcting mechanism, but through the effects of rising housing costs in the suburbs rather than through an overly extended journey to work:

> The city could hardly compete with the suburbs where vast areas of open land were still available for fringe building. The cost of putting new housing on this undeveloped land is increasing each year. Furthermore, the rapid rise in taxes necessary to provide schools and other community facilities has made the suburban housing burden heavier than many house buyers had anticipated. As suburban land and housing become even more costly, and taxes even higher in the future, attractive city dwellings within a reasonable price range might well exert an appeal which has been lacking in the past. Indeed, it may not be going too far to suggest that the traditional housing situation of scarce and expensive city land, compared with ample and low-cost suburban land, may eventually — through competition for outlying properties — equalize if not reverse itself.[31]

Raymond Vernon also speculates on the possibility that peripheral growth will create a shortage of land in outlying locations and thus stimulate central redevelopment to obtain building sites:

> . . . if urban land were to prove an acutely scarce resource at some point in the future . . . pressure to recapture the "underused" gray areas for living space might be so strong as to generate vast expenditures to that end. But it is one of the paradoxes of urban growth today that the increase in the supply of urban land is probably outstripping the demand. At the edges of most urban masses, farmers are shrinking their land use, on the whole, faster than developers are taking the land up. . . .
>
> Eventually, of course, this will change. Urban land will become scarce again as sheer population growth fills up the empty spaces. But the land promises to grow more plentiful before it grows scarce again. And for several decades, we are likely to see suburban developments making more and more profligate use of the land.[32]

Vernon's assertions about the rate of growth of the supply of urban land are not directly testable. Much depends upon future transportation systems and their ability to provide acceptable conditions of access from outlying vacant land to employment centers; the future location of employment centers is thus an additional factor in determining the effective supply of urban land. The other equilibrium concepts are more readily testable, and both have been investigated in the three case studies.

Characteristics of the Declining Areas

Different conceptions of the problems of declining areas emerge from the foregoing analyses of public preferences and market factors influencing the location of new housing. These conceptions have contrasting implications for government policies seeking to promote the rebuilding of old areas, and they delineate some of the important issues confronting policymakers.

Declining demand and depressed land values characterize Hoyt's conception of Chicago's areas of population loss in 1933. Successive waves of immigrants occupied these areas in the past; with the ending of large-scale immigration after World War I, demand for housing in the blighted areas declined, and the population thinned out. Miles Colean also emphasizes the role of immigration in maintaining old and blighted housing. During the period of mass immigration, Colean explains that owners of obsolete structures saw opportunities for profit in crowding them with newcomers rather than replacing them. Impoverished immigrants created a constant demand for old housing; as a result, old areas that might have been improved were bypassed by new development and left to deteriorate. When the flow of immigration stopped, these areas were far removed from new development, and they had reached a scale where individual efforts at rebuilding could not cope with the problem of blighted surroundings.[33]

Hoyt's land value analysis of Chicago showed a relative depression in the blighted areas corresponding to their decline in population. Before 1900, land values resembled a pyramid with its peak at the Loop and steeply sloping sides. From 1900 to 1928, the pyramid shape disappeared: land values in outlying areas rose to levels aproximating those in the Loop, and values between the core and the fringe formed valleys on either side of the Loop. In a historical analysis of land values in the old areas (settled before 1873), Hoyt found that their values had increased only slightly after 1890. He suggests that the difference in land values between old and new areas reflects not only the different numbers of occupants but other characteristics as well: the limited purchasing power available in the blighted areas, resulting from low individual incomes and declining population density; losses in rent collection; and a substantial rate of property deterioration caused by neglect and vandalism.[34]

If Hoyt's conception is accurate, land values in the declining areas will be low, both because of falling housing demand and because of characteristics of the resident population. If so, acquisition costs of old property may not constitute a serious obstacle to redevelopment.

The "Gray Areas" Problem: Declining Demand and High Acquisition Prices

The New York Metropolitan Region Study dramatized the subject of residential decline with an incisive characterization of the "gray areas." Hoover and Vernon see the problem in New York essentially as a situation of declining demand for gray area locations for any purpose:

> What is least clear in the [future] prospect is the trend of development in the "gray" areas that comprise most of the less central parts of the core, and their counterparts in the older large cities elsewhere in the region. The aging multifamily housing of those areas suffers most of the drawbacks of congestion and high redevelopment cost that prevail in still more central areas, but lacks their unique access advantage. In terms of access, its appeal is to the subway commuters, a group now beginning to shrink in numbers. Employment opportunities within the gray areas themselves are unlikely to grow. On the other hand, the supply of obsolescent housing is likely to grow at record rates. The increasing fraction of the region's population who work outside the core will generally look farther out for their homes, while the shift of inner-core dwellers into the gray areas may well fall far short of maintaining demand for all of the low-grade housing that will exist there. Renewal projects will accommodate more and more people in the inner core itself, perhaps even at slightly higher densities per square mile if past Manhattan experience is a guide; and those who leave the inner core will have a great deal more freedom to move into the single-family residential neighborhoods beyond the gray areas than they had in the past.[35]

Hoover and Vernon foresee some potential for redevelopment in the innermost parts of the gray areas, near the central business district, where special access advantages are available. Farther

194

out, they estimate that redevelopment costs are as high as in central gray area locations, but the high prices do not bring corresponding access advantages. This study has investigated their assumptions: Is the demand for central locations a discontinuous one, strong near the core and very much weaker elsewhere in the gray areas, or does it resemble a gradient extending across the gray areas without a precipitous decline as one leaves the central business district? Are site acquisition costs relatively constant within the old areas, or do they decline with increasing distance from the center?

The Conflict of Market Standards with Social Criteria

In a separate article, Vernon describes the problem of the gray areas not merely as a lack of demand for building sites but as a demand blocked by high acquisition costs:

> One can picture the development of a gray ring around the central portions of some of our major cities — a ring consisting of structures abandoned by the low-income groups and unwanted by others at the costs involved in converting the area to other purposes.

The obstacle of excessive acquisition costs for re-use purposes arises again in this view. Vernon goes on to raise the question of social costs arising from increasing abandonment of gray areas:

> The social costs of maintaining the ring would be high. The ring would lengthen the journeys-to-work of those whose business lay in the central city. It could needlessly lengthen the mileage of mass transit facilities. Underused though it was, it would still demand fire and police protection, schools, water and sewers. And the eyesore it presented would be a constant source of revulsion to those who passed through it.[36]

Chester Rapkin also sees the gray areas problem as a conflict arising from the clash of economic standards of the housing market against noneconomic social criteria. Vernon sees a lack of effective market demand for gray area locations at prevailing costs; Rapkin sees the high acquisition costs of gray area sites as reflections of a housing market that fails to provide sufficient low-income alternatives. Rapkin phrases the problem of the gray areas as the question, "What shall we do with physical assets that retain economic value long after they cease to serve social purposes judged by other than

195

market criteria?"[37] The approach that he suggests is to promote measures that will reduce the economic value of obsolete housing. Basically, the way to lower acquisition costs in the gray areas is to maintain a rate of new housing construction in excess of the rate of net family formation. He cites Philadelphia as a city where these conditions have been achieved; the results have been increased vacancies in lower quality housing and a reduction in site acquisition costs.

The key elements of these conceptions of the gray areas concern the demand for gray area locations and the costs of site acquisition. Some analyses of the problem emphasize the weakness of demand; others emphasize the high costs of redevelopment. The approach of this study has been to investigate both sides of the problem in order to determine how wide the gap is between site costs and re-use values. The regions chosen for study illustrate different types of metropolitan structure. The analysis has been designed to search out the structural factors that influence demand and cost levels, in an effort to establish guidelines for public policies concerned with rebuilding the declining sections of cities.

NOTES

CHAPTER ONE

1 The "gray areas" hypothesis is most fully developed in the work of Raymond Vernon cited in Appendix C, but see also the work of Homer Hoyt and Chester Rapkin in Appendix C and the general interpretations of Paul N. Ylvisaker, "The Deserted City," *Journal of the American Institute of Planners,* Vol. 25 (February 1959), pp. 1–6, and "Opening Minds and Expanding Cities," in *Ends and Means of Urban Renewal* (Philadelphia: Philadelphia Housing Association, 1961), pp. 7–21.

2 See Gardner F. Derrickson, "Recent Homebuilding Trends in Major Metropolitan Areas," *Construction Review,* Vol. 6 (September 1960), pp. 5–10. Of the eleven areas cited, five had more than 15,000 new multifamily units (in 5-or-more family structures) in 1958 and 1959, and the remainder had more than 5,000 new multifamily units in this two-year period.

CHAPTER TWO

1 Philip Roth, *Goodbye, Columbus* (New York: Meridian Fiction, 1960), p. 90.

2 U.S. Bureau of the Census, *Current Population Reports: Population Estimates,* P-25, No. 247, "Estimates of the Components of Population Change by Color, for States: 1950 to 1960," April 2, 1962. For a general discussion, see Paul F. Coe, "The Nonwhite Population Surge to our Cities," *Land Economics,* Vol. 25 (August 1959), pp. 195–210; and Harry Sharp and Leo F. Schnore, "The Changing Color Composition of Metropolitan Areas," *Land Economics,* Vol. 28 (May 1962), pp. 169–185.

3 See U.S. Department of Justice Immigration and Naturalization Service, *Report of the Commissioner of Immigration and Naturalization, 1960,* Table 13; Max L. Margolis and Alexander Marx, *A History of the Jewish People* (New York: Meridian Books, 1958), pp. 701, 719.

4 See Oscar Handlin, *The Newcomers* (Cambridge: Harvard University Press, 1959), p. 141; and Clarence Senior, *Strangers — Then Neighbors* (New York: Freedom Books, 1961), p. 22.

5 Source: See Figure 2.2.

6 Calculated from *U.S. Census of Housing: 1950,* Vol. 1, *General Characteristics,* Part 1: U.S. Summary, Table 28; and *U.S. Census of Housing: 1960,* Advance Reports, *Housing Characteristics: States,* HC(A1) Series, Table 1. Substandard units are those classified as dilapidated or lacking one or more plumbing facilities.

7 *U.S. Census of Housing: 1960,* Advance Reports, *Housing Characteristics: States,* HC(A1) — 52, United States Summary, Table 2. Substandard housing includes units classified as dilapidated or lacking one or more plumbing facilities.

8 Information for 1940 and 1950 from Davis McEntire, *Residence and Race* (Berkeley: University of California Press, 1960), Table A-2, p. 366. Information for 1960 calculated from *U.S. Censuses of Population and Housing: 1960, Census*

Tracts, Final Report PHC(1)–166, Washington, D. C.–Md.–Va. Standard Metropolitan Statistical Area, Table P-1.

[9] See McEntire, *op. cit.,* Table A.2, pp. 366–367, for information through 1950.

[10] See *ibid.,* pp. 148–156.

[11] Lorraine Hansberry, *A Raisin in the Sun* (New York: Signet Books, 1961), p. 61.

[12] Population changes, migration estimates, and natural increase for New York City reported in Department of City Planning *Newsletter,* September 1961, p. 2. Growth of Puerto Rican population in Newark and Jersey City reported in "Jersey Drive Set by Puerto Ricans," *The New York Times,* January 22, 1962, p. 25.

[13] See "Negroes Shifting from Manhattan to all Boroughs," *The New York Times,* July 9, 1961, p. 1. Suburban increases in Negro population discussed in "Negro Faces Housing Test in Major Shift to Suburbs," *The New York Times,* May 21, 1961, p. 1.

[14] Information on Negro residential patterns within New York City from an address by Henry Cohen (Deputy City Administrator, Office of the Mayor) to the Association of Fair Housing Committees, September 23, 1961. For information on 1950 patterns, see McEntire, *op. cit.,* Table A.2, p. 366.

[15] Department of City Planning *Newsletter,* June 1959, p. 4.

[16] John R. White and Edna L. Hebard, *The Manhattan Housing Market* (New York: Brown, Harris, Stevens, Inc., 1959), p. 70.

[17] J. Anthony Panuch, *Building a Better New York: Final Report to Mayor Robert F. Wagner* (March 1, 1960), p. 75.

[18] *Ibid.,* p. 37; *U.S. Census of Housing: 1960,* Advance Reports, *Housing Characteristics: States,* HC(A1)–31, *New Jersey,* and HC(A1)–33, *New York,* Table 1.

[19] Edgar M. Hoover and Raymond Vernon, *Anatomy of a Metropolis* (Cambridge, Massachusetts: Harvard University Press, 1959), p. 203.

[20] Los Angeles County Commission on Human Relations. "A Comparative Statistical Analysis of Minority Group Population for Los Angeles County from April, 1950 to July 1, 1959."

[21] Calculated for communities within the City of Los Angeles; data from Los Angeles County Commission on Human Relations, "A Comparative Statistical Analysis of Population by Race for Incorporated Cities of Los Angeles County Covering the Years 1950–1956–1960."

[22] City of Los Angeles, *Population Estimate by Communities,* Bulletin 1960–4 (October 1, 1960).

[23] *Ibid.*

[24] Information made available by City of Los Angeles Department of City Planning for area west of Figueroa Street in Central City Study Area.

[25] Calculated from *U.S. Census of Population: 1950,* Vol. 3, *Census Tract Statistics,* Bulletin P-D23, Hartford, Connecticut and Adjacent Area; *U.S. Censuses of Population and Housing: 1960, Census Tracts,* Final Report PHC(1)–61, Hartford, Conn. Standard Metropolitan Statistical Area.

[26] City of Hartford Commission on the City Plan, "Population and Housing Changes in Hartford from 1950 to 1960 by Census Tract" (September 1960).

[27] *U.S. Census of Housing: 1960,* Advance Reports, *Housing Characteristics: States,* HC(A1)–5, *California;* HC(A1)–7, *Connecticut;* HC(A1)–33, *New York;* Table 1.

CHAPTER THREE

[1] Chester Rapkin, "Trends in the Philadelphia Area," in Philadelphia Housing Association, *Ends and Means of Urban Renewal* (Philadelphia, 1961), p. 78.

[2] Louise P. Lerdau, "Same Facets of the Region's Consumer Trade and Service Activities," in Robert M. Lichtenberg, *One-Tenth of a Nation* (Cambridge, Massachusetts: Harvard University Press, 1960), p. 234.

3 A few exceptions occur in the Hartford region where some units built between 1947–1950 were included in the 20–29 minute time zone to supplement a very small sampling of post-1950 development.

4 Sources: for New York, City of New York Department of City Planning, New York Transit Authority timetables; for Westchester County, timetables of commuter railroads (average of three fastest times for trains departing from 42nd Street between 5:00 p.m. to 6:00 p.m.); for Los Angeles, Automobile Club of Southern California, *Los Angeles Metropolitan Peak-Hour Driving Study* (June 1960) — travel times measured from interchange of Hollywood Freeway and Harbor Freeway; for Hartford, Hartford Area Transportation Study, Connecticut Highway Department, and Wilbur Smith and Associates, *Mass Transportation in the Capitol Region,* prepared for the Capitol Region Planning Agency (December 1960) — travel times measured from corner of Market Street and State Street. Walking rate from subway station in New York and bus line in Hartford to apartment house estimated at 3 miles per hour. New York housing over 3,000 feet from subway station excluded from sample.

5 Source: James Felt and Co., New York.

6 In a study of the downtown housing market in Philadelphia, Rapkin and Grigsby mention that similar new apartments rent for $40 a room close to downtown and $35 a room in outlying parts of the Philadelphia area. Core employment in Philadelphia accounts for 20 to 25 per cent of the total for the region, and substantial time savings are possible from central locations. Chester Rapkin and William Grigsby, *Residential Renewal in the Urban Core* (Philadelphia: University of Pennsylvania Press, 1960), pp. 51, 56.

7 California Department of Employment, community labor market surveys as of July 1960, reported September 1960. Nearby districts included in the total are Van Nuys and Inglewood.

8 *U.S. Census of Business: 1958,* Vol. 7, Central Business District Report, Los Angeles — Long Beach, California Area — BC58–CBD43, Tables 1A, 7. San Fernando Valley shopping areas included: North Hollywood, Valley Plaza, Van Nuys, Sherman Oaks.

9 Information prepared by Hartford Area Transportation Study, Connecticut Highway Department.

10 Measuring general accessibility to all jobs and shopping in the region (and ideally to entertainment and recreation facilities as well) is a superior way of gauging access advantages of particular housing locations. An index of this type is not available for most metropolitan areas, however, and considerable time and expense are required to prepare one. The alternate approach used in this study requires measuring the *proportion* of employment and retailing in the downtown core rather than gauging the theoretical pulling power of the core by means of the *absolute* amount of employment and retailing located downtown. The rental patterns of Los Angeles and Hartford can be understood in terms of the relative weakness of downtown Los Angeles and the relative strength of downtown Hartford. Any judgment based on absolute quantities of core employment and retailing would fail to take account of jobs and retail facilities in nondowntown locations.

11 Nelson N. Foote *et al., Housing Choices and Constraints* (New York: McGraw-Hill, 1960), pp. 439–444.

12 Residential Research Committee of Southern California, *Residential Research Report,* Fourth Quarter, 1960, p. 43. Source: Los Angeles Department of Water and Power, Southern California Edison Company, City of Pasadena Light Department, Burbank Public Service. Average of quarterly vacancy rates for 1959 and 1960 in 12,400 apartments.

13 State of New York Temporary Housing Rent Commission, "Report on the Survey of the Rental and Housing Market" (January 19, 1961), p. 10.

14 Real Estate Board of New York, cited in State of New York Temporary

State Housing Rent Commission, "Report on the Survey of the Rental and Housing Market," *op. cit.*, p. 13.

[15] *U.S. Census of Housing: 1960,* Advance Reports, *Housing Characteristics: States,* HC(A1)–33, *New York,* Table 1. Vacant units available for rent with all plumbing facilities as percentage of total rental units with all plumbing facilities in New York Standard Metropolitan Statistical Area.

[16] *U.S. Census of Housing: 1960,* Advance Reports, *Housing Characteristics: States,* HC(A1)–7, *Connecticut,* Table 1. Vacant units available for rent with all plumbing facilities as percentage of total rental units with all plumbing facilities, in Hartford Standard Metropolitan Statistical Area, towns of East Hartford, Hartford, West Hartford, Wethersfield.

[17] American Public Health Association Committee on the Hygiene of Housing, *Planning the Neighborhood* (Chicago: Public Administration Service, 1948), p. 39.

CHAPTER FOUR

[1] Edgar M. Hoover and Raymond Vernon, *Anatomy of a Metropolis* (Cambridge, Massachusetts: Harvard University Press, 1959), p. 175.

[2] Information from Abram Barkan, James Felt and Co.; William Lese, Pease and Elliman; Jacob Perlow; Frederick Rose, David Rose and Associates.

[3] Land cost information based upon sales in 1958–1960 reported by Walter Lampe, Chief Appraiser, Federal Housing Administration, New York, and the following New York realtors: Abram Barkan, James Felt and Co.; Jacob Perlow; Frederick Rose, David Rose and Associates. Further information on land costs derived from report by Peter Stone for New York Metropolitan Region Study, November 1957, on file at Regional Plan Association.

[4] Land prices in redevelopment areas given in City of New York Committee on Slum Clearance, *Title I Progress* (January 29, 1960), pp. 24–25. Prices include planning and land acquisition costs, converted to square foot costs for gross project area. Traveltimes from the core have been calculated on the basis described in Chapter 3, footnote 4.

[5] Land prices for public housing projects given in New York City Housing Authority, *Project Statistics* (December 31, 1960); prices used are land costs per square foot of private property, for projects completed after 1950. Information on the character of each site prior to acquisition was obtained separately from the Housing Authority; land that was predominantly vacant is excluded from this discussion of land costs.

[6] In addition to interview sources cited above in footnote 3, information has been made available by Charles Abrams, and by Frank Kristof of the New York Housing and Redevelopment Board. Published cost estimates appear in "How A Builder Figures," *Fortune,* Vol. 61 (February 1960), pp. 243–246; New York City Planning Commission, *Urban Renewal: A Report on the West Side Urban Renewal Study* (1958); and the following reports of the New York City Committee on Slum Clearance: *Lincoln Square* (1956), *Hammels-Rockaway* (1956), *Penn Station South* (1957), *Riverside-Amsterdam* (1958), *Soundview* (1959). Tax rates are those cited on the bottom of p. 76; Rent and density data sources cited in Chapter 3. Most analyses of this kind are based on costs and rents per rental room — a measure which introduces difficulties of comparison when the mix of apartment sizes varies from building to building. For illustrative purposes in comparing costs and returns at different densities, data in this chapter are given for one-bedroom apartments with variations in floor area noted explicitly.

[7] A further source of profit for the developer that I have excluded from this investment framework consists of income tax advantages resulting from deductions during the construction period and from depreciation allowances after the building is completed. For a discussion of tax advantages in apartment development, see Daniel M. Friedenberg, "The Coming Bust in the Real Estate Boom," *Harpers,* Vol. 222 (June 1961), pp. 29–40.

8 Land cost estimates have been obtained for apartment sites in the sector of Los Angeles surrounding Wilshire Boulevard, extending the full length of the Boulevard, from downtown Los Angeles to the Pacific coast at Santa Monica. Sites for which prices were obtained lie predominantly within a one-mile belt on either side of Wilshire Boulevard; all estimates are based on recent sales to apartment developers. Sources were interviews with Claude Cunningham, Assistant Chief, Land Division, Los Angeles County Assessor; R. Douglas Burrows, Vice-President and Chief Appraiser, Security First National Bank; Charles Shattuck and Kurt Shelger, Appraisers; Robert Filley, Vice-President, Western Real Estate Research Corporation; Nelson Smith, Prudential Insurance Co.; Hal Wiseman, Norman Construction Co.

9 Information on Bunker Hill and Temple Projects from Los Angeles Community Redevelopment Agency.

10 Interview sources are those cited in footnote 8. Additional information from Federal Housing Administration, Los Angeles, and the following published studies: Henry A. Babcock, *Report on the Economic Phases of the Bunker Hill Renewal Project, Los Angeles, California* (Community Redevelopment Agency of the City of Los Angeles, May 15, 1956); and Stanford Research Institute (James H. Forbes, Jr., Frederick P. Lyte, Emil L. de Graeve), *Feasibility of a Residential Rental Development in the Bunker Hill Urban Renewal Project* (Community Redevelopment Agency of the City of Los Angeles, May, 1957).

11 Land cost information for the Hartford region consists of prices paid in recent transactions and prices asked in recent sales offerings for sites in the same general locations used for the rental survey in Chapter 3. Most of these locations are in a sector extending west of downtown Hartford in a one-mile band on either side of Farmington Avenue in Hartford and West Hartford. Information on sales prices and offerings from John Rowlson, Rowlson Real Estate and Insurance, Hartford; and Robert Weisberg, Suburban Associates, Bloomfield.

12 Sources of information on cost levels and densities were the Federal Housing Administration, Hartford (John B. Maylott, Director); Robert Stone, Goldberg and Stone, Manchester; John Rowlson, Rowlson Real Estate and Insurance, Hartford.

CHAPTER FIVE

1 For sources and details of land utilization calculations for New York, Los Angeles, and Hartford, see Appendix B.

2 "City Planning Billion in Housing for 250,000 Within Few Years," *The New York Times,* April 7, 1961, p. 19.

3 Edgar M. Hoover, "Demographic Projections for the Region as a Whole," in Barbara R. Berman, Benjamin Chinitz, and Edgar M. Hoover, *Projection of a Metropolis: Technical Supplement to the New York Metropolitan Region Study* (Cambridge, Massachusetts: Harvard University Press, 1961), pp. 57–75.

4 See Figures 3.1 to 3.3.

5 Real Estate Research Corporation, *Rental Housing Market Analysis: Downtown Hartford* (prepared for Department of Housing, City of Hartford, 1959).

6 U.S. Housing and Home Finance Agency, *Housing Statistics, Historical Supplement* (October 1961), p. 12; *Housing Statistics* (October 1961), p. 7.

7 Louis Winnick, *Rental Housing: Opportunities for Private Investment* (New York: McGraw-Hill, 1958).

CHAPTER SIX

1 John W. Dyckman and Reginald R. Isaacs, *Capital Requirements for Urban Development and Renewal* (New York: McGraw-Hill, 1961), p. 88.

2 George Orwell, *The Road to Wigan Pier* (New York: Berkley Publishing Corp., 1961) (first published 1937), p. 69.

[3] J. Anthony Panuch, *Relocation in New York City: Special Report to Mayor Robert F. Wagner* (December 15, 1959), p. 18.

[4] See, for example, Elinor G. Black, *Manhattantown Two Years Later* (New York: Women's City Club of New York, Inc., April 1956); Marc Fried and Peggy Gleicher, "Some Sources of Residential Satisfaction in an Urban 'Slum'," *Journal of the American Institute of Planners,* Vol. 27 (November 1961), pp. 305–315; Herbert J. Gans, *The Urban Villagers* (New York: Free Press of Glencoe, 1962); Sidney Goldstein and Basil G. Zimmer, *Residential Displacement and Resettlement of the Aged* (Providence: Rhode Island Division on Aging, 1960); Peter Marris, *Family and Social Change in an African City* (Chicago: Northwestern University Press, 1962); J. M. Mogey, *Family and Neighbourhood* (London: Oxford University Press, 1956); John R. Seeley, "The Slum: Its Nature, Use, and Users," *Journal of the American Institute of Planners,* Vol. 25 (February 1959), pp. 7–14; Peter Townsend, *The Family Life of Old People* (London: Routledge and Kegan Paul, 1957); United Community Services of Metropolitan Boston, *Housing Preferences of Older People, Follow-up Study No. 2: West End Couples* (January 1962); Charles Vereker and John Barron Mays, *Urban Redevelopment and Social Change* (Liverpool: Liverpool University Press, 1961); Michael Young and Peter Wilmott, *Family and Kinship in East London* (Glencoe: Free Press, 1957).

[5] U.S. Housing and Home Finance Agency, Urban Renewal Administration, *Urban Renewal Project Characteristics* (June 30, 1961), Table 3.

[6] "Elegant Name Proposed for Third Avenue," *The New York Times,* July 12, 1961, p. 33.

[7] Information on the West End from *U.S. Census of Population: 1910* and *U.S. Census of Population: 1950,* Boston tracts H-1, H-2, H-3, H-4; Gordon Gottsche, "Relocation: Goals, Implementation, and Evaluation of the Process with Reference to the West End Redevelopment Project in Boston, Massachusetts," unpublished master's dissertation, Massachusetts Institute of Technology, Department of City and Regional Planning, 1960.

[8] Information on the Lower East Side from Leo Grebler, *Housing Market Behavior in a Declining Area* (New York: Columbia University Press, 1952).

[9] *Ibid.,* p. 143.

[10] Walter Firey, *Land Use in Central Boston* (Cambridge: Harvard University Press, 1947), Chapter 5, pp. 170–225.

[11] John R. Seeley, *op. cit.*

[12] See U.S. Housing and Home Finance Agency, Urban Renewal Administration, *op. cit.,* "Characteristics Directory of Projects as of June 30, 1961."

[13] See City of New York Committee on Slum Clearance, *Title I Progress* (January 29, 1960), p. 25; J. Anthony Panuch, *Relocation in New York City: Special Report to Mayor Robert F. Wagner* (December 15, 1959), p. 24; "30,000 Families Face Relocation," *The New York Times,* June 26, 1961, p. 17.

[14] See "Luxury Housing Limited by City," *The New York Times,* March 6, 1962, p. 1; Milton Mollen (Chairman, City of New York Housing and Redevelopment Board), "For Urban Renewal," letter to the editor, *The New York Times,* March 17, 1962, p. 24; "More Low-Cost Housing Added to Plan for West Side Renewal," *The New York Times,* June 22, 1962, p. 11; Harris L. Present, "To Halt Destruction of Buildings," letter to the editor, *The New York Times,* February 9, 1962, p. 28. For a general review of urban renewal in New York, see "Title I and Slum Clearance: A Decade of Controversy," *The New York Times,* June 29, 1959, p. 1; and succeeding articles on June 30, July 1, and July 2, 1959.

[15] See J. Anthony Panuch, *Building a Better New York: Final Report to Mayor Robert F. Wagner* (March 1, 1960), pp. 68–69; Gertrude Samuels, "To Brighten the 'Gray Areas,'" *The New York Times Magazine,* October 22, 1961, pp. 48, 72, 74; and "City to Spur Slum Conversions by Liberalizing Tax Benefits," *The New York Times,* July 6, 1962, p. 26.

[16] Much of the following discussion is based on an interview with Louis Winnick,

Director, Planning and Program Research Division, City of New York Housing and Redevelopment Board, March 10, 1961. See also policy recommendations in John R. White and Edna L. Hebard, *The Manhattan Housing Market* (New York: Brown, Harris, Stevens, Inc., 1959), pp. 103–104.

[17] Information on West Side renewal area from New York City Planning Commission, *Urban Renewal: A Report on the West Side Urban Renewal Study to Mayor Robert F. Wagner and the Board of Estimate of the City of New York, and to the Urban Renewal Administration* (New York: 1958). Plan proposals cited are those of Plan A.

[18] See J. Anthony Panuch, *Building a Better New York, op. cit.,* pp. 47–48, 59.

[19] City of New York Committee on Slum Clearance, *op. cit.,* p. 25.

[20] *Ibid.*

[21] For a summary of central business district proposals, see Los Angeles Central City Committee and Los Angeles City Planning Department, "Economic Survey: Los Angeles: Centropolis 1980" (December 12, 1960), p. 36. Mass transit proposals are described in Daniel, Mann, Johnson, and Mendenhall, *Los Angeles Metropolitan Transit Authority Rapid Transit Program* (June 27, 1960). The full program described in this report was subsequently modified to an initial proposal for a single transit line; this immediate program is described in *The Los Angeles Times,* August 13, 1961, Section C.

[22] Information on Los Angeles renewal projects from Community Redevelopment Agency of the City of Los Angeles; financial estimates as of April 1961.

[23] Information on Ocean Park Project from Redevelopment Agency of the City of Santa Monica; financial estimates are those of February 1, 1961.

[24] For a description of the code enforcement program, see City of Los Angeles Department of Building and Safety, *Conservation: A New Concept of Building Law Enforcement* (Los Angeles: 1958).

[25] Information from an interview with Fred Hoppe, Conservation Bureau, City of Los Angeles Department of Building and Safety, April 26, 1961.

[26] Information on minority housing from Fred E. Case, "The Housing Status of Minority Families: Los Angeles, 1956" (University of California at Los Angeles Real Estate Research Program, January 1958); Los Angeles County Commission on Human Relations, Statement of John A. Buggs, Executive Secretary, January 16, 1960; Remi Nadeau, *Los Angeles: From Mission to Modern City* (New York: Longmans, Green, 1960), p. 247.

[27] Information from an interview with Arnold A. Wilken, Area Representative, Housing and Home Finance, Los Angeles, May 4, 1961.

[28] Financial data for Hartford urban renewal projects from Rogers, Taliaferro, and Lamb, *Renewal Program for Downtown Hartford, Connecticut* (1960); and U.S. Housing and Home Finance Agency, Urban Renewal Administration, *Urban Renewal Project Characteristics* (December 31, 1960).

[29] One recent study has made a notable start on this subject, setting forth a useful conceptual framework and interpreting the operation of the housing market in four racially mixed areas of Philadelphia. See Chester Rapkin and William G. Grigsby, *The Demand for Housing in Racially Mixed Areas* (Berkeley: University of California Press, 1960).

APPENDIX B

[1] Source: New York Department of City Planning.

[2] Information from New York Department of City Planning.

[3] See City of New York Department of City Planning *Newsletter,* January 1958, p. 4, for the range of residential densities within the different boroughs as of 1955–1956. A study of renewal prospects for part of the West Side of Manhattan gives information on densities for different types of structures within the area; these structural types are also to be found at similar densities in deteriorated

areas elsewhere in New York. The average density for walk-up tenements (primarily old-law tenements built prior to 1901) is 240 dwelling units per net acre. For all brownstone structures, including those converted to rooming houses, the average density is 224 dwelling units per net acre. For brownstones that have not been converted to rooming houses — a housing type more representative of the outer boroughs — the average density is 139 dwelling units per net acre in the West Side study area. Source: New York City Planning Commission, *Urban Renewal: A Report on the West Side Urban Renewal Study to Mayor Robert F. Wagner and the Board of Estimate of the City of New York, and to the Urban Renewal Administration* (New York: 1958).

[4] City of New York Department of City Planning *Newsletter,* October 1958, p. 1. The average density of all old-law tenements reported in the West Side renewal study is 246 units per net acre; those used for single-room occupancy had an average density of 619 units per acre. A study by the Regional Plan Association lists densities of 350 to 400 units per acre as typical for old-law tenements: Regional Plan Association, *Bulletin Number 87,* "People, Jobs and Land in the New Jersey–New York–Connecticut Metropolitan Region 1955–1975" (June 1957), p. 38.

[5] Source: Los Angeles County Regional Planning Commission, net increases for 35 statistical areas within the county.

[6] Real Estate Research Corporation, *Rental Housing Market Analysis: Downtown Hartford* (prepared for Department of Housing, City of Hartford, 1959).

APPENDIX C

[1] Homer Hoyt, *One Hundred Years of Land Values in Chicago* (Chicago: University of Chicago Press, 1933), p. 295.

[2] Homer Hoyt, *The Structure and Growth of Residential Neighborhoods in American Cities* (Washington, D. C.: Federal Housing Administration, 1939), p. 102.

[3] Hoyt, *One Hundred Years, op. cit.,* p. 295.

[4] Some recent analyses of density as a function of distance from the core: Hans Blumenfeld, "The Tidal Wave of Metropolitan Expansion," *Journal of the American Institute of Planners,* Vol. 20 (Winter 1954), pp. 3–14; Warren S. Thompson, *Growth and Changes in California's Population* (Los Angeles: Haynes Foundation, 1955), pp. 263–264; John R. Hamburg and Roger L. Creighton, "Predicting Chicago's Land Use Pattern," *Journal of the American Institute of Planners,* Vol. 25 (May 1959), pp. 67–72; Edgar M. Hoover and Raymond Vernon, *Anatomy of a Metropolis* (Cambridge, Massachusetts: Harvard University Press, 1959), pp. 185–186; Wilbur Smith and Associates, *Future Highways and Urban Growth* (New Haven: 1961), pp. 16–17.

[5] Richard M. Hurd, *Principles of City Land Values* (New York: The Record and Guide, 1924) (first published 1903), p. 11.

[6] Hoyt, *One Hundred Years, op. cit.,* pp. 24–25.

[7] Robert Murray Haig, "Toward an Understanding of the Metropolis: II. The Assignment of Activities to Areas in Urban Regions," *Quarterly Journal of Economics,* Vol. 40 (May 1926), pp. 420–421.

[8] *Ibid.,* p. 423.

[9] Richard U. Ratcliff, "Efficiency and the Location of Urban Activities," in Robert Moore Fisher, ed., *The Metropolis in Modern Life* (Garden City, New York: Doubleday, 1955), p. 125.

[10] Walter Firey, *Land Use in Central Boston* (Cambridge, Massachusetts: Harvard University Press, 1947), pp. 324–325.

[11] Robert B. Mitchell and Chester Rapkin, *Urban Traffic: A Function of Land Use* (New York: Columbia University Press, 1954). The following discussion is

based primarily on Chapter 7, "The Influence of Movement on Land Use Patterns," pp. 104–133.

12 William Alonso, "A Model of the Urban Land Market: Location and Densities of Dwellings and Businesses," unpublished Ph.D. dissertation, University of Pennsylvania, 1960; summarized in William Alonso, "A Theory of the Urban Land Market," *Regional Science Association Papers and Proceedings,* Vol. 6 (1960), pp. 149–157.

13 Hoover and Vernon, *op. cit.,* pp. 169–170.

14 Lowdon Wingo, Jr., *Transportation and Urban Land* (Washington, D. C.: Resources for the Future, 1961).

15 Wingo, *op. cit.,* p. 91.

16 *Ibid.*

17 Hoyt, *One Hundred Years, op. cit.,* Figure 81, p. 356.

18 *Ibid.,* p. 353.

19 *Ibid.,* p. 356.

20 *Ibid.,* p. 336.

21 Hans Blumenfeld, *op. cit.*

22 Hoover and Vernon, *op. cit.,* p. 190.

23 See Amos H. Hawley, *The Changing Shape of Metropolitan America* (Glencoe: Free Press, 1956), pp. 14–16; Warren S. Thompson, *op. cit.,* pp. 263–264; John R. Hamburg and Robert Sharkey, "Chicago's Changing Land Use and Population Structures," *Journal of the American Institute of Planners,* Vol. 26 (November 1960), pp. 317–323.

24 *U.S. Census of Population: 1960,* Supplementary Reports, PC(S1)–7, "Rank of Cities of 100,000 or More: 1960" (June 16, 1961); PC(S1)–1, "Population of Standard Metropolitan Statistical Areas: 1960 and 1950" (April 10, 1961).

25 Hoyt, *One Hundred Years, op. cit.,* p. 355.

26 For a general summary, see Nelson L. Foote, Janet Abu-Lughod, Mary Mix Foley, Louis Winnick, *Housing Choices and Housing Constraints* (New York: McGraw-Hill, 1960), pp. 329–330.

27 Chester Rapkin and William G. Grigsby, *Residential Renewal in the Urban Core* (Philadelphia: University of Pennsylvania Press, 1960), p. 117.

28 Janet Abu-Lughod, "A Survey of Center-City Residents," in Nelson L. Foote *et al., op. cit.,* p. 391.

29 Hoyt, *The Structure and Growth, op. cit.,* p. 118. For a fuller statement of Hoyt's views, see pp. 116–119, and *One Hundred Years, op. cit.,* pp. 361–365.

30 Homer Hoyt, "Expressways and Apartment Sites," *Traffic Quarterly,* Vol. 12 (April 1958), pp. 263–268.

31 Nelson L. Foote *et al., op. cit.,* p. 77.

32 Raymond Vernon, "The Economics and Finances of the Large Metropolis," *Daedalus,* Vol. 90 (Winter 1961), pp. 46–47.

33 Miles L. Colean, *Renewing Our Cities* (New York: Twentieth Century Fund, 1953), pp. 13–15.

34 Hoyt, *One Hundred Years, op. cit.,* Figure 87, p. 361; Figure 59, p. 318; and pp. 355–356.

35 Hoover and Vernon, *op. cit.,* pp. 237–238. The core includes Manhattan, the Bronx, Queens, Brooklyn, and Hudson County, New Jersey.

36 Raymond Vernon, "Some Reflections on Urban Decay," *Confluence,* Vol. 7 (Summer 1958), pp. 139–140.

37 Chester Rapkin, letter in *Journal of Housing,* Vol. 17 (May 1960), p. 191.

INDEX

207